Time and Money

Can we accept or find practical use for a macroeconomics

- in which consumption and investment always move together in the short run
- in which these two magnitudes must move in opposition to change the economy's rate of growth, and
- for which the long run emerges as a seamless sequence of short runs?

It is increasingly recognized that the weakness in modern macroeconomic theorizing is the lack of any real coupling of short- and long-run aspects of the market process. In the short run, the investment and consumption magnitudes move in the same direction, either both downward into recession or both upward toward full employment and even beyond in an inflationary spiral. But for a given period and with a given technology, any change in the economy's growth rate must entail consumption and investment magnitudes that move, initially, in opposition to one another.

Roger W. Garrison claims that modern Austrian macroeconomics, which builds on the early writings of F.A. Hayek, can be comprehended as an effort to reinstate the capital-theory core that allows for a real coupling of short- and long-run perspectives. Although the macroeconomic relationships identified are largely complementary to the relationships that have dominated the thinking of macroeconomists for the past half century, *Time and Money* presents a fundamental challenge to modern theorists and practitioners who overdraw the short-run/long-run distinction. The primary focus of this text is the intertemporal structure of capital and the associated set of issues that have long been neglected in the more conventional labor- and money-based macroeconomics. This volume puts forth a persuasive argument that the troubles that characterize modern capital-intensive economies, particularly the episodes of boom and bust, may best be analyzed with the aid of a capital-based macroeconomics.

Roger W. Garrison is Professor of Economics at Auburn University, Alabama, USA.

Foundations of the market economy

Edited by Mario J. Rizzo, *New York University*
Lawrence H. White, *University of Georgia*

A central theme in this series is the importance of understanding and assessing the market economy from a perspective broader than the static economics of perfect competition and Pareto optimality. Such a perspective sees markets as causal processes generated by the preferences, expectations and beliefs of Economic agents. The creative acts of entrepreneurship that uncover new information about preferences, prices and technology are central to these processes with respect to their ability to promote the discovery and use of knowledge in society.

The market economy consists of a set of institutions that facilitate voluntary cooperation and exchange among individuals. These institutions include the legal and ethical framework as well as more narrowly "economic" patterns of social interaction. Thus the law, legal institutions and cultural and ethical norms, as well as ordinary business practices and monetary phenomena, fall within the analytical domain of the economist.

Time and Money

The macroeconomics of capital structure

Roger W. Garrison

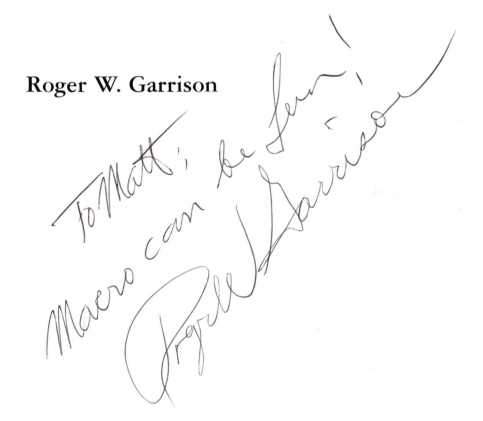

To Matt; Macro can be fun! Roger W. Garrison

London and New York

First published 2001
by Routledge
2 Park Square, Milton Park, Abingdon, Oxon, OX14 4RN

Simultaneously published in the USA and Canada
by Routledge
270 Madison Ave, New York NY 10016

Reprinted 2001 (twice), 2002 (twice)

Transferred to Digital Printing 2006

Routledge is an imprint of the Taylor & Francis Group

© 2001 Roger W. Garrison

Typeset in Garamond by
Florence Production Ltd, Stoodleigh, Devon

British Library Cataloguing in Publication Data
A catalogue record for this book is available from
the British Library

Library of Congress Cataloging in Publication Data
Garrison, Roger W.
   Time and money: the macroeconomics of capital structure /
Roger W. Garrison.
     p.   cm. – (Foundations of the market economy)
   Includes bibliographical references and index.
     1. Money.   2. Capital.   3. Macroeconomics.
   I. Title.   II. Foundations of the market economy series
HG220.A2 G37 2001
339.5'3–dc21   00–029106

This book has been sponsored in part by the Austrian Economics
Program at New York University.

ISBN10: 0–415–07982–9 (hbk)
ISBN10: 0–415–77122–6 (pbk)

ISBN13: 978–0–415–07982–2 (hbk)
ISBN13: 978–0–415–77122–1 (pbk)

To Karen and Jimmy

Contents

Figures

Preface

My venture into macroeconomics has not been a conventional one. In the mid-1960s, I took a one-semester course in microeconomic and macroeconomic principles in partial fulfillment of the social-studies requirement in an engineering curriculum. The text was the sixth edition (1964) of Samuelson's *Economics*. It was several years later that I returned on my own to reconsider the principles that govern the macroeconomy, having stumbled upon Henry Hazlitt's *Failure of the "New Economics"* (1959). The first few chapters of this critique of Keynes's *General Theory of Employment, Interest and Money* (1936) were enough to persuade me that I could not read Hazlitt's book with profit unless I first read Keynes's. I had no idea at the time what actually lay in store for me.

In his own preface, Keynes does warn the reader that his arguments are aimed at his fellow economists, but he invites interested others to eavesdrop. As it turned out, even the most careful reading of the *General Theory*'s 384 pages and the most intense pondering of its one solitary diagram were not enough to elevate me much beyond the status of eavesdropper. But Keynes made me feel that I was listening in on something important and mysterious. The ideas that investment is governed by "animal spirits" and that the use of savings is constricted by the "fetish of liquidity" do not integrate well with more conventional views of the free-enterprise system. Keynes's notion that the rate of interest could and should be driven to zero seemed puzzling, and his call for a "comprehensive socialization of investment" was cause for concern.

With Keynes's mode of argument – though not the full logic of his system – fresh in my mind, Hazlitt's book was intelligible, but his virtual page-by-page critique came across as the work of an unreceptive and hostile eavesdropper. Keynes's vision of the macroeconomy – in which the market tends toward depression and instability and in which the government assumes the role of stimulating and stabilizing it until social reform can replace it with something better – was never effectively countered. Hazlitt did point to the Austrian economists as the ones offering the most worthy alternative vision. There were a double handful of references to Friedrich A. Hayek's writings and twice that many to those of Ludwig von Mises.

My self-directed study expanded to include Mises's *Theory of Money and Credit* ([1912] 1953), Hayek's *Prices and Production* ([1935] 1967), and, soon enough, Murray Rothbard's *America's Great Depression* ([1963] 1972).

After a diet of Keynes, contra-Keynes, and then Austrian economics, I returned to my old principles text to see how I had failed to come to any understanding at all during my undergraduate experience with macro-economics. In Samuelson's chapters on the macroeconomy, I found a total gloss of the issues. The fundamental questions of whether, how, and in what institutional settings a market economy can be self-regulating were eclipsed by a strong presumption that self-regulation is not possible and by simplistic exercises showing how in a failure-prone macroeconomy the extent of labor and resource idleness is related to the leakages from – and injections into – the economy's streams of spending.

In the early 1970s I entered the graduate program at the University of Missouri, Kansas City, where I learned the intermediate and (at the time) advanced versions of Keynesianism. Having read and by then reread the *General Theory*, the ISLM framework struck me as a clever pedagogical tool but one that, like Samuelson's gloss, left the heart and soul out of Keynes's vision of the macroeconomy. It was at that time that I first conceived of an Austrian counterpart to ISLM – with a treatment of the fundamental issues of the economy's self-regulating capabilities emerging from a com-parison of the two contrasting graphical frameworks.

Initially drafted as a term paper, my "Austrian Macroeconomics: A Dia-grammatical Exposition," was presented at a professional meeting in Chicago in 1973. In 1976 I rewrote it for a conference on Austrian Economics spon-sored by the Institute for Humane Studies and held at Windsor Castle, after which it appeared in the conference volume titled *New Directions in Austrian Economics* (Spadaro, 1978). This early graphical exposition had a certain lim-ited but enduring success. It was published separately as a monograph by the Institute for Humane Studies and was excerpted extensively in W. Duncan Reekie's *Markets, Entrepreneurs and Liberty: An Austrian View of Capitalism* (1984: 75–83). It continues to appear on Austrian economics reading lists, was the basis for some discussion in a interview published in Snowden *et al.* (1994), and tends to get mentioned in histories of the Austrian School, such as in Vaughn (1994), and in survey articles, such as in Kirzner (1997).

Though largely compatible with the graphical exposition offered in the present volume, this earlier effort was inspired by Mises's original account of boom and bust – an account that was anchored in classical modes of thought:

> The period of production . . . must be of such a length that exactly the whole available subsistence fund is necessary on the one hand and suffi-cient on the other for paying the wages of the labourers throughout the duration of the productive process.
>
> (Mises, [1912] 1953: 360)

This classical language got translated into graphical expression as the supply and demand for dated labor – with the production period being represented by the time elapsing between the employment of labor and the emergence of consumable output. While this construction served its purpose, it placed undue emphasis on the notion of a period of production and put an undue burden on the reader of interpreting the graphics in the light of the more modern language of Austrian macroeconomics.

Resuming my graduate studies – at the University of Virginia – I dropped the graphical framework but continued to deal with the conflict of visions that separated the Keynesian and Austrian Schools. From my dissertation came two relevant articles, "Intertemporal Coordination and the Invisible Hand: An Austrian Perspective on the Keynesian Vision" (1985a) and "Austrian Capital Theory: The Early Controversies" (1990). Bellante and Garrison (1988), together with the two dozen or so of my singly authored articles that appear in the bibliography, undergird or anticipate to one extent or another the theme of the present volume.

Since 1978, when I joined the faculty at Auburn University, I have taught courses in macroeconomics at the introductory, intermediate, and graduate levels. During the summers I have lectured on business cycle theory and on related issues in teaching seminars sponsored by such organizations as the Institute for Humane Studies, the Ludwig von Mises Institute, and the Foundation for Economic Education. I hit upon the interlocking graphical framework presented in Chapter 3 while teaching intermediate macro-economics in 1995. Since that time I have used this framework in other courses and have presented it at conferences and teaching seminars with some success. At the very least, it helps in explaining just what the Austrian theory is. But because the interlocking graphics impose a certain discipline on the theoriz-ing, they help in demonstrating the coherence of the Austrian vision. For many students, then, the framework goes beyond exposition to persuasion.

My final understanding of Keynesianism comes substantially from my own reading of Keynes's *General Theory* together with his earlier writings, but it owes much to two of Keynes's interpreters – Allan Meltzer and Axel Leijonhufvud. In 1986 I had the privilege of participating in a Liberty Fund Conference devoted to discussing Allan Meltzer's then-forthcoming book, *Keynes's Monetary Theory: A Different Interpretation* (1988). Though called a "different interpretation," Meltzer had simply taken Keynes at his word where other interpreters had been dismissive of his excesses. The notions of socializing investment to avoid the risks unique to decentralized decision making and driving the interest rate to zero in order that capital be increased until it ceases to be scarce were given their due. Meltzer had put the heart and soul back into Keynesianism. My subsequent review article (1993a) substantially anticipates the treatment of these essential aspects of Keynes's vision in Chapter 9.

Leijonhufvud, who was also a participant at the conference on Meltzer's book, has influenced my own thinking in more subtle – though no less substantial – ways. Leijonhufvud (1968) is a treasure-trove of Keynes-inspired insights into the workings of the macroeconomy, and Leijonhufvud (1981b) links many of those insights to the writings of Knut Wicksell in a way that the Austrian economists, who themselves owe so much to Wicksell, cannot help but appreciate. Though Leijonhufvud has often been critical of Austrian theory, he sees merit in emphasizing the heterogeneity of capital goods and the subjectivity of entrepreneurial expectations (1981b: 197) and has recently called for renewed attention to the problems of intertemporal coordination (1998: 197–202). I have dealt only tangentially with Leijonhufvud's views of Keynes and the Austrians (Garrison, 1992a: 144–5), including, though, a mild chiding for his reluctance to integrate Austrian capital theory into his own macroeconomics (1992a: 146–7, n. 10). A late rereading of Leijonhufvud (1981b), and the recent appearance of Leijonhufvud (1999), however, revealed that my treatment in Chapter 8 of Keynes's views on macroeconomic stimulation and stabilization is consistent in nearly all important respects to Leijonhufvud's reconstruction of Keynesian theory.

My understanding of Monetarism reflects the influence of Leland Yeager, though in ways he may not appreciate. In fact, had I taken his blunt and frequent condemnations of Austrian business cycle theory to heart, I would never have conceived of writing this book. But as professor and dissertation director at the University of Virginia and as colleague and friend at Auburn University, he has influenced me in many positive ways. For one, Yeager's graduate course in macroeconomics focused intensely on Don Patinkin's *Money, Interest, and Prices* (1965). Having profited greatly from that course, I show, in Chapter 10, that Patinkin's account of interest-rate dynamics complements the more conventional Monetarist theory in a way that moves Monetarism in the direction of Austrianism. For another, his exposition and development of Monetary Disequilibrium Theory have persuaded me, as I explain in Chapter 11, that pre-Friedman Monetarism is an essential complement to the Austrian theory – though Yeager himself sees the Austrian theory as an embarrassingly poor substitute for Monetary Disequilibrium Theory.

I had occasion to learn from and interact with Ludwig Lachmann in the early 1980s when he was a visiting professor at New York University and I was a postdoctoral fellow there. As recounted in Chapter 2, Lachmann's ideas about expectations and the market process served as an inspiration for many of my own arguments.

Though I met and talked with Friedrich Hayek on several occasions, I can hardly claim to have known him. However, the reader will not fail to notice his influence in virtually every chapter – and in virtually every graph – of this book. His writings fueled my interest in the early years and in later years provided the strongest support for my own rendition of Austrian macroeconomics. It is to Hayek, then, that I owe my greatest intellectual debt.

Roger W. Garrison
January 2000

Acknowledgments

The author and publisher would like to thank the following publishers and journals for granting permission to incorporate previously published material in this work:

The Edwin Mellen Press for permission to incorporate into Chapter 1 a reworking of material drawn from my foreword to John P. Cochran and Fred R. Glahe, *The Hayek-Keynes Debate: Lessons for Current Business Cycle Research* (1999). *The South African Journal of Economics* for permission to include as Chapter 2 an adaptation of "The Lachmann Legacy: An Agenda for Macroeconomics" (1997), *South African Journal of Economics*, 65(4). This paper was originally presented as the Fourth Ludwig Lachmann Memorial Lecture at the University of the Witwatersrand in August 1997. Routledge for permission to incorporate into Chapter 6 material drawn from my "Hayekian Triangles and Beyond," which originally appeared in J. Birner and R. van Zijp (eds) *Hayek, Coordination and Evolution: His Legacy in Philosophy, Politics, Economics, and the History of Ideas* (1994). The Free Market Foundation of Southern Africa for permission to incorporate into Chapter 6 material drawn from my *Chronically Large Federal Budget Deficits*, which originally appeared as FMF Monograph No. 18 (1998). *Critical Review* for permission to incorporate into Chapter 9 material drawn from my "Keynesian Splenetics: From Social Philosophy to Macroeconomics" (1993), *Critical Review*, 6(4). The MIT Press for permission to use as Figure 10.1 a graph that is analytically equivalent to Figure X-4 in Don Patinkin's *Money, Interest, and Prices: An Integration of Monetary and Value Theory*, 2nd edn, abridged (1989). Aldine Publishing Company for permission to use as Figure 10.3b a graph that resembles in all critical respects Figure 12.6 in Milton Friedman, *Price Theory* (New York: Aldine de Gruyter) Copyright © 1962, 1976 by Aldine Publishing company, New York. *Economic Inquiry* for permission to incorporate into Chapter 11 material drawn from my "Friedman's 'Plucking Model': Comment" (1996), *Economic Inquiry*, 34(4).

The author would like to thank Routledge Editor Robert Langham as well as Alan Jarvis, who preceded Mr Langham in that post, and especially Editorial Assistant Heidi Bagtazo for their efficiency and goodwill in seeing this book project through to completion. The helpful guidance in the final stages from Susan Leaper and Simon Dennett (of Florence Production Ltd) was much appreciated. A warm thanks is also extended to the Series Editors, Mario J. Rizzo and Lawrence H. White, for their patience and helpfulness. The author is indebted to many others who provided encouragement and helpful feedback at various stages of production: John Cochran, Robert Formaini, Randall Holcombe, Steven Horwitz, Roger Koppl, Thomas and Donna McQuade, Michael Montgomery, Ivo Sarjanovic, Larry Sechrest, George Selgin, Mark Skousen, Sven Thommesen, and John Wells. The author alone, of course, is responsible for all remaining errors.

Part I

Frameworks

1 The macroeconomics of capital structure

The long and the short of it

In early 1997 a small group of world-class economists, serving as panelists in a session of the American Economics Association meetings, addressed themselves to the question "Is there a core of practical macroeconomics that we should all believe?" Their listeners could hardly imagine that a second group of economists were gathered across the hall to answer a similar question about microeconomics. Dating from the marginalist revolution of the 1870s, microeconomics has had a readily recognizable core – and one that has grown increasingly solid over the past century. By contrast, the Keynesian revolution that began in the 1930s ushered in a macroeconomics that was – at least from one important point of view – essentially coreless. The capital theory that underlay the macroeconomics being developed by the Austrian School was nowhere to be found in the new economics of John Maynard Keynes.

"One major weakness in the core of macroeconomics," as identified by AEA panelist Robert Solow (1997a: 231f.), "is the lack of real coupling between the short-run picture and the long-run picture. Since the long run and the short run merge into one another, one feels that they cannot be completely independent." Ironically, when the same Robert Solow (1997b: 594) contributed an entry on Trevor Swan to *An Encyclopedia of Keynesian Economics*, he took a much more sanguine view: "[Swan's writings serve] as a reminder that one can be a Keynesian for the short run and a neoclassical for the long run, and that this combination of commitments may be the right one."

The present volume takes Solow's more critical assessment to be the more cogent. The weakness, or lacking, in modern macroeconomic theorizing can most easily be seen by contrasting Keynes's macroeconomics with Solow's own economics of growth. In the short run, the investment and consumption magnitudes move in the same direction – both downward into recession or both upward toward full employment and even beyond in an inflationary spiral. The economics of growth, which also allows investment and consumption to increase together over time, features the fundamental trade-off faced in each period between current consumption and investment. We can increase investment (and hence increase future consumption) if and to the extent we are willing to forgo current consumption. For a given period and with a given technology, any change in the economy's growth rate must entail consumption and investment magnitudes that move, initially, in opposition to one another.

So, can we accept or find practical use for a macroeconomics (1) in which consumption and investment always move together in the short run; (2) in which these two magnitudes must move in opposition to change the economy's rate of growth; and (3) for which the long run emerges as a seamless sequence of short runs?

Keynes (1936: 378), whose demand-dominated theory offered us nothing in the way of a "real coupling," simply refocused the profession's attention on the short-run movements in macroeconomic magnitudes while paying lip service to the fundamental truths of classical economics: "if our central controls succeed in establishing an aggregate volume of output corresponding to full employment as nearly as is practicable, the classical theory comes into its own again from this point onward." This statement comes immediately after his claim that the "tacit assumptions [of the classical theory] are seldom or never satisfied."

The classical economists, or so Keynes's caricature of them would lead us to believe, focused their attention exclusively on the long-run relationships, as governed by binding supply-side constraints, and relied on Say's Law ("Supply creates its own Demand," in Keynes's rendering) to keep the Keynesian short run out of the picture.

If Keynes focused on the short-run picture, and the classical economists focused on the long-run picture, then the Austrian economists, and particularly Friedrich A. Hayek, focused on the "real coupling" between the two pictures. The Hayekian coupling took the form of capital theory – the theory of a time-consuming, multi-stage capital structure envisioned by Carl Menger ([1871] 1981) and developed by Eugen von Böhm-Bawerk ([1889] 1959). Decades before macroeconomics emerged as a recognized subdiscipline, Böhm-Bawerk had molded the fundamental Mengerian insight into a macroeconomic theory to account for the distribution of income among the factors of production. Dating from the late 1920s, Hayek ([1928] 1975a and [1935] 1967), following a lead provided by Ludwig von Mises ([1912] 1953), infused the theory with monetary considerations. He showed that credit policy pursued by a central monetary authority can be a source of economy-wide distortions in the intertemporal allocation of resources and hence an important cause of business cycles.

Tellingly, Robert Solow, as revealed in an interview with Jack Birner (1990: n. 28), found Hayek's arguments to be "completely incomprehensible." A major claim in the present book is that Hayek's writings – and those of modern Austrian macroeconomists – can be comprehended as an effort to reinstate the capital-theory "core" that allows for a "real coupling" of short-run and long-run aspects of the market process. Hayek was simply observing an important methodological maxim, as later articulated by Mises (1966: 296):

> [W]e must guard ourselves against the popular fallacy of drawing a sharp line between short-run and long-run effects. What happens in the short run is precisely the first stages of a chain of successive transformations which tend to bring about the long-run effects.

The question addressed by the AEA panelists in 1997 is but an echo of a lingering question about the nature of macroeconomic problems posed by John Hicks (1967: 203) three decades earlier: "[Who] was right, Keynes or Hayek?" The most recent answer to Hicks's question is offered by Bruce Caldwell in his introduction to *Contra Keynes and Cambridge* (vol. 9 of the *Collected Works* of F. A. Hayek). According to Caldwell (1995: 46), "neither was right. Both purported to be supplying a general theory of the cycle, and in this, neither was successful." This verdict can be called into question on two counts. First, Chapter 22 of Keynes's *General Theory*, "Notes on the Trade Cycle," is not advertised as a general theory of the cycle, and the remainder of Keynes's book is concerned primarily with secular unemployment and only secondarily if at all with cyclical variations. Second, although Hayek's *Prices and Production* and related writings *were* concerned primarily with cyclical variation, applicability took priority over generality. Hayek's focus ([1935] 1967: 54) on a money-induced artificial boom reflects the fact that, as an institutional matter and as an historical matter, money enters the economy through credit markets. Hence, it impinges, in the first instance, on interest rates and affects the intertemporal allocation of resources. He recognized that a fully general theory would have to encompass other institutional arrangements and allow for other possible boom–bust scenarios.

But there is a greater point that challenges Caldwell's answer. The major weakness that Solow saw in modern macroeconomics has as its counterpart in Austrian macroeconomics a major strength. There *is* a real coupling between the short run and the long run in the Austrian theory. The fact that the Austrian economists feature this coupling is the basis for an alternative answer to Hicks's question: Hayek was right – as argued by O'Driscoll (1977b) and most recently by Cochran and Glahe (1999). More substantively, identifying the relative-price effects (and the corresponding quantity adjustments) of a monetary disturbance, as compared to tracking the movements in macroeconomic aggregates that conceal those relative-price effects, gives us a superior understanding of the nature of cyclical variation in the economy and points the way to a more thoroughgoing capital-based macroeconomics.

What's in a name?

The subtitle of this book, *The Macroeconomics of Capital Structure*, is intended
to suggest that the macroeconomic relationships identified and explored
here are, to a large extent, complementary to the relationships that have
dominated the thinking of macroeconomists for the past half century.
Arguably, the macroeconomics of labor, which is the focus of modern
income–expenditure analysis, and the macroeconomics of money, which gets
emphasis in the quantity-theory tradition, have each been pushed well into
the range of diminishing marginal returns. If further pushing toward a
fuller macroeconomic understanding is to pay, it may well involve paying
attention to the economy's intertemporal capital structure.

In a more comprehensive and balanced treatment of the issues, we might
want to present a macroeconomics of labor, capital, and money. This trilogy
is sequenced so as to parallel the title chosen by Keynes: *The General Theory
of Employment, Interest, and Money*. Capital does not appear in his trilogy,
but its shadow, interest, does. The lack of conformability in Keynes's identification of the objects of study – employment (of labor), capital's shadow,
and money – should alert us at the outset to the enduring perplexities that
theorizing about capital and interest entails. Classical economists saw the
rate of interest, also known as the rate of profit, as the price of capital.
Keynes, who clearly rejected this view, would have us believe that the
shadow is actually being cast by money. Keynes's critics, particularly the
members of the Austrian School, took the rate of interest to reflect a systematic discounting of future values – whether or not capital was involved in
creating them or money was involved in facilitating their exchange. Decades
of controversy have demonstrated that the interest rate's relationship to
capital and to money is not a simple one. In the present study, capital –
or, more pointedly, the intertemporal structure of capital – is the primary
focus. The centrality of the interest rate derives from its role in allocating
resources – and sometimes in misallocating them – within the economy's
capital structure.

Undeniably, claims can be made to justify each of the three candidates
(labor, capital, and money) as an appropriate basis, or primary focal point,
for macroeconomic theorizing. The rationale for labor-based macroeconomics
and for money-based macroeconomics are more often assumed than actually spelled out. The case for capital-based macroeconomics, however, is at
least equally compelling and has a special claim on our attention because
of its relative neglect.

Labor-based macroeconomics

The employment of labor is logically and temporally prior to the creation
of capital. Capital goods, after all, are produced by labor. Even the macroeconomic theorists who have devoted the most attention to capital have

typically identified labor, together with natural resources, as the "original" means of production. And although the employment of labor in modern economies is facilitated by a commonly accepted medium of exchange, the use of money is not fundamentally a prerequisite to employment. The employment of labor can take place in a barter economy, and self-employment in a Crusoe economy.

Employee compensation accounts for a large portion – more than 70 percent – of national income even in the most capital-intensive economies. The earning and spending by workers, then, dominate in any circular-flow construction. The occasional widespread unemployment in modern economies is the most salient manifestation of a macroeconomic problem. And cyclical variation in economic activity is conventionally charted in terms of changes in the unemployment rate. The pricing of labor even in markets that may otherwise be characterized by flexibility can be affected by attitudes about fairness, implications for worker morale, and considerations of firm-specific human capital. Hence, changes in labor-market conditions can result in quantity adjustments and/or price adjustments not fully accounted for by simple supply-and-demand analysis. All these considerations give employment a strong claim to being the primary focus for macroeconomic theorizing.

Money-based macroeconomics

It is the use of money that puts the macro in macroeconomics. In the context of a barter system, it is difficult even to imagine – unless we think of a widespread natural disaster – that the economy might experience variations in market conditions that have systematic economy-wide repercussions. But, with trivial exceptions, money is on one side of every transaction in modern economies. Unavoidably, however, the medium of exchange is also a medium through which difficulties in any sector of the economy – or difficulties with money itself – get transmitted to all other sectors. Further, the provision of money even in the most decentralized economies is – not to say must be – the business of a central authority. This institutionalized centrality translates directly into a central concern of macroeconomists. Money comes into play both as a source of difficulties and as a vehicle for transmitting those difficulties throughout the economy. Using terminology first introduced by Ragnar Frisch (1933), we can say that money matters both as "impulse" and as "propagation mechanism." So involved is money that macroeconomics and monetary theory have, in some quarters, come to be thought of as two names for the same set of ideas. Monetarism, broadly conceived, is simply money-based macroeconomics.

Capital-based macroeconomics

What, then, is the case for capital-based macroeconomics? Considerations of capital structure allow the time element to enter the theory in a fundamental yet concrete way. If labor and natural resources can be thought of as original means of production and consumer goods as the ultimate end toward which production is directed, then capital occupies a position that is both logically and temporally intermediate between original means and ultimate ends. The goods-in-process conception of capital has a long and honorable history. And even forms of capital that do not fit neatly into a simple linear means–ends framework, such as fixed capital, human capital, and consumer durables, occupy an intermediate position between some relevant production decisions and the corresponding consumption utilities.

This temporally intermediate status of capital is not in serious dispute, but its significance for macroeconomic theorizing is rarely recognized. Alfred Marshall taught us that the time element is central to almost every economic problem. The critical time element manifests itself in the Austrian theory as an intertemporal capital structure. The scope and limits to structural modifications give increased significance to monetary disturbances. Simply put, capital gives money time to cause trouble. In a barter economy, there is no money to cause any trouble; in a pure exchange economy, there is not much trouble that money can cause. But in a modern capital-intensive economy, . . .

The macroeconomic significance of the fact that production takes time suggests that, for business cycle theory, capital and money should get equal billing. The nature and significance of money-induced price distortions in the context of time-consuming production processes were the basis for my early article "Time and Money: The Universals of Macroeconomic Theorizing" (1984) – and for the title of the present book. Macroeconomic theorizing, so conceived, is a story about how things can go wrong – how the economy's production process that transforms resources into consumable output can get derailed. Sometime subsequent to the committing of resources but prior to the emergence of output, the production process can be at war with itself; different aspects of the market process that governs production can work against one another. Thus, the troubles that characterize modern capital-intensive economies, particularly the episodes of boom and bust, may best be analyzed with the aid of a capital-based macroeconomics.

An exercise in comparative frameworks

This book was originally conceived as a graphical exposition of boom and bust as understood by the Austrian School. In its writing, however, the horizon was extended in two directions. First, a theory of boom and bust became capital-based macroeconomics. The relationships identified in pursuit of the narrower subject matter proved to be a sound basis for a more encompassing theory, one that sheds light upon such topics as deficit spending, credit controls, and tax reform. The general analytical framework that emerges from the insights of the Austrian School qualifies as a full-fledged

Austrian macroeconomics. Chapter 3 sets out the capital-based framework; Chapter 4 employs it to depict the Austrian perspective on economic growth and cyclical variation; Chapter 5 extends the analysis from monetary matters to fiscal and regulatory matters; Chapter 6 offers a variation on the Austrian theme by introducing risk and uncertainty and making a distinction – in connection with the distribution of risk and the exposure to uncertainty – between preference-based choices and policy-induced choices.

Second, the task of setting out and defending a capital-based (Austrian) macroeconomics requires a conformable labor-based (Keynesian) macroeconomics with which to compare and contrast it. The comparison was not well facilitated by the existing renditions of conventional macroeconomics – the Keynesian cross, ISLM, and Aggregate-Supply/Aggregate-Demand. Fortunately, it was possible to create a labor-based macroeconomic framework that remains true to Keynes (truer, arguably, than the more conventional constructions) and that contains important elements common to both (Keynesian and Austrian) frameworks. The resulting exercise in comparative frameworks requires a second set of core chapters. Chapter 7 sets out the labor-based framework; Chapter 8 employs it to depict the Keynesian view of cyclical variation and of counter-cyclical policies; Chapter 9 shifts the focus from stabilization policy to social reform.

As it turns out, money-based macroeconomics is virtually framework-independent. Any framework that tracks the quantity of money, the economy's total output, and the price level can be used to express the essential propositions of Monetarism. However, two separate strands of Monetarism can be identified – one that offers a theory of boom and bust and one that denies, on empirical grounds, that the boom–bust sequence has any claim on our attention. Both strands can be set out with the aid of either the labor-based framework (we're all Keynesians, now) or the capital-based framework (a close reading of Milton Friedman reveals elements of Austrianism). Chapter 10 deals with the Monetarists' view of boom and bust; Chapter 11 deals with depression as monetary disequilibrium.

The intertemporal structure of capital gets a strong emphasis throughout the book – an emphasis that some might judge to be unwarranted. But this book emphasizes the structure of capital in the same sense and in the same spirit that Friedman's work emphasizes the quantity of money or that the New Classical economists emphasize expectations. We tend to emphasize what we judge to have been unduly neglected in earlier writings. Chapter 12 summarizes and puts capital-based macroeconomics into perspective.

The emphasis in macroeconomics during the final quarter of the twentieth century has clearly been – not on labor, not on capital, not on money – but on expectations, so much so that theories tend to be categorized and judged primarily in terms of their treatment of expectations. Static expectations are wholly inadequate; adaptive expectations are only marginally less so. The assumption of rational expectations has become a virtual prerequisite for having any other aspect of a macroeconomic construction taken seriously. There is something troubling, however, about the notion of an expectations-based macroeconomics. Readers of Lewis Carroll and Dennis Robertson will sense a certain grin-without-the-cat flavor to modern treatments of expectations. Chapter 2 of the present book deals head on with the issue of expectations in the context of the development of macro-economics over the last three-quarters of a century and argues that there has been an overemphasis on expectations in modern theory which is ultim-ately attributable to the corelessness of modern macroeconomics, to the lack of "real coupling," as identified by Solow, between short-run and long-run macroeconomic relationships, or – more concretely – to the failure to give due attention to the economy's intertemporal capital structure.

Point of departure and style of argument

F. A. Hayek's contribution to the development of capital theory is commonly regarded as his most fundamental and path-breaking achievement (Machlup, 1976). His early attention to "Intertemporal Price Equilibrium and Movements in the Value of Money" (1928; English translation in Hayek, 1984) provided both the basis and inspiration for many subsequent contri-butions. The widely recognized but rarely understood Hayekian triangle, introduced in his 1931 lectures at the London School of Economics, were subsequently published (in 1931 with a second edition in 1935) as *Prices and Production*. The triangle, described in the second lecture (Hayek, [1935] 1967: 36–47), is a heuristic device that gives analytical legs to a theory of business cycles first offered by Ludwig von Mises ([1912] 1953: 339–66). Triangles of different shapes provide a convenient but highly stylized way of describing changes in the intertemporal pattern of the economy's capital structure.

In retrospect, we see that the timing of Hayek's invitation to lecture at the University of London takes on a special significance. We learn from the preface of the subsequent book that had the invitation come earlier, he couldn't have delivered those lectures; had it come later, he probably wouldn't have delivered them.

> [The invitation] came at a time when I had arrived at a clear view of the outlines of a theory of industrial fluctuations but before I had elabo-rated it in full detail or even realized all the difficulties which such an elaboration presented.
>
> (Hayek, [1935] 1967: vii)

Hayek mentions plans for a more complete exposition and indicates that his capital theory would have to be developed in much greater detail and adapted to the complexities of the real world before it could serve as a satis-factory basis for theorizing about cyclical fluctuations.

A decade after the London lectures the more complete exposition took form as *The Pure Theory of Capital* (1941). In this book Hayek fleshed out the earlier formulations and emphasized the centrality of the "capital problem" in questions about the market's ability to coordinate economic activities over time. The "pure" in the title meant "preliminary to the introduction of monetary considerations." Though some 450 pages in length, the book achieved only the first half of the original objective. The final sixty pages of the book did contain a "condensed and sketchy" (p. viii) treatment of the rate of interest in a money economy, but the task of retelling the story in *Prices and Production* in the context of the *Pure Theory of Capital* was put off and ultimately abandoned. The onset of the war was the proximate reason for cutting the project short; Hayek's exhaustion and waning interest in the business-cycle issues – and his heightened interest in the broader issues of political philosophy – account for his never returning to the task. In later years he acknowledged that Austrian capital theory effectively ended with his 1941 book and lamented that no one else has taken up the task that he had originally set for himself (Hayek, 1994: 96).

More fully developing the Austrian theory of the business cycle came to be synonymous with writing the follow-on volume to Hayek's *Pure Theory*. Many a graduate student has imagined himself undertaking this very project, only to abandon the idea even before the enormity of the task was fully comprehended. Thus, while the comparatively simple relationships of capital-free Keynesian theory captured the attention of the economics profession, the inherently complex relationships of Austrian theory languished.

Time and Money is not the sequel to Hayek's *Pure Theory*. Rather, the ideas and graphical constructions in the present volume take the original Hayekian triangle of *Prices and Production* to be the more appropriate point of departure for creating a capital-based macroeconomics. The trade-off between simplicity and realism is struck in favor of simplicity. Hayek's triangles allow us to make a graphical statement that there is a capital structure and that its intertemporal profile can change. This statement enables the Austrian theory to make a quantum leap beyond the competing theories that ignore capital altogether or that treat capital as a one-dimensional magnitude.

It is true, of course, that the triangles leave much out of account, but so too – despite their complexity – do the *Pure Theory*'s warped pie-slice figures that are intended to make some allowance for durable capital (Hayek, 1941: 208, 211). Degrees of realism range from K (for capital) to an aerial photograph of the Rust Belt. K is too simple; everything from the *Pure Theory* to the aerial photograph is too realistic for use in a macroeconomic framework. The Hayekian triangle is just right. It is comparable in terms of the simplicity/realism trade-off to the Keynesian cross; and it is comparable in this same regard to other graphical devices (the production-possibilities frontier, the market for loanable funds, and markets for labor) that make up the capital-based framework. Sophomores in their first economics course sometimes complain about all the considerations that the simple Marshallian supply and demand curves fail to capture. As they reel off a list of particulars, the professor waits patiently to deliver the news: "What's remarkable about supply and demand curves is not that they leave so much out of account but that they account for so much on the basis of so little." The same point is an appropriate response to those critical of Hayekian triangulation.

The style of argument in *Time and Money* may appear to some as strangely anachronistic – as theory from the 1930s and pedagogy from the 1960s. This appearance is not without significance. The theory is from the 1930s because it was during that period that capital theory was dropped out of macroeconomics. The pedagogy is reminiscent of the 1960s because Austrian macroeconomics is missing the stage of development that the alternative (Keynesian) macroeconomics was pacing through during that decade. The sequence of frameworks from the Keynesian cross to ISLM to Aggregate-Supply/Aggregate-Demand has no counterpart in Austrian macroeconomics. Instead, we have the Hayekian triangle accompanied by critical assessments and apologetic defenses, followed in time with the *Pure Theory*, which was an unfinished task and strategic miscue, followed by years of neglect. In recent years there has been a scatter of restatements of the Austrian theory, many of which are contorted by the near-obligatory attention to the current concerns of mainstream macroeconomics, such as expectations and lag structure. Not surprisingly, there can be only limited success in reintroducing the old Austrian insights into a macroeconomics whose development over the past half-century has followed an alternative course. Accordingly, if the constructions and argumentation in *Time and Money* are pedagogical throwbacks, partially remedial in nature, they are unapologetically so.

The modern Austrian School is fairly well defined in terms of axiomatic propositions and methodological precepts, but there are significant differences in judgment about the appropriate research agenda. Some members of the school have long turned a blind eye to the issues of business cycles and to macroeconomics more broadly conceived. *Classics in Austrian Economics: A Sampling in the History of a Tradition*, edited by Israel Kirzner (1994), gives little or no hint that the Austrian economists ever asked a macroeconomic question, let alone offered answers that show great insight and much promise for development. And while Kirzner himself has contributed importantly to the development of capital theory, primarily in his *Essays on Capital and Interest: An Austrian Perspective* (1996), he has steered clear of macroeconomics. His introductory essay includes a brief assessment of the developments on this front: "[R]ecent Austrian work on Hayekian cycle theory [and presumably on Austrian macroeconomics generally] seems, on the whole, to fail to draw on the subjectivist, Misesian, tradition which the contemporary Austrian resurgence has done so much to revive" (ibid.: 2). Similarly, Nicolai Foss's *The Austrian School of Modern Economics: Essays in Reassessment* (1994) gives no clue of the existence of a modern Austrian macroeconomics. Karen Vaughn's *Austrian Economics in America: The Migration of a Tradition* (1994) leaves the impression that macroeconomics never reached – or possibly shouldn't have reached – the American shore. And in her recent reflections on the development of the Austrian tradition (1999), she hints that progress is to be measured in part by the school's distancing itself from the issues associated with the business cycle.

The capital-based macroeconomics offered in this volume is intended to help put capital back in macro and help put macro back in modern Austrian economics. This undertaking is bolstered by the judgment of Machlup that Hayek's contribution to capital theory was both fundamental and path-breaking and by the belief that a macroeconomic framework that features the Austrian theory of capital can compare favorably to the alternative frameworks of mainstream macroeconomics.

A readers' guide

The five parts and twelve chapters of this book are arranged to accommodate a variety of backgrounds and interests. Chapter 2 is aimed primarily at fellow macroeconomists and students of macroeconomics who are already familiar with the various modern schools of thought, such as New Classicism and New Keynesianism. These and related schools have become so focused on "expectations" as virtually to require an up-front discussion of the implicit assumptions or understandings about the role of expectations in the performance of the economy and in the effectiveness of macroeconomic policy. Readers not so steeped in the modern tradition of macroeconomics may want to skip Chapter 2 – or possibly save it for a later reading.

The original conception of the book – as a graphical exposition of the Austrian theory of the business cycle – has its realization in Part II, especially Chapters 3 and 4. The ideas in these two chapters – with or without the extensions offered in Chapters 5 and 6 – stand on their own. (Although Chapter 6 is offered as a variation on an Austrian theme, the discussion there breaks loose from the strict confines of the graphical model and discusses risk-related aspects of boom–bust cycles.)

Readers interested in the Keynes–Hayek debate will want to compare the macroeconomics of Chapters 3 and 4 with the macroeconomics of Chapters 7 and 8. These two sets of core chapters, which give shape to Parts II and III, are designed to allow Keynes and Hayek to go head-to-head.

Though designed with the Keynes–Hayek debate in mind, the labor-based framework set out in Chapter 7 allows for revealing perspective on the Keynes–Keynes debate. Conflicting interpretations of Keynes's *General Theory* are partially reconciled by a first-order distinction between policy issues (Chapter 8) and issues of social reform (Chapter 9).

Readers who are interested in the relationship between the Austrian theory and the competing theories of other market-friendly schools of macroeconomic thought will want to pay special attention to Chapters 10 and

11, which make up Part IV and deal with the various forms and outgrowths of Monetarism. The money-based macroeconomics of these political allies, however, is presented with the aid of both the labor-based macroeconomics of Part III and the capital-based macroeconomics of Part II and therefore cannot be read separately from the earlier chapters.

The final chapter can be read in its turn or – for those who read novels this way – in conjunction with the introductory chapter.

2 An agenda for macroeconomics

Adopting a means-ends framework for macroeconomic theorizing is a way of emphasizing the critical time dimension – the time that elapses between the employment of means and the achievement of ends. In a modern, decentralized, capital-intensive economy, the original means and the ultimate ends are linked by the myriad decisions of intervening entrepreneurs. As the market process moves forward, each entrepreneur is guided by circumstances created by the past decisions of all entrepreneurs and by expectations about the future decisions of consumers and of other entrepreneurs. These are the decisions associated with what Ludwig Lachmann (1986: 61) has called a network of plans. The concretization of these plans gives rise to a capital structure, which we will call – to emphasize the time dimension – the intertemporal structure of capital.

Austrian macroeconomics, then, concerns itself with two critical aspects of economic reality: the intertemporal capital structure and entrepreneurial expectations. Mainstream macroeconomics has long ignored the first-mentioned aspect but has become keenly attentive – almost obsessively attentive – to the second. On my interpretation, Lachmann's writings argue for a better balance of attention and suggest that the mainstream's overemphasis of expectations is directly related to its underemphasis of capital structure.

What about expectations?

There is some dispute concerning the Austrian School's attention to expectations as evidenced by conflicting perspectives on the writings of Ludwig von Mises: "Mises always emphasized the role of expectations" (Phelps, 1970b: 129); "Mises hardly ever mentions expectations" (Lachmann, 1976: 58). Is it possible that these seemingly opposing pronouncements are somehow both true? The "always" and even the "hardly ever" (Lachmann didn't say "never") make us suspect that both involve overstatement. But the validity of each derives from the different alternative treatments of expectations to which Misesian economics is being compared. Phelps was providing a contrast to the 1960s view of the trade-off between inflation and unemployment. The idea that this trade-off is a stable one and that it provides a menu of social choice for policy-makers requires a wholesale neglect of expectations. Lachmann was providing a contrast to the 1930s view of investment in an uncertain world. Equilibration, according to the Swedish economists, involves a play-off between expected and realized values of the level of investment; persistent disequilibrium, according to Keynes, is attributable to the absence of any relevant and timely connection between long-term expectations and underlying economic realities. In comparison with Keynes and even the Swedes, Mises underemphasized expectations. This was Lachmann's judgment.

In a letter of August 1989, Lachmann posed to me a direct question about Mises's and Hayek's neglect of expectations (a neglect he referred to in a subsequent letter as "a simple matter of historical fact"). "Do you agree with me that in the 1930s Hayek and Mises made a great mistake in neglecting expectations, in failing to extend Austrian subjectivism from preferences to expectations?" His particular phrasing of this question links it directly to his 1976 article, in which he traced the development of subjectivism "From Mises to Shackle." Also, Lachmann's question was a leading question, followed immediately with "What, in your view, are the most urgent tasks Austrians must now address?" Lachmann himself had spent several decades grappling with expectations. He recognized in an early article ([1943] 1977) that expectations in economic theorizing present us with a unique challenge. They cannot be regarded as exogenous variables. We must be able to give some account of "why they are what they are" (ibid.: 65). But neither can expectations be regarded as endogenous variables. To do so would be to deny their inherent subjectivist quality. This challenge always emphasized but never actually met by Lachmann has been dubbed the "Lachmann problem" by Roger Koppl (1998: 61).

My response to Lachmann did not deal head-on with the Lachmann problem but focused instead on Hayek and Keynes and derived from considerations of strategy. Hayek was trying to counterbalance Keynes, whose theory featured expectations but neglected capital structure. Without an adequate theory of capital, expectations became the wild card in Keynes's arguments. Guided by his "vision" of economic reality, a vision that was set in his mind at an early age, he played this wild card selectively – ignoring expectations when the theory fit his vision, relying heavily on expectations when he had to make it fit. Hayek's countering strategy is made clear in his *Pure Theory of Capital* (1941: 407ff.): "[Our] task has been to bring out the importance of the real factors [as opposed to the psychological factors], which in contemporary discussion are increasingly disregarded." But in countering Keynes's "expectations without capital theory," Hayek produced – or so it could be argued – a "capital theory without expectations." In response to Lachmann's question about the most urgent tasks, I suggested that we need to put capital theory (with expectations) back into macroeconomics and that my inspiration for working in this direction was Lachmann's own writings.

What I saw then as inspiration I see now as legacy. Though exhibiting increasing emphasis on the uncertain future and decreasing confidence that the market's equilibrium tendencies will prevail, Lachmann's writings – from his 1943 "Role of Expectations" article, to his 1956 *Capital and Its Structure*, to his 1986 *The Market as An Economic Process* – were focused sharply on both capital and expectations. During the three decades that separated the two books, his own thinking grew ever closer to Shackle's. The macroeconomy to him became the kaleidic society. The existence of equilibrating forces was not in doubt. But neither was the existence of dis-equilibrating forces. And there was no way to know which, in the end, would win out. Among Austrian economists, Lachmann was virtually alone in his agnosticism about the ability of the market economy to coordinate.

If Lachmann's legacy is to bear fruit, today's Austrian macroeconomists will have to allow their thinking to be guided by the question "What about capital?" But as a preliminary task, they will have to respond effectively to the question that has become the litmus test for modern macroeconomic theorizing: "What about expectations?"

So: what about expectations in today's macroeconomics? In earlier decades, this question could be asked out of concern about emphasis – too little or too much? But more recently the question is posed impishly – with serious doubts that any theory that does not feature so-called rational expectations can survive a candid response. The question has gotten the attention in recent years of defenders as well as critics of Austrian theory and particu-larly of the Austrian theory of the business cycle. But as we have seen, the challenge itself is not new to the Austrians. Hayek ([1939] 1975d) dealt early on with "Price Expectations, Monetary Disturbances, and Malinvest-ments." Lachmann ([1943] 1977 and 1945) raised the issue anew – and with a hint of impishness – arguing that the treatment (or neglect) of expectations in Mises's account of business cycles constitutes the Achilles' heel of the Austrian theory. Mises's glib response (1943), in which he acknowledged an implicit assumption about expectations (their being fairly elastic), suggested that he did not take Lachmann's critical assessment to be a particularly hard-hitting one. More recently, however, critics within the Austrian School (e.g. Butos, 1997) have charged that modern Austrian macroeconomists ignore expectations or, at least, do not deal adequately with them.

Modern defenders of the Austrian theory are often put on the spot to respond to these critics in a way that (1) recognizes the treatment of expec-tations as the *sine qua non* of business cycle theory it has come to be in modern macroeconomics; (2) reconciles the Austrian view with the kernel of truth in the rational expectations theory; and (3) absolves modern expos-itors of Austrian business cycle theory for not giving expectations their due. There is no direct answer, of course, that will satisfy the modern critic who issues the challenge in the form of the rhetorical question: "What about expectations?" – hence the impish tone with which it is posed.

While my response to Lachmann in 1989 focused on the strategic considerations made by Hayek in his battle with Keynes, my reply to the imps
of the 1990s hinges on the fact that Hayek lost the battle. Reflection reveals
that this question, or, more accurately, the context in which it is asked, is
wholly anachronistic. Modern treatments of expectations, which can be
understood only in the context of the macroeconomics that grew out of the
Keynesian revolution, cannot simply be grafted onto the Austrian theory,
whose origins predate Keynes and whose development entailed an explicit
rejection of Keynes's aggregation scheme. Accordingly, a brief history of
macroeconomic thought is prerequisite to a satisfactory answer to any question about the role of expectations in the Austrian theory of the business
cycle.

The Keynesian spur

It was in the 1930s that macroeconomics and, with it, business cycle theory,
broke away as a separate subdiscipline. To describe the breakaway, some
writers use terms such as "Keynesian detour" or "Keynesian diversion,"
which suggest that the path of development was, for a time, less direct
than it might have been; my "Keynesian spur" (analogous to a spur line of
a railway) suggests development in the direction of a dead end. As
Keynesianism worked its way through the profession, macroeconomics came
to be defined not as a set of issues concerning the overall performance of
the economy but as a particular way of theorizing about the economy. For
purposes of gauging the economy's ability to employ resources, the new
macroeconomics focused on the aggregate demand for output relative to the
economy's potential output. For purposes of dealing with the issue of
stability and charting the dynamic properties of the economy (such as those
implied by the multiplier-accelerator process), the output of investment
goods was separated from the output of consumption goods: investment is
the unstable component, and consumption is the stable component of aggregate demand. The summary treatment of inputs was even more severe.
Consistent with the strong labor-market orientation, inputs were treated
as if they consisted exclusively of labor or could be reckoned in labor-
equivalent terms. The structure of capital was assumed fixed, the extent of
its actual utilization changing in virtual lockstep with changes in the
employment of labor. Income earned by workers was reckoned as the going
wage rate times the number of (skill-adjusted) worker hours, and changes
in labor income were taken to imply proportional changes in total income.

Dropping out of the macroeconomic picture was any notion that labor
income may move against other forms of income, as the classical economists had emphasized, as well as the notion that changes in the structure
of capital – more of some kinds, less of other kinds – may figure importantly in the economy's overall performance. These changes in relative
magnitudes, by virtue of their being relative changes, were no part of the

new macroeconomics. In fact, it was the masking of all the economic forces that assert themselves *within* the designated aggregate magnitudes, particularly those that are at work within the investment aggregate, that allowed macroeconomics to make such a clean break from the pre-Keynesian modes of thought.

Analytical simplicity was achieved in part by the aggregation *per se* and in part by the fact that the featured input aggregate was labor rather than capital. All the thorny issues of capital – involving unavoidable ambiguities in defining it, measuring it, and theorizing about it – were set aside as the simpler issues of labor became the near-exclusive focus. The pre-eminence of labor in this regard seemed almost self-justifying not only on the grounds of its relative simplicity but also on the grounds that it is our concern for workers, after all, and their periodically falling victim to economy-wide bouts of unemployment that justify our study of macroeconomic phenomena. Despite its being descriptively accurate, "labor-based macroeconomics" is a term not in general use today but only because virtually all modern macroeconomics *is* labor-based.

A few noncontroversial propositions about spending on consumption goods as it relates to aggregate income are enough to establish a clear dependence of aggregate demand and hence aggregate income on investment spending, which – absent capital theory – seems to be rooted in psychology rather than in economics (Keynes, 1936: 161–3). It follows in short order that an economy dominated by such a dependency and constricted by an assumed fixity of the wage rate is inherently unstable. Movements in the investment aggregate, up or down, give rise to magnified movements – in the same direction – of income and consumption. Classical theory is reduced to the minimal role of identifying the level of income that constitutes full employment, implying that changes in the Keynesian aggregates are real changes for levels below full employment and nominal changes for levels above.

A comparison of the Keynesian analytics with those that predate the breakaway of macroeconomics confirms that what counts in classical theorizing is the interplay among landlords, workers, capitalists, and entrepreneurs. Relative and sometimes opposing movements of the incomes associated with these four categories give the economy its stability. For Keynes, all such relative movements were downplayed or ignored. It is as if an automotive engineer, in his quest for analytical simplicity, had modeled a four-wheeled vehicle as a wheelbarrow and then declared it inherently unstable. To impose stability on the Keynesian wheelbarrow, some external entity would have to have a firm grip on both handles. Those handles, of course, took the form of fiscal policy and monetary policy. The mixed economy, whose market forces are continually countered by policy activism, could achieve a level of performance that a wholly private macroeconomy could never be able to achieve on its own. If sufficiently enlightened about the inherent flaws of capitalism, the fiscal and monetary authorities could keep the Keynesian wheelbarrow between the hedgeposts of unemployment and inflation.

Although simple in the extreme, highly aggregative, labor-based macroeconomics was ripe for development. Questions about each of the aggregates and their relations to one another gave rise to virtually endless variations on a theme. What about consumer behavior? Beyond the simple linear relationship with current income, consumers may behave in accordance with the relative-income hypothesis (Duesenberry), the life-cycle hypothesis (Modigliani), or the permanent-income hypothesis (Friedman). What about the interest elasticity of the demand for money and of the demand for investment funds? Different assumptions, as might apply in the short run and the long run, allowed for some reconciliation between Keynesian and Monetarist views. What about wealth effects? What about investment lags? What about differential stickiness between wages and prices?

The "what-about" questions served to enrich the research agenda of macroeconomics in all directions. The highly aggregative, labor-based macroeconomics survived them all, even thrived on them, by providing answers that set the stage for still more what-about questions. Even the critical question, "What about the real-cash-balance effect?", whose answer initially separated the Keynesians from the classicists, ultimately worked in favor of policy activism. The Keynesians embraced the notion that the economy could settle into an equilibrium characterized by persisting unemployment. Critics such as Haberler, Pigou, and eventually Patinkin argued that falling wages and prices would increase the real value of money holdings and that the spending out of these real cash balances would restore the economy to full employment. That is, even with all the other equilibrating forces buried deep in Keynes's macroeconomic aggregates, there remained a single margin (between money and output) on which to achieve a full-employment equilibrium. Real cash balances became, in effect, a balancing act that allowed the market economy to ride the Keynesian wheelbarrow as if it were a unicycle! Keynesians could concede the theoretical point while making the classically oriented critics look impractical if not downright foolish. If the critics willingly accepted Keynes's aggregation scheme, they would have to accept the policy implication of his theory as well. Considerations of practicality strongly favor a policy activism that takes the macroeconomy to be a Keynesian wheelbarrow rather than a policy of *laissez-faire* that presumes it to be a classical unicycle.

The one exception to the agenda-expanding queries was the question that eventually came to be dreaded by practitioners of the new macroeconomics: What about expectations? In the face of the Monetarist counter-revolution and particularly the introduction of the expectations-augmented Phillips curve, it was no longer acceptable to assume that workers expect stable prices even as their real wage rate is being continually and dramatically eroded by inflation. The notion of a stable downward-sloping Phillips curve was no longer possible to maintain. Allowing workers to adjust their expectations of next year's rate of inflation on the basis of last year's experience did not much improve the theory's logical consistency or preserve its policy implications. The short-run Phillips curve was not exploitable in any welfare-enhancing sense. Even half-serious attempts to answer the question about expectations led to a contraction rather than an expansion of the research program. Logically consistent and rigorous answers led to a virtual implosion. If macroeconomists could provide simple answers to the what-about questions, why couldn't market participants? Some entrepreneurs and speculators could literally figure out the same things that the macroeconomists had figured out. Others could mimic these macro-savvy market participants, and still others could eventually catch on if only by stumbling around in an economy where the highest profits go to those most in the know. Any theory about systematic macroeconomic relationships and certainly any policy recommendation would have to be based on the assumption of rational expectations.

Embracing the rational-expectations theory had the effects of bringing long-run conclusions into the short run (Maddock and Carter, 1982), denying the possibility of using fiscal and monetary policy to stimulate or stabilize the economy (Sargent and Wallace, 1975 and 1976), and – despite the fact that these ideas were an outgrowth of Monetarism – questioning the importance of money in theorizing about the macroeconomy (Long and Plosser, 1983). The sequential attempts to deal with expectations became more and more directed towards preserving the internal logic of macroeconomics at the expense of maintaining a link between macroeconomic theory and macroeconomic reality. All too soon, the very idea of business cycles was purged of any meaning that might connect this term with actual historical events.

Macroeconomics in the hands of the New Classical economists, who tend to judge all other macroeconomic theories in terms of their treatment of expectations, lost the flavor but not the essence of its highly aggregative forerunners. The 1970s witnessed a search by macroeconomists for their microeconomic moorings. That is, recognizing that macroeconomics had pulled anchor in the 1930s and had been adrift for four decades, they sought to re-anchor it in the fundamentals. The actual movement back to the fundamentals, however, affected form more than substance. The macroeconomic aggregates were replaced by representative agents. But the illusion of these agents forming expectations, making choices and otherwise doing their own thing is just that, an illusion. Kirman (1992: 119) refers to this mode of theorizing as "primitive [and] fundamentally erroneous."

What the representative agent represents is the aggregate. Further, the things that the agent is imagined to be doing leave little scope for theorizing at either a microeconomic or a macroeconomic level. Phelps (1970a: 5), who pioneered this search for microfoundations, clearly recognized the nature of the New Classical theorizing: "On the ice-covered terrain of the Walrasian economy, the question of a connection between aggregate demand and the employment level is a little treacherous." The terrain is featureless, and the individuals, aka agents, are indistinguishable from the representative agent. (One is reminded of the once-popular poster showing ten thousand penguins dotting an ice-scape – with an anonymous penguin in the back ranks belting out the title bar of *I Gotta Be Me*.) In typical New Classical models, the ice-scape is an especially bleak one, allowing for the existence of only one commodity. And to rule out such considerations as decisions about storing the commodity, leasing it, or capitalizing the value of its services, the single commodity is itself conceived as a service indistinguishable from the labor that renders it. This construction eliminates the need to distinguish even between the input and the output. In order to keep such an economy from degenerating into autarky, with each penguin rendering the service to himself, we are to think in terms of some particular service which, due to technological – or anatomical – considerations, one penguin has to render to another. "Back-scratching services" is offered as the paradigm case (Barro, 1981: 83).

In their zeal to isolate the issue of expectations and elevate it to the status they believe it deserves in macroeconomics, the New Classical economists have produced models whose sterility is matched by no other. Theorizing centers on the question of whether or not a change in the demand for the commodity is a real change or only a nominal change. The expectation that a change will prove to be only a nominal one implies that no real supply-side response is called for; the expectation that a change will prove to be a real one implies the need for a corresponding reallocation of the representative penguin's time – between scratching backs and consuming leisure.

In order even to raise the issue of cyclical variation in output, New Classical macroeconomists, whose models are constructed to deal explicitly and rigorously with expectations, must contrive some time element between (1) the observation of a change in demand and (2) the realization of the true nature (nominal or real) of the change. A construction introduced by Phelps (1970a: 6) involves a multiplicity of islands, each with its own underlying economic realities but all under the province of a single monetary authority. (Here, we overlook the fact that the very existence of money on the New Classical ice-scape presents a puzzle in its own right.) In accordance with the fundamental truth in the quantity theory of money, a monetary expansion has a lasting influence only on nominal variables. Thus, in Phelps's construction, real changes are local; nominal changes are global. The representative penguin on a given island observes instantly each change in demand for the service but discovers only later (on the basis of information from distant islands) whether the change is nominal or real. The microeconomics of maximizing behavior in the face of uncertainty allows us to conclude that even before discovering the true nature of the change in demand, the penguins will respond to the change as if it were at least partially real. Monetary manipulation, then, can cause temporary changes in real magnitudes. This is the model that underlies the New Classical monetary misperception theory of the business cycle.

An alternative development of New Classicism, one that avoids the contrived and theoretically troublesome notion of monetary misperception, simply denies the existence of business cycles as conventionally conceived – or as modeled with the aid of the distinction between local and global information. According to real business cycle theory, what appear to be cyclical variations in macroeconomic magnitudes are actually nothing more than market adjustments to randomly occurring technology shocks to the economy – even if the shocks themselves cannot always be independently identified. Changes in the money supply have nothing to do with these adjustments (or are an effect rather than a cause of them). Further, the adjustments take place at an optimum, or profit-maximizing, pace (Nelson and Plosser, 1982 and Prescott, 1986). Whereas conventional macroeconomics attempts to track the cyclical variation of the economy's output around its trend-line growth path, real business cycle theory denies that trend-line growth can be meaningfully defined. It holds that actual variations in output reflect variations in the economy's potential. According to this strand of New Classicism (and despite its being labeled real business cycle theory), movements in the macroeconomy's input and output magnitudes are not actually cyclical in any economically relevant sense.

Still another alternative development closely tied to the idea of rational expectation is one that recognizes the possibility of macroeconomic downturns but denies any role to misperceptions. The variations in output can be attributed to certain obstacles (costs) that prevent the instant adjustment of nominal magnitudes. Technology shocks need not be the only source of change. Changes in the money supply can affect the economy, too. There are no significant information lags, but penguins cannot translate changes in demand instantaneously into the appropriate changes in nominal magnitudes. Prices are sticky. The stickiness, however, can be explained in terms of optimizing behavior and rational expectations. So-called menu costs (the costs of actually producing new menus, catalogs, and price tags) stand in the way of instantaneous price adjustments. These are the ideas of new Keynesian theory (Ball *et al.*, 1988) – "Keynesian" because of price stickiness; "new" because the stickiness is not indicative of irrational behavior. (We will argue in Chapter 11 that new Keynesian ideas in the context of a complex decentralized capital-intensive economy are worthy of attention.)

In response to the question "What about expectations?", we get New Classical monetary misperception theory, real business cycle theory, and new Keynesian theory. This is the state of modern macroeconomics. While each of these theories include rigorous demonstrations that the assumptions about expectations are consistent with the theory itself, none are accompanied by persuasive reasons for believing that there is a connection between the theoretical construct and the actual performance of the economy over a sequence of booms and busts. Applicability has been sacrificed to rigor. The Keynesian spur has led us to this dead end.

Meeting the challenge to the Austrian theory

The very fact that the Austrian theory of the business cycle is offered as a theory applicable to many actual episodes of boom and bust – from the Great Depression to the Bush recession – seems to raise the suspicions of modern critics. If the theory has maintained its applicability, it obviously has not suffered the implosion that follows from the attempt to deal adequately – rigorously – with expectations. The critic imagines that he can stand flat-footed in front of an Austrian business cycle theorist, ask "What about expectations?" and then step back to watch the Austrian theory degenerate into some story about back-scratching penguins. The questioner expects that the Austrian theorist will first grapple ineffectively for an acceptable answer and then finally realize the true significance of this implosion-inducing question.

Some modern Austrians (Butos and Koppl, 1993) have argued that dealing effectively with expectations may be a matter of doing the right kind of cognitive psychology. They suggest that Hayek's *The Sensory Order* (1952), which deals with sensory data in the context of the structure of the human mind, may be relevant here. In this view, dealing with expectations consists not of choosing among alternative hypotheses (static, adaptive, rational) but of providing a theoretical account of the mental process through which expectations are formed and then integrating this theory with the theory of the business cycle. It is as if we must begin our story with photons striking the retinas of the entrepreneurs and end it with the ticker tape reporting the consequent capital gains and losses. This interdisciplinary exercise may well have some pay-offs. But surely it is doubtful that such a merging of cognitive psychology and macroeconomics would provide answers that would satisfy the critics for whom rational expectations have become a bedrock assumption.

In light of the evolution of modern macroeconomic thought (from its break with the rest of economics and particularly with capital theory, to its simplification on the basis of the now conventional macroeconomic aggregates, to its blossoming in the hands of practitioners exploring the many variations on a theme, to its eventual implosion in the face of embarrassing questions about expectations), the Austrians are ill-advised to take the question about expectations at face value. "What about expectations?" proved to be an embarrassing question for conventional macroeconomists; it need not be an embarrassing one for Austrian economists, whose theory has not suffered the same evolutionary fate. Further, the Austrians can hardly be expected to resist embarrassing the modern business cycle theorists by simply turning the impish question around and asking: "Expectations about what?" About changes in the overall levels of prices and wages? About price and quantity changes in a one-commodity world as perceived by a representative agent? About real and nominal changes in the demand for back scratching? It should go without saying that a satisfactory answer to the

"Expectations about what?" question is a strict prerequisite to a satisfactory answer to the "What about expectations?" question. And for the Austrians, the prerequisite question is to be answered in terms of the macroeconomics that predates its breaking away from the fundamentals.

In the Austrian view, the issues of macroeconomics are inextricably bound up with the issues of microeconomics and particularly with capital theory. The entrepreneurs, no one of whom is representative of the economy as a whole, influence and are influenced by one another as they bid for resources with which to carry out or possibly to modify their production plans. Conflicting plans involving the provision of immediately consumable services, such as Barro's back scratching, can be quickly reconciled as potential consumers make decisions about whether to purchase this service or to consume leisure and as they choose among the alternative providers of it. If an economy could be usefully modeled as the market for a single service provided by a representative supplier, there would not likely be any issues that would give macroeconomics a distinct subject matter. Important macroeconomic issues arise precisely to the extent that the economics of back scratching is *not* the paradigm case, which is to say, to the extent that inputs and outputs are not temporally coincident. If resources must be committed well before the ultimate satisfaction of consumer demand, then capital goods in some form must exist during the period that spans the initial expectations of the entrepreneur and the final choices of consumers. These capital goods can be conceived to include human capital as well as capital in the more conventional sense and to include durable capital goods as well as capital in the sense of goods in process.

It is useful to think of the production process as being divided into stages of production such that the output of one stage is sold as input to a subsequent stage. Hayek ([1935] 1967) employed a simple right triangle to depict the capital-using economy – which gave him a leg up on Keynes, who paid no attention to production time. This little piece of geometry will become a key element of our capital-based macroeconomic model in Chapter 3. One leg of the triangle represents consumer spending, the macroeconomic magnitude that had the attention of both Keynes and Hayek; the other leg tracks the goods-in-process as the individual plans of producers transform labor and other resources into the goods that consumers buy. In Hayek's construction, human capital and durable capital are ruled out for the sake of keeping the theory tractable and developing a heuristic model, leaving us with the relatively simple conception of capital as goods in process with a sequence of entrepreneurs having command over these goods as they mature into consumable output. Still, there is a nontrivial answer to the "Expectations about what?" question. Complicating matters, however, is the fact that the sequence of stages is far from linear: there are many feedback loops, multiple-purpose outputs, and other instances of nonlinearities. Further, each stage may also involve the use of durable – but depreciating – capital goods, relatively specific and relatively nonspecific capital goods, and capital goods that are related with various degrees of substitutability and complementarity to the capital goods in other stages of production. These are the complications emphasized by Lachmann in his *Capital and Its Structure*.

It is this context in which the Austrians can address the "Expectations about what?" question. The proximate objects of entrepreneurial expectations relevant to a particular stage of production include prices of inputs, which are the outputs of earlier stages, and prices of outputs, which are inputs for subsequent stages. The expected price differentials (between inputs and outputs) have to be assessed in the light of current loan rates and of alternative uses of existing capital goods. And judgments have to be made about possible changes in credit conditions and in the market conditions for the eventual consumer goods to which a particular stage of production contributes. Price, wage, and interest-rate changes will have an effect on entrepreneurs' decisions, and their decisions will have an effect on prices, wages, and interest rates. This interdependency is what justifies the general conception of the market as an economic process.

The market process facilitates the translation of the underlying economic realities – resource availabilities, technology, and consumer preferences (including intertemporal preferences) – into production decisions guided by the expectations of the entrepreneurs. The process plays itself out differently depending upon whether the interest rate on which it is based is a faithful reflection of consumers' time preferences or, owing to credit expansion by the central bank, a distortion of those preferences. In the first case, the economy experiences sustainable growth; in the second, it experiences boom and bust. This, the essence of the Austrian theory of the business cycle (Mises *et al.*, [1978] 1996; Garrison, 1986a), will be presented graphically in Chapter 4.

Two "assumptions" (a more appropriate term here might be "understandings") about expectations are implicit in the Austrian theory: (1) the entrepreneurs do not already know – and cannot behave *as if* they already know – the underlying economic realities whose changing characteristics are conveyed by changes in prices, wages, and interest rates; and (2) prices, wages, and interest rates tend to facilitate the coordination of economic decisions and to keep those decisions in line with the underlying economic realities. Thinking broadly in terms of a market solution to the economic problem, we see that a violation of the first assumption implies a denial of the problem, while a violation of the second assumption implies a denial that the market is a viable solution. Taken together, these two assumptions do not allow us to categorize the Austrians' treatment of expectations as static, adaptive, or rational, as these terms have come to be used. But they do allow for a treatment of expectations that is consistent with the view that there *is* an economic problem and that the market *is*, at least potentially, a viable solution to that problem. And dealing with expectations in the context of a market process does give us some basis for a partial solution to the Lachmann problem identified early in this chapter. Expectations can be regarded as endogenous in a special sort of way when the market process has been set against itself by policies that affect the intertemporal allocation of resources.

Consistency provides a standard by which the alternative treatments of expectations can be compared. After all, the idea of rational expectations stemmed from the recognition that the assumptions of static expectations and even of adaptive expectations were often inconsistent with the theories in which they were incorporated. Lucas (1987: 13) refers to the rational expectation hypothesis as a consistency axiom for economics. As such, the adjective "rational" refers neither to a characteristic of the market participant whose expectations are said to be rational nor to a quality of the expectations *per se*. It refers only to the relationship between the assumption about expectations and the theory in which it is incorporated. The New Classical assumption of rational expectations may well be consistent with the monetary misperception theory as set out in a Barro-style back-scratching model. But note that both the assumption and the model are inconsistent with there being a significant economic problem for which the market might provide a viable solution. Accordingly, a rational-expectations assumption plucked from a New Classical formulation and inserted into Austrian theory – or into any other pre-Keynesian theory that affirms the existence of an economic problem – would involve an *in*consistency, and hence, by the standard of consistency, would no longer be "rational." That is, it is not logically consistent to claim (1) that there is a representative agent who already has (or behaves as if he or she already has) the information about the underlying economic realities independent of current prices, wage rates and interest rates *and* (2) that it is prices, wage rates and interest rates that convey this information.

The distinction between local and global information together with the information lag that attaches to global information allows for a telling point of comparison of New Classical and Austrian views. In the New Classical construction, this knowledge problem is contrived for the sake of modeling misperception. The representative agent sees changes in money prices immediately but sees evidence of changes in the money supply only belatedly. The agent does not know immediately, then, whether the change in the money prices reflects a real change or only a nominal change. In the Austrian theory, the treatment of the knowledge problem rests upon a different distinction between two kinds of knowledge – a distinction introduced by Hayek for the purpose of calling attention to the nature of the economic problem broadly conceived. Hayek (1945b) distinguishes between the knowledge of the particular circumstances of time and place and knowledge of the structure of the economy. Roughly, the distinction is one between market savvy and theoretical understanding. It is not a contrivance for the purposes of modeling misperception but rather an acknowledgment of the fundamental insight most commonly associated with Adam Smith:

the market economy works without the market participants themselves having to understand just how it works.

The strong version of rational expectations employed by New Classicism exhibits a certain symmetry with the notion of rational planning conceived by advocates of economic centralization. The notions of both rational expectations and rational planning fail to give adequate recognition to Hayek's distinction between the two kinds of knowledge. Both employ the term "rational" to suggest, in effect, that reasonable assumptions about one kind of knowledge can (rationally) be extended to the other kind. Central planning could be an efficient means of allocating resources if the planners, who, we will assume, have a good theoretical understanding of the calculus of optimization, also had (or behaved as if they had) the knowledge that is actually dispersed among a multitude of entrepreneurs and other market participants. Symmetrically, monetary policy would have no systematic effect on markets if entrepreneurs and other market participants, whose knowledge of the particular circumstances of time and place are mobilized by those markets, also had (or behaved as if they had) a theoretical understanding of macroeconomic relationships. To recognize Hayek's distinction and its significance is simply to acknowledge that central planning is, in fact, not efficient and that monetary policy can, in fact, have systematic effects.

Dealing with expectations in the context of Hayek's distinction rather than in the context of the contrived distinction between global and local knowledge adds a dimension to Austrian economics that can be no part of New Classicism. While the global/local distinction is stipulated to separate two mutually exclusive kinds of knowledge, the two kinds of knowledge identified by Hayek exhibit an essential blending at the margin. Market participants must have *some* understanding of how markets work, if only to know that lowering a price is the appropriate response to a surplus and raising a price is the appropriate response to a shortage. Suppliers of particular products as well as traders in organized markets have a strong incentive to understand much more about their respective markets – about current and expected changes in market conditions and the implications for future prices. They know enough to make John Muth's (1961) treatment of expectations as applied to the hog market seem not only "rational" but eminently plausible. Symmetrically, economists-cum-policy-makers must have some knowledge about the particulars of the economy in order to apply their theories to various existing circumstances. And to prescribe policies aimed at a particular goal, such as a specific unemployment rate or inflation rate, they would have to have a substantial amount of market information – about how changes in actual market conditions affect, for instance, the demand for labor and the demand for money.

Further, the extent of the overlap is itself a matter of costs and benefits as experienced differentially by policy-makers and by market participants. For policy-makers, additions to their theoretical understanding are likely to be strongly complementary to existing understandings and may even have synergistic effects, while additional knowledge of the particular circumstances of time and place would likely involve high costs and low benefits. A symmetrical statement can be made about entrepreneurs with respect to costs and benefits of increased market savvy as compared to increased theoretical understanding. In general, specialists in one kind of knowledge experience sharply rising costs of – and sharply declining benefits to – the other kind of knowledge. Putting the matter in terms of costs and benefits suggests that the actual and/or perceived costs and benefits can change. Undoubtedly, the extent to which policy-makers and market participants make use of *both* kinds of knowledge is dependent on the institutional setting and the policy regime. A change in the direction of increased policy activism on the part of the central bank, for instance, will increase the benefits to entrepreneurs and other market participants of their understanding the short- and long-run relationships linking money growth to interest rates, prices, and wages. Stated negatively, entrepreneurs who experience a sequence of episodes in which the central bank is implementing stabilization policy or attempting to "grow the economy" may face a high cost of *not* understanding how money-supply decisions affect the market process.

There is an overlap between the two kinds of knowledge and the extent of the overlap is itself a result of the market process. These aspects of Austrian theory have no counterpart in New Classical theory. Expectations will be based on the knowledge of particular circumstances of time and place *plus* the understanding that corresponds to the overlap. Expectations are not rational in the strong sense of that term, but they do become more rational with increased levels of policy activism and with cumulative experience with the consequences of it. Equivalently stated, expectations are adaptive, but they adapt not just to changes in some particular price, wage rate, or interest rate, but also to the changing level of understanding that corresponds to the overlap. Finally and significantly, further development of the issue of expectations in the context of two kinds of knowledge and the market as an economic process will involve an expansion rather than an implosion of the Austrian research program.

What about capital?

If we think in terms of market solutions to economic problems, we must accord expectations a crucial role. But that role is overplayed if it is assumed that expectations come ready-made on the basis of information that is actually revealed only as the market process unfolds; it is underplayed if it is assumed that expectations are and forever remain at odds with economic realities despite the unfolding of the market process. Either assumption would detract from the equally crucial role played by the market process itself, which alone can continuously inform expectations. On reflection, we see that the near-obsessive focus on expectations in modern labor-based macroeconomics owes much to the sterility of the theoretical constructions. There is simply not much of anything else to focus upon.

What about capital? Much of Austrian theory is aimed – either directly or indirectly – at providing a satisfying answer to this question. And macro-economists who think in terms of entrepreneurial decisions in the context of a complex intertemporal capital structure have at the same time written much "about" expectations – even if that very word does not appear in their every sentence. Ludwig Lachmann's attention to expectations was always explicit as was his attention to capital and its structure. Accordingly, we can credit him for setting an important agenda for macroeconomics. As the following chapters are designed to show, capital-based macroeconomics with due attention to entrepreneurial expectations and the market process can achieve a richness, a relevance and a plausibility that are simply beyond the reach of the modern labor-based macroeconomics and its assumption of rational expectations.

Part II
Capital and time

3 Capital-based macroeconomics

Macroeconomics in the Austrian tradition owes its uniqueness to the Austrian capital theory on which it is based. This is the central message of Chapter 2. But as hinted in Chapter 1, there are critics within the tradition who take "Austrian Macroeconomics" to be a term at war with itself. The Austrian label usually denotes (1) subjectivism, as applied to both values and expectations; and (2) methodological individualism with its emphasis on the differences among individuals – differences that account for the give and take of the marketplace and for the very nature of the market process. These essential features of Austrianism stand in contrast to the features of the macroeconomics that has evolved over the last several decades.

Conventional macroeconomics has developed a reputation for abstracting from individual market participants and focusing primarily, if not exclusively, on aggregate magnitudes, such as the economy's total output and its employment of labor. Even when the incentives and constraints relevant to individuals are brought into view, the focus is on the so-called representative agent, which deliberately abstracts from the interactions among the different agents and hence represents, if anything, the averages or aggregates of conventional macroeconomics.

The graphical analysis presented in this chapter allows us to deal with the enduring issues of macroeconomics without losing sight of the market process that gives rise to them. To base macroeconomics on capital theory – or, more precisely, to base it on a theory of the market process in the context of an intertemporal capital structure – is to maintain a strong link to the ideas of the Austrian School. Entrepreneurs operating at different stages of production make decisions on the basis of their own knowledge, hunches and expectations, informed by movements in prices, wages, and interest rates. Collectively, these entrepreneurial decisions result in a particular allocation of resources over time.

The intertemporal allocation may be internally consistent and hence sustainable, or it may involve some systematic internal inconsistency, in which case its sustainability is threatened. The distinction between sustainable and unsustainable patterns of resource allocation is, or should be, a major focus of macroeconomic theorizing. Systematic inconsistencies can cause the market process to turn against itself. If market signals – and especially interest rates – are "wrong," inconsistencies will develop. Movements of resources will be met by "countermovements," as recognized early by Ludwig von Mises ([1912] 1953: 363). What initially appears to be genuine economic growth can turn out to be a disruption of the market process attributable to some disingenuous intervention on the part of the monetary authority.

Though committed to the precepts of methodological individualism, the Austrian economists need not shy away from the issues of macroeconomics. Some features of the market process are macroeconomic in their scope. Production takes time and involves a sequence of stages of production; exchanges among different producers operating in different stages as well as sales at the final stage to consumers are facilitated by the use of a common medium of exchange. Time and money are the common denominators of macroeconomic theorizing. While the causes of macroeconomic phenomena can be traced to the actions of individual market participants, the consequences manifest themselves broadly as variations in macroeconomic magnitudes. The most straightforward concretization of the macroeconomics of time and money is the intertemporal structure of capital – hence, capital-based macroeconomics.

Capital-based macroeconomics rejects the Keynes-inspired distinction between macroeconomics and the economics of growth. This unfortunate distinction, in fact, derives from the inadequate attention to the intertemporal capital structure. Conventional macroeconomics deals with economy-wide disequilibria while abstracting from issues involving a changing stock of capital; modern growth theory deals with a growing capital stock while abstracting from issues involving economy-wide disequilibria. With this criterion for defining the subdisciplines within economics, the thorny issues of disequilibrium and the thorny issues of capital theory are addressed one at a time. Our contention is that economic reality mixes the two issues in ways that render the one-at-a-time treatments profoundly inadequate. Economy-wide disequilibria in the context of a changing capital structure escape the attention of both conventional macroeconomists and modern growth theorists. But the issues involving the market's ability to allocate resources over time have a natural home in capital-based macroeconomics. Here, the short-run issues of cyclical variation and the long-run issues of secular expansion enjoy a blend that is simply ruled out by construction in mainstream theorizing.

The elements of capital-based macroeconomics

Three elementary graphical devices serve as building blocks for an Austrian-oriented, or capital-based, macroeconomics. Graphs representing (1) the market for loanable funds; (2) the production possibilities frontier; and

(3) the intertemporal structure of production all have reputable histories. The first two are well known to all macroeconomists; the third is well known to many Austrian economists. The novelty of the capital-based macroeconomics presented in this and the two succeeding chapters is in their integration and application. Auxiliary graphs that link markets for capital goods and markets for labor can extend the analysis and help establish the relationship between our capital-based macroeconomics and the more conventional labor-based macroeconomics.

The fundamentals of capital-based macroeconomics is set forth with the aid of a three-quadrant, interlocking graphical framework. Once assembled, our graphical construction can be put through its paces to deal with issues of secular growth, changes in resource endowments and in technology, intertemporal preference changes, booms and busts, and more. These graphics are not offered as a first step towards the determination of the equilibrium values of the various macroeconomic magnitudes. Rather, this framework is intended to provide a convenient basis for discussing the market process that allocates resources over time. (A framework and the discussion of the issues stand in the same relationship to one another as a hat rack and the hats.)

The explicit attention to intertemporal allocation of resources allows for a sharp distinction between sustainable and unsustainable growth. The underlying consistency (or inconsistency) between consumer preferences and production plans will determine whether the market process will play itself out or do itself in. Our graphical framework demonstrates the coherence of the Austrian macroeconomics that was inspired early in the last century by Mises, who drew ideas from still earlier writers. It also sheds light on contemporary political debate. Nowadays candidates for the presidency and other high offices vie with one another for votes on the basis of their pledges to "grow the economy"; opposing candidates differ primarily in terms of just how they plan to grow it. The political rhetoric overlooks the fundamental issues of the very nature of economic growth. Is growth something that simply happens when the economy is left to its own devices? Or, is it something that a policy-maker does to the economy? Is the verb "to grow," as used in economic debate, an intransitive verb or a transitive verb? Capital-based macroeconomics provides us with reasons for associating this fundamentally intransitive verb with sustainable growth and its transitive variant with unsustainable growth. That is, the economy grows, but attempts to grow it can be self-defeating.

Our graphical framework serves also to demonstrate the essential unity between the Austrian theory of the business cycle, which is typically set out with reference only to the Hayekian triangle, and other implications of the Austrian macroeconomic relationships. The inclusion of the market for loanable funds allows us to deal with the consequences of the policy of deficit finance. The implications of mainstream theories that the method of financing government spending is largely if not wholly irrelevant (the Ricardian

Equivalence Theorem) and even the summary judgments of Austrian economists to this same effect will be called into question. The inclusion of the
production possibilities frontier allows us to deal with certain aspects of
tax reform. These and related issues are discussed in Chapter 5. We turn now
to the individual elements of the graphical construction.

The market for loanable funds

"Loanable funds" is a commonly used generic term to refer to both sides
of the market that is brought into balance by movements of the interest
rate broadly conceived. The supply of loanable funds, which represents the
willingness to lend at different interest rates, and the demand for loanable
funds, which represents the eagerness to borrow, are shown in Figure 3.1.
For use in macroeconomics, two modifications to this straightforward interpretation are needed, both of which are common to macroeconomic
theorizing. First, consumer lending is netted out on the supply side of this
market. That is, each instance of consumer lending represents saving on
the part of the lender and dissaving on the part of the borrower. Net
lending, then, is saving in the macroeconomically relevant sense. It is the
saving by all income earners made available to the business community to
finance investment, to facilitate capital accumulation, to maintain and
expand the economy's capital structure. Second, though narrowed to exclude
consumer loans, the lending and borrowing represented in the supply and
demand for loanable funds are broadened to include retained earnings and
saving in the form of the purchasing of equity shares. Retained earnings
can be understood as funds that a business firm lends to (and borrows from)
itself. Equity shares are included on the grounds of their strong family
resemblance, macroeconomically speaking, to debt instruments. The distinction between debt and equity, which is vitally important in a theory of the
structure of finance, is largely dispensable in our treatment of the structure
of capital. The supply of loanable funds, then, represents that part of total
income not spent on consumer goods but put to work instead earning
interest (or dividends).

Böhm-Bawerk, who drew heavily on the classical tradition, thought of
the loanable funds market as the market for "subsistence" – a term that is
avoided here only because of the classical inclination to take the subsistence
fund as fixed and to see it as a stock of consumption goods for sustaining
the labor force during the production period. In view of the netting out of
consumer lending and the broadening to include retained earnings and
equity shares, "loanable funds" may be better understood as "investable
resources," a term that emphasizes the purpose of the borrowing. This understanding is consistent with that of Keynes (1936: 175): "[According to the
classical theory], investment represents the demand for investable resources
and saving represents the supply, whilst the rate of interest is the 'price'
of investable resources at which the two are equated."

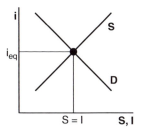

Figure 3.1 The market for loanable funds (or for investable resources).

Beyond the adjustments mentioned above, we should recognize that there remains a small portion of income which is neither spent nor lent. The possibility for holding funds liquid puts some potential slippage into our construction. Money holdings constitute saving in the sense of their not being spent on current consumption, but this form of saving translates only in an indirect way into loanable funds. Our graphical construction can easily allow for variation in liquidity preferences and hence in the demand for money: to the extent that an increase in saving is accompanied by an increase in liquidity preferences, it does not substantially increase the supply of loanable funds and hence has little effect on the rate of interest. However, in contrast to its role in Keynesian macroeconomics, this particular slippage is not a primary focus of the analysis.

Consistent with our understanding of the supply of loanable funds, the demand for loanable funds represents the borrowers' intentions to participate in the economy's production process. Investment in this context refers not to financial instruments but to plant and equipment, tools and machinery. More broadly, it refers to the means of production, which include goods in process as well as durable capital goods and human capital. In some contexts investment could include even consumer durables (automobiles and refrigerators), in which case, only the services of those consumer durables would count as consumption. However, to align the market for loanable funds with other elements in the graphical analysis, consumer durables themselves are categorized as consumption rather than investment (see pp. 47–8). While our graphical apparatus is most straightforwardly interpreted on the basis of a goods-in-process conception of investment goods, our discussion often allows for alternative conceptions.

The demand for loanable funds reflects the willingness of individuals in the business community operating in the various stages of production to pay input prices now in order to sell output at some (expected) price in the future. With consumers spending part of their incomes on the output of the final stage of production and saving the rest, the market for loanable funds facilitates the coordination of production plans with consumer preferences. Individual investment decisions in the business community tend to bring into uniformity the interest rate available in the loan market more narrowly conceived and the interest rates implicit in the relative prices of outputs in comparison with inputs of the stages of production. The market process that allocates resources intertemporally consists precisely of individuals taking advantage of profit opportunities in the form of interest-rate discrepancies implied by the existing pattern of input and output prices. And, of course, exploiting the intertemporal profit opportunities reduces the discrepancies. In the limit and with the unrealistic assumption of no change in the underlying economic realities, all wealth holders would be earning the market rate of interest.

In reality, of course, some amount of discoordination is inherent in the very nature of the market process. The market for loanable funds registers the expected rate of return net of the losses that this discoordination entails. For this reason, the loan rate of interest is not a "pure" rate. It reflects more than the underlying time preferences of market participants. On the demand side, changes in the level of "expected losses from discoordination" are identified in conventional macroeconomics as changes in the level of "business confidence." But business confidence, or, alternatively, business optimism and pessimism – or the waxing and waning of "animal spirits," to use Keynes's colorful phrase – seem to call for a psychological explanation. In capital-based macroeconomics, the expected losses from discoordination call for an economic explanation. Thus, the normal assumption will be: no change in the general level of business confidence (of expected loss from discoordination), except in circumstances where our analysis of the market process suggests that there is a basis for such a change.

On the supply side of the market for loanable funds, a similar contrast between conventional macroeconomics and capital-based macroeconomics can be made. Savers, who can partially insulate themselves through diversification from particular instances of discoordination in the business community, may nonetheless be concerned about the general health of the economy. Diversified or not, savers who want to put their savings at interest must bear a lenders' risk. What manifests itself on the demand side of the loan market as a loss of business confidence manifests itself on the supply side as an increase in liquidity preference. Savers may prefer, sometimes more so than others, to hold their wealth liquid rather than to put it at interest. But like business confidence, liquidity preference – or, all the more, Keynes's fetish of liquidity – seems to call for a psychological explanation. By contrast, lenders' risk, which is the more appropriate term in capital-based macroeconomics, calls for an economic explanation. The normal assumption, especially in the light of opportunities for diversification, will be: no change in lenders' risk – except, again, in circumstances where our analysis of the market process suggests that there is a basis for such a change.

This interplay between the market for loanable funds and markets for investment goods, the discussion of which anticipates other elements of our graphical analysis, is brought into view here so as to warn against too narrow a conception of the interest rate. In the broadest sense, the equilibrium rate of interest is simply the equilibrium rate of intertemporal exchange, which manifests itself both in the loan market and in markets for (present) investment goods in the light of their perceived relationship to (future) consumer goods. The market for loanable funds, however, warrants special attention. The most direct and obvious manifestation of intertemporal exchange, the loan rate that clears this market is vital in translating the intertemporal consumption preferences of income earners into intertemporal production plans of the business community. And, significantly, this same loan rate is also crucial in translating stimulation policies implemented by the monetary authority into their intended – and their unintended – consequences.

The supply and demand for loanable funds, shown in Figure 3.1, identify a market-clearing, or equilibrium, rate of interest i_{eq}, at which saving (S) and investment (I) are brought into equality. This is the conventional understanding of the loanable-funds market. In application, however, one feature of this market, critical to its incorporation into capital-based macroeconomics, involves an understanding that is not quite conventional. Mainstream theorizing relies on two separate and conflicting constructions – one for the short run and one for the long run. In macroeconomics as well as in growth theory, "to save" simply means "not to consume." Increased saving means decreased consumption. Resources that could have been consumed are instead made available for other purposes – for investment, for expanding the productive capacity of the economy. In long-run growth theory, where problems of disequilibria are assumed away, the actual utilization of saving for expanding capacity and hence increasing the growth rate of output (of both consumer goods and investment goods) is not in doubt. In the conventional macroeconomics of the short run – especially in Keynesian macroeconomics, where economy-wide disequilibrium (the Keynesians would say unemployment equilibrium) is the normal state of affairs – the actual utilization of saving by the investment community is very much in doubt. Decreased consumption now is likely to be taken by members of the business community as a permanently lower level of consumption. Saving can depress economic activity all around. The well-known "paradox of thrift" is based squarely on this all-but-certain cause-and-effect relationship between increased saving and decreased economic activity. This particular contrast between the short-run effect and the long-run effect of an increase in saving is undoubtedly what Robert Solow, as quoted in Chapter 1, had in mind when identified as a major weakness in modern macroeconomics the lack of real coupling between the short run and the long run.

Significantly, our understanding of saving in capital-based macroeconomics lies somewhere between the understandings of neoclassical growth theory and of Keynesian macroeconomics. As in many other issues, the

Austrians adopt a middle-ground position (Garrison, 1982). People do not just save (S); they save-up-for-something (SUFS). Their abstaining from present consumption serves a purpose; saving implies the intent to consume later. SUFS, our unaesthetic acronym (which we will resist employing repeatedly throughout this volume), stands in contrast to the conventional distinction between "saving," the flow concept (so much per year – from now on?) and "savings," the corresponding stock concept (the accumulation of so many years of saving – to what end?). Saving in capital-based macroeconomics means the accumulation of purchasing power to be exercised sometime in the future. It is true, of course, that individual savers do not indicate by their acts of saving just what they are saving for or just when they intend to consume. (They may not know these things in any detail themselves.) But this is only to say that the economy is not a clockwork. Future consumer demands are not determinate. The future is risky, uncertain, unknowable. The services of entrepreneurs, each with his or her own knowledge about the present and expectations about the future, are an essential requirement for the healthy working of the market economy. Increased saving now means increased consumption sometime in the future and hence increased profitability for resources committed to meet that future consumption demand.

The market process does not work "automatically," as commonly assumed in growth theory, and it does not "automatically" fail, as implied by the Keynesian paradox of thrift. To help identify instances in which the market process works – or fails to work – requires the perspective offered by the production possibilities frontier, which is the second element in capital-based macroeconomics.

The production possibilities frontier

The production possibilities frontier (PPF) appears in all introductory textbooks but is never integrated into either Keynesian or classical macroeconomic analysis. Typically, the PPF makes its appearance only in the preliminary discussions of scarcity. Following Samuelson, the older texts (and some new ones) identify the alternative goods to be produced as guns and butter. In its simplicity, the guns-and-butter construction allows us to see that we can have more wartime goods but only if we make do with fewer peacetime goods. The two alternative outputs are negatively related to one another. And while some of the economy's resources are suitable for producing either output, some are better suited to meeting our wartime needs, some to meeting our peacetime needs. When it becomes necessary for the economy to change its mix of outputs, it must use resources better suited for one output for producing the other. Hence, we must forego ever-increasing amounts of peacetime goods in order to produce additional amounts of wartime goods. Figure 3.2 shows a guns-and-butter PPF with its increasingly negative slope.

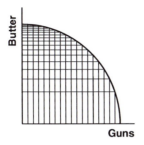

Figure 3.2 The production possibilities frontier (guns and butter).

The PPF is sometimes used for comparing different countries in terms of their economic performances over time. For this purpose, the fundamental trade-off between consumer goods and capital goods is presented in a PPF format. In this application, we simply call attention to the fact that the economy grows to the extent that it uses its resources for the production of capital goods rather than for the production of consumer goods. While the trade-off in any given year is made on the basis of that year's PPF, the year-to-year expansion of the PPF itself depends on just how that trade-off is made. For instance, postwar Japan, whose location on the PPF reflected a considerable sacrifice of consumer goods in favor of capital goods (or exportable goods), grew rapidly from the mid-1950s through the mid-1970s, as depicted by large year-to-year outward shifts in the frontier itself; the United States, whose location on the PPF reflected sacrifices in the other direction, grew more slowly. Compare in Figure 3.3 the location of Japan and the United States on their respective (and normalized) PPFs with the corresponding rates of expansion.

The same PPF that illustrates the possibilities of growth in the face of scarcity can easily be adapted for use in our capital-based macroeconomics. Any one year's production of capital goods is simply the amount of gross investment for that year. Accordingly, our PPF shows the trade-off between consumption (C) and investment (I). This construction allows for an obvious link with the supply and demand for loanable funds, and it also gives us a link to the more conventional macroeconomic theories which use these same aggregates, (C, I, and S) as their building blocks.

Unlike the investment magnitude in conventional constructions, however, our investment is measured in gross terms, allowing for capital maintenance as well as for capital expansion. There is some point on the frontier, then, for which gross investment is just enough to offset capital depreciation. With no net investment, we have a stationary, or no-growth, economy. Combinations of consumption and investment lying to the south-east of the no-growth point imply an expansion of the PPF; combinations lying

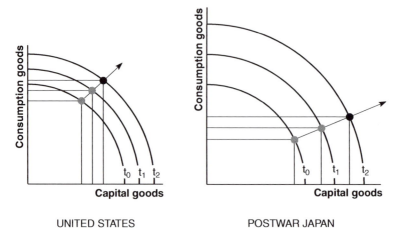

UNITED STATES   POSTWAR JAPAN

Figure 3.3 Capital and growth (the United States and postwar Japan)

to the north-west imply a contraction. Contraction, stationarity, and expansion are shown in Figure 3.4.

Applying the PPF to a mixed economy requires us to make room for government spending (G) and taxes (T). In conventional macroeconomics, which is based on the Keynesian aggregates, total expenditures (E) in a mixed economy is written as the sum of three components: $E = C + I + G$. Consumption is the stable component; investment is the unstable component; and government spending is the stabilizing component. Keynesian theory hinges importantly on a separation of consumption, which exhibits a strong and stable dependence on current after-tax income, and the other two components (I and G), which are not directly related to current income. Investment in the simplest Keynesian construction is largely "autonomous" and government spending is a key policy variable. This conceptualization leads almost immediately to the conclusion that if unpredictable and disruptive changes in investment spending are countered by changes (equal in magnitude and opposite in direction) in government spending, then the mixed economy will enjoy a stability that a wholly private economy could not have achieved on its own. The level of taxation (T), which affects disposable income and hence consumption spending, can serve as an alternative policy variable – or as a companion policy variable – in the policy-maker's prescriptions for stabilizing the economy.

How do G and T fit into capital-based macroeconomics? The PPFs of Figures 3.3 and 3.4 are drawn on a set of axes labeled C and I, suggesting that they apply to a wholly private economy. But there is some scope for extending the analysis to apply to a mixed economy, one that includes both a private sector and a public sector. Adapting our PPF to deal with relevant

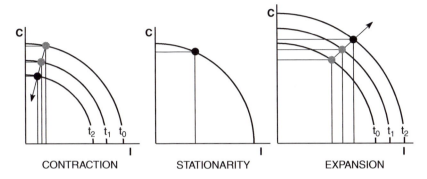

Figure 3.4 Gross investment and growth (contraction, stationarity, and expansion).

aspects of the public sector involves considerations quite different from those just mentioned. In the simplest – and most implausible – case, where the government imposes a lump-sum tax (a head tax), spends the revenues in ways that are wholly unrelated to private-sector activities, and maintains a balanced budget (G = T), the PPF simply applies to the private sector of a mixed economy. It represents the production possibilities after the government has extracted a certain portion of the economy's resources for use in the public sector.

More generally, drawing the PPF net of tax-financed government spending will involve more than simply scaling down the PPF. Just how the shape of the PPF might change (gross-to-net) and just where on the net PPF the economy might find itself will depend importantly on the particular design of the tax system and the particular use of the revenues. An income tax would have a different effect than a consumption tax would have (reform in the direction of a consumption tax is discussed in Chapter 5), and a tax-financed food-stamp program would have a different effect than a tax-financed airport-construction project. Strong arguments can be made that, in large part, the US economy is pushed towards increased consumption and the Japanese economy is pushed away from it by the two countries' respective policies that govern taxing and spending. Just how far the net PPF for either country lies inside the corresponding PPFs that would have been relevant in the absence of a large public sector involves arguments and judgments that go beyond the scope of our analysis.

The gross-to-net adjustment discussed above pertains to a public sector whose budget is balanced or, more generally, to tax-financed government spending. However, a portion of government spending, namely that portion financed by borrowing, adds to the demand for loanable funds and hence can be represented more explicitly in our graphics. That is, to allow for public-sector borrowing, we can relabel the horizontal axis in the market for loanable funds $I + G_d$, where G_d is deficit-financed government spending, or (ignoring here the possibility of inflationary finance) simply $G - T$. Note that private-sector investment and the deficit-financed portion of the public sector are taken to be additive both in conventional macroeconomics and in capital-based macroeconomics – but for different reasons. They are additive conventionally by virtue of their being two components (along with consumption and the tax-financed portion of the public sector) of total spending. In the present analysis, they are additive because of their being two components of the demand for loanable funds. Both components impinge on the rate of interest, which affects the intertemporal allocation of resources. Deficit finance and the Ricardian Equivalence Theorem are discussed in Chapter 5.

In some cases, where the government spending is almost wholly unrelated to spending in the private sector (think of the construction of monuments or of conducting remote military operations), we may choose to employ a PPF that excludes this public-sector activity. In other cases, the relabeling of the horizontal axis of the loanable-funds market may apply as well to the horizontal axis of the PPF. That is, in certain applications, we might find it helpful to represent a part of the government's appropriation of resources as a distance along the horizontal axis of the PPF diagram. Consider, for instance, a nationalized industry, where the government issues bonds and competes with the private sector for resources. In this instance, we can add public investment to private investment. The similarities between the two types of investment are captured in the PPF, while the critical differences are captured elsewhere in the analysis. These alternative treatments of deficit-financed government spending, depending on the particular nature of the spending, will find application in Chapter 5.

As applied to a wholly private economy or to the private sector of a mixed economy for which $G = T$, the (net) PPF represents *sustainable* combinations of consumption and investment and implies a fully employed economy. Combinations of consumption and investment inside the frontier involve unemployment – of labor and of other resources. Such widespread unemployment, according to Keynes, is characteristic of a market economy. In circumstances of pervasive unemployment, it is possible for consumption and investment to move in the same direction. Idle resources can be mobilized to allow for more of each. Scarcity is not a binding constraint. The trade-off is not between consumption and investment but between output of both kinds and idleness. The object of Keynesian policy, of course, is to drive the economy to some point on the frontier and keep it there. Any point is consistent with Keynesian principles, although Keynes himself was partial to investment.

Keynes clearly recognized that once full employment has been established, the classical theory (in which he included Austrian theory) comes into its own. The purpose of featuring the PPF in capital-based macroeconomic analysis is to give full play to those classical and Austrian relationships. The PPF for a given year constrains consumption and invest-ment to move in opposite directions along the frontier. More strictly speaking, comparative-statics analysis entails combinations of consumption and investment that lie on a given PPF. But as we shall see, the actual movement from one combination to the other, however, may involve a bubbling up above the frontier or a dipping down into its interior.

The constraint represented by the PPF, for capital-based analysis as well as for macroeconomic applications generally, is not absolute. Consumption and investment can move together beyond the frontier but only temporarily; in real terms, points beyond are not sustainable. And, of course, in conditions where malfunctioning markets have economy-wide consequences, consump-tion and investment can move together inside the frontier; where scarcity is not binding, idleness can be traded for more of both kinds of output.

Using the PPF as an elementary component of capital-based macro-economics leaves unspecified (within a wide range) the particular temporal relationship between this year's investment and the corresponding consump-tion of future years. In a simple two-period framework, an increase in investment of ΔI in period 1 permits an increase in consumption of $\Delta C = (1 + r)\Delta I$ in period 2, where r is the real rate of return on capital. In an equally simple stock-flow framework, in which infinitely-lived invest-ment goods yield a stream of consumption services, an increase in investment of ΔI in period 1 permits an increase in consumption of $\Delta C = r\Delta I$ for each and every successive year.

Neither of these overly simple conceptions of intertemporal transforma-tion gives adequate play to capital in the sense of a collection of heterogeneous capital goods that can be combined in different ways to yield consumable output at various future dates. In neither is there any non-trivial meaning to the notion of a capital structure or any scope for a restructuring of capital. To allow for the sort of problems that make the Austrian approach to macroeconomics worthwhile, a substantial portion of the economy's capital goods must be remote from consumable output, some more so than others. Capital must be heterogeneous, and the different capital goods must be related to one another by various degrees of complemen-tarity and substitutability. The expression for intertemporal transformation in capital-based macroeconomics is itself changeable and lies somewhere in the intermediate range between the simple two-period conception and the simple stock-flow conception. Dealing more specifically with possible patterns and likely patterns of movements of, along, beyond, and within the frontier requires a specific account of the intertemporal structure of production, which is the third element of capital-based macroeconomics.

The intertemporal structure of production

Attention to the intertemporal structure of production is unique to Austrian macroeconomics. Elementary textbooks on macroeconomics all contain some mention of a sequence of stages of production, but only to warn against double counting in constructing the more aggregate national income accounts. The farmer sells grain to the miller; the miller sells flour to the baker; the baker sells cases of bread to the grocer, and the grocer sells individual loaves to the consumer. The emphasis in such examples is on the value dimension of the production process and not on the time dimension. One method of calculating total output is to subtract the value of the inputs from the value of the output for each stage to get the "value added" and then to sum these differences to get the total value of final output. Simply adding the outputs of the farmer, the miller, the baker, and the grocer would entail some double, triple, and quadruple counting.

Capital-based macroeconomics gives play to both the value dimension and the time dimension of the structure of production. The relationship between the final, or consumable, output of the production process and the production time that the sequence of stages entails is represented graphically as the legs of a right triangle. In its strictest interpretation, the structure of production is conceptualized as a continuous-input/point-output process. The horizontal leg of the triangle represents production time. The vertical leg measures the value of the consumable output of the production process. Vertical distances from the time axis to the hypotenuse represent the values of goods-in-process. The value of a half-finished good, for instance, is systematically discounted relative to the finished good – and for two reasons: (1) further inputs are yet to be added; and (2) the availability of the finished good lies some distance in the future. Alternatively stated, the slope of the hypotenuse represents value added (by time and factor input) on a continuous basis. The choice of a linear construction here over an exponential one maintains a simplicity of exposition without significant loss in any other relevant regard.

Although the goods-in-process example is the most straightforward way to conceptualize the triangle, our interpretation of this Hayekian construction can be extended to include all forms of capital that make up the economy's structure of production. We can take into account the fact that mining operations are far removed in time from the consumer goods that will ultimately emerge as the end result of the time-consuming production process, while retail operations are in relative close temporal proximity to final output. Figure 3.5 shows the Hayekian triangle and identifies five stages of production as mining, refining, manufacturing, distributing, and retailing. The identification of the individual stages is strictly for illustrative purposes. The choice of five stages rather than six or sixty is strictly a matter of convenience of exposition. To choose two stages would be to collapse the triangle into the two-way distinction between consumption and investment – the distinction that gets emphasis in the PPF. To choose more than five stages would be to add complexity for the sake of complexity. Five gives us the just the appropriate degree of flexibility: a structural change that shifts consumable output into the future, for instance, would

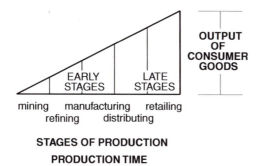

Figure 3.5 The structure of production (continuous-input/point-output).

involve an expansion of the early stages (with the first stage expanding more than the second), a contraction of the late stages (with the fifth stage contracting more than the fourth), and neither expansion nor contraction of the (third) stage that separates the early and late stages.

The time dimension that makes an explicit appearance on the horizontal leg of the Hayekian triangle has a double interpretation. First, it can depict goods in process moving through time from the inception to the completion of the production process. Second, it can represent the separate stages of production, all of which exist in the present, each of which aims at consumption at different points in the future. This second interpretation allows for the most straightforward representation of the relationships of capital-based macroeconomics. The first interpretation comes into play during a transition from one configuration to another. The double labeling of the horizontal axis in Figure 3.5 is intended to indicate the double interpretation: "Production Time" connotes a time-consuming process; "Stages of Production" connotes the configuration of the existing capital structure.

To illustrate the time element in the structure of production with an reference to the so-called smoke-stack industries may seem counter to trends in economic development over the past few decades. Mining and manufacturing may be in (relative) decline and the service and information industries on the rise. The mix of goods and services may be changing in favor of services, and human capital may have more claim on our attention than does heavy equipment. But as long as we think in terms of the employment of means, the achievement of ends, and the time element that separates the means and the ends, the Hayekian triangle remains applicable.

The continuous-input/point-output process that is depicted by the Hayekian triangle takes time into account but only as it relates to production. Adopting the point-output configuration gives us a straightforward link to the consumption magnitude featured in our PPF quadrant. But point output implies that consumption takes no time. Explicit treatment of consumer durables would involve extending the time dimension beyond

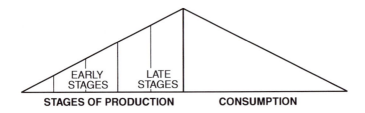

Figure 3.6 The structure of production (continuous-input/continuous-output).

the production phase of such durable goods. A second triangle representing the structure of consumption could be abutted onto the triangle representing the structure of production as shown in Figure 3.6. William Stanley Jevons offered this depiction of the investment process in his *Theory of Political Economy* ([1871] 1965: 231). The vertical distance to the hypotenuse of the second triangle might be interpreted as representing the capacity of consumer durables to provide services. The fact that these services, measured in value terms, decline over time is attributable to two considerations. First, consumer durables wear out, some more quickly than others, and old consumer durables provide less valuable services than new ones provide. Second, the time discount applies to consumption activities no less than to production activities. That is, the services to be provided in the remote future are discounted relative to the same services provided in the present. (Similarly, explicit treatment of durable capital goods employed in the various stages of production would require additional complicating modifications to the configuration.)

The notion of stages of consumption has much more limited interpretation than the corresponding stages of production. We might think of used-car lots, second-hand furniture stores, and junk shops as separating the stages. Although the allowance for consumption time as well as production time may constitute a move in the direction of realism, there is little to be gained analytically by replacing the multistage Hayekian triangle with the Jevonsian investment figure. Durable consumption goods and durable capital goods are obvious and, in some applications, important features of the market process. But to include these features explicitly would be to add complexity while clouding the fundamental relationships that are captured by the simpler construction. Instead, we avoid this graphical complication and rely on informal discussion to qualify our applications of the simple capital-based framework.

Conventional macroeconomics makes a first-order distinction between consumption and investment; capital-based macroeconomics owes many of its insights to the special attention to the time dimension in the investment sector, the temporal structure of production. The graphical depiction of a linear sequence of stages is not intended to suggest that the production process is actually that simple. There are many feedback loops, multiple-purpose outputs, and other instances of nonlinearities. Each stage may also involve the use of durable – but depreciating – capital goods, relatively specific and relatively nonspecific capital goods, and capital goods that are related with various degrees of substitutability and complementarity to the capital goods in other stages of production. Insights involving these and other complexities are best dealt with by careful and qualified application of Hayek's original construction.

Even in the simple triangular construction, however, the reckoning of production time is anything but simple. While the vertical and horizontal dimensions of the triangle are intended to represent value and time separately, the relevant time dimension is not measured in pure time units. Instead, the time dimension measures the extent to which valuable resources are tied up over time. Production time itself, then, has both a value dimension and a time dimension. Two dollars worth of resources tied up in the production process for three years amounts to six dollar-years (neglecting compounding) of production time. The complex unit of dollar-years is not foreign to capital theory. It measures Gustav Cassel's (1903) "waiting" and underlies Böhm-Bawerk's ([1889] 1959) roundaboutness. These two related concepts have come in for much misunderstanding and criticism. The dimensional complexity of an intertemporal production process is what gave play to the technique-reswitching and capital-reversing debates of the 1960s and accounts for most of the thorny and controversial issues of capital theory. It was precisely these thorny issues that underlay the eagerness of macroeconomists in the 1930s to drop capital theory out of macroeconomics.

If our objective was to set out the issues of the 1960s controversy, we would have to forego the simple Hayekian triangle in favor of an exponential function to allow for the compounding of interest, without which the controversies do not emerge. Thus, the key element of capital-based macroeconomics, the Hayekian triangle, is not intended to rid capital theory of its thorniness but rather to put those thorns aside in order to highlight the macroeconomic aspects of intertemporal equilibrium and intertemporal disequilibrium. Nor is it intended to help determine quantitatively the precise amount of waiting or the precise degree of roundaboutness that characterizes the structure of production. Rather, it is intended to indicate the general pattern of the allocation of resources over time and the general nature of changes in the intertemporal pattern. To this end, the still-unresolved – and possibly unresolvable – issues of capital theory can be kept at bay. The focus, instead, is on the most fundamental interrelationships among the separate elements of capital-based macroeconomics.

The macroeconomics of capital structure

Having accounted separately for each of the three elements of capital-based macroeconomics, the basic interconnections among these elements follow

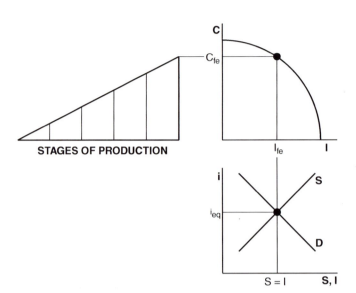

Figure 3.7 The macroeconomics of capital structure.

almost without discussion. Figure 3.7 represents a wholly private economy or the private sector of a mixed economy whose public-sector budget is in balance. It shows just how the supply and demand for loanable funds, the production possibility frontier, and the intertemporal structure of production relate to one another. The loanable-funds market and the PPF are explicitly connected by their common axes measuring investment. The PPF and the structure of production are explicitly connected by their common axes measuring consumption.

A critical connection between the structure of production and the loanable funds market is not quite as explicit as the others. The slope of hypotenuse of the Hayekian triangle reflects the market-clearing rate of interest in the market for loanable funds. "Reflects" is as strong a connection as can be made here. With a continuous-input construction, the slope of the hypotenuse reflects more than the interest rate. The value-differential across any given stage is partly attributable to inputs being added in that stage and partly attributable to the change in temporal proximity to final output. However, as applied to the private sector and under given institutional arrangements, the slope of the hypotenuse and the market-clearing rate of interest will move in the same direction. That is, a lower (higher) rate of interest will imply a shallower (steeper) slope. The qualifications suggest that public-sector spending can upset this relationship as can institutional reform, such as the replacement of an income tax with a consumption tax. These applications will be dealt with in Chapter 5.

The rate of interest – or rate of return on capital – could be depicted more explicitly by adopting an alternative construction. A point-input/point-output production process could be represented by a truncated Hayekian triangle, a trapezoid – with the shorter vertical side measuring input, the longer one measuring output. The trapezoid would depict a single input which would then mature with time into consumable output. Aging wine is the paradigm case. The rate of interest in this case, neglecting compounding, would be *equal* to the slope of a line that connects the value of the input to the value of the output. This construction together with the supply and demand for dated labor was used in my more classically oriented "Austrian Macroeconomics" (1978). However, the point-input construction does violence to the notion of a production process. Continuous input, divided for heuristic purposes into a number of stages, seems more in the spirit of Austrian capital theory.

The location of the economy on the PPF implies full employment, or, equivalently, the "natural" rate of unemployment. The mutual compatibility of the three elements implies that the market-clearing interest rate is the "natural" rate of interest. (Note that the natural rate of interest cannot be defined solely in terms of the loanable-funds market.) In its simplest interpretation, Figure 3.7 represents a fully employed, no-growth economy, such as depicted in terms of the PPF alone in Figure 3.4. Resources devoted to gross investment, I_{fe}, are just sufficient to offset capital depreciation. This investment is distributed among the various stages of production so as to allow each stage to maintain its level of output. There is no net investment. Income earners continue to consume C_{fe} and to save an amount that just finances the gross investment. The rate of interest reflects the time preferences of market participants. These steady-state interrelationships provide a macroeconomic perspective on Mises's Evenly Rotating Economy and constitute a macroeconomic benchmark for the analysis of secular growth and cyclical fluctuations.

Figure 3.7 looks dramatically different, to say the least, from the diagrammatics of conventional macroeconomics. The specific relationship between capital-based macroeconomics and, say, ISLM analysis or Aggregate-Supply/Aggregate-Demand analysis is not readily apparent. To compare and contrast Austrian macroeconomics with its Anglo-American counterpart in any comprehensive way would take our discussion too far afield. A few particular points of contrast, however, will help to put the differences into perspective.

First, unlike ISLM analysis, the graphics in Figure 3.7 do not include a market for money. Neither the money supply nor money demand are explicitly represented. Both in reality and in our analysis of it, money has no market of its own. Understanding the broadest implications of this truth sets the research agenda for monetary disequilibrium theory, which we take up in Chapter 11. Austrians, too, recognize the uniqueness of money in this respect. With trivial exceptions, money appears on one side of every exchange. Money, by definition, is the medium of exchange. But neither the transactions demand for money, as embedded in the classical equation of exchange, nor the speculative demand for money, as conceived by Keynes, make a direct appearance in the Austrian-oriented construction. Consistent with Hayek's understanding, capital-based macroeconomics treats money as a "loose joint" in the economic system. As Hayek ([1935] 1967: 127) indicated early on, "the task of monetary theory [is] nothing less than to cover a second time the whole field which is treated by pure theory under the assumption of barter." The three-quadrant construction in Figure 3.7 can be taken to depict, if not actually a barter system, a tight-jointed system. That is, money is assumed to allow market participants to avoid the inefficiencies of barter – without introducing any inefficiencies of its own. So interpreted, the interrelationships shown in Figure 3.7 belong to the realm of pure theory.

To deny money its own diagram and even its own axis is not to downplay or ignore monetary considerations. Money is actually on *every* axis of *every* diagram. Monetary phenomena in the context of capital-based macroeconomics are to be accounted for by allowing for some looseness in the market process that governs the intertemporal allocation of resources. Monetary theory entails the identification of possible instances in which the system is out of joint, instances in which the intermediation of money allows misallocations to persist long enough to cause a macroeconomic problem. The Austrian theory of boom and bust, which presupposes an essential loose-jointedness, identifies a systematic misallocation of resources that could not possibly characterize a tight-jointed system. Policy-induced intertemporal disequilibrium is the essence of the unsustainable boom. Thus, despite our explicit focus on saving, investment, consumption, and production time, the theory of boom and bust (to be presented in Chapter 4) is, root and branch, a monetary theory.

Second, unlike AggS/AggD analysis, Figure 3.7 does not keep track of changes in the price level. Keeping the equation of exchange in the background is not to deny the kernel of truth in the quantity theory of money. But intertemporal allocation is not governed primarily by (actual or anticipated) changes in the price level. It is governed by changes in relative prices within the capital structure. Tracking changes in the general level of prices as well as in relative prices would complicate the theory without adding substantially to it. Hayek was critical of pre-Keynesian monetary theorists for their nearly-exclusive attention to the relationship between money and the general level of prices. There are other relationships in his view that have a stronger claim on our attention.

It is true, of course, that a falling price level in conditions of less-than-full employment increases the real value of money. If market participants engage in additional spending because of the increase in value of their money balances, the economy will move in the direction of full employment. This aspect of the equilibrating process, which gets emphasis in

Monetarist constructions and became the focus of attention during the protracted debates between Keynes and the Classics, is treated in Chapter 10. The significance of the real-balance effect is very different for Keynesian theory than for Austrian theory. In Keynesian theory, the real-balance effect was the only prospect – and a dim prospect it was, in Keynes's judgment – for the successful market solution to the problem of depression. In the absence of a viable real-cash-balance effect, the Keynesians had the argument won. There was no other effect in contention. If real balances didn't push the economy towards full employment, the economy could settle into an unemployment equilibrium. And even with a real-balance effect the Keynesians could concede defeat but only as a matter of strict theory. As a practical matter – a policy matter – the adjustment of demand to prevailing price level could be favored over allowing the price level to adjust to prevailing market demands.

In Austrian theory, the existence of the real-balance effect is not in dispute, and the strength of the real-balance effect is not at issue. But there *is* another effect that has a claim on our attention, namely, the capital-allocation effect. Capital-based macroeconomics is designed to show that quite independent of any movements in the general price level, the adjustments of relative prices within the capital structure can bring the intertemporal allocation of resources into line with intertemporal consumption preferences without idling labor or other resources. To factor in price-level changes and their significance for the performance of the macro-economy would be to detract from the unique aspects of the Austrian theory. Austrian-oriented treatments of price-level changes (induced alternatively by real and by monetary forces) can be found in Selgin (1991), Garrison (1996a), and Horwitz (2000).

Finally, unlike ISLM analysis, in which the employment of labor is assumed to move in lockstep with output and income, and unlike AggS/AggD analysis, in which aggregate supply is firmly based on the supply of and demand for labor, our capital-based analysis does not feature the labor market. Labor, of course, counts as an important input for each and every stage of production. But the fact that capital-based macro-economics allows for allocation of inputs among stages implies that thinking in terms of *the* labor market is inadequate. Changes in the rate of interest will cause the demand for labor in some stages to increase and the demand for labor in other stages to decrease. When the allocation of labor is at issue, auxiliary diagrams will be added at the different stages of production to show the relative movements in labor demands and wage rates.

ISLM analysis and AggS/AggD analysis are too far removed from the issues of capital-based macroeconomics and from the issues that interest most modern macroeconomists to make an extended treatment of these frameworks worthwhile. The chapters in Part III will offer a labor-based macroeconomics that is more faithful to its origins and more directly comparable with the capital-based macroeconomics offered here.

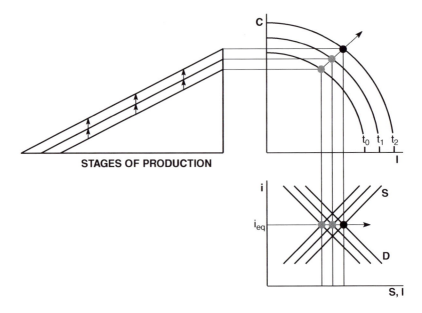

Figure 3.8 Secular growth (with assumed interest-rate neutrality).

The macroeconomics of secular growth

While a no-growth economy allows for the simplest and most straightfor-ward application of our graphical analysis, an expanding economy is the more general case. Secular growth occurs without having been provoked by policy or by technological advance or by a change in intertemporal prefer-ences. Rather, the ongoing gross investment is sufficient for both capital maintenance and capital accumulation. The macroeconomics of secular growth is depicted in Figure 3.8, which shows an initial configuration (t_0) plus two successive periods (t_1 and t_2).

As in Figure 3.4, the growth in Figure 3.8 is depicted by outward shifts in the PPF – from t_0 to t_1 to t_2. But we now see what must be happening with the other two elements of the interlocking construction. The right-ward shifts in both the supply and the demand for loanable funds are consistent with the absence of any intertemporal preference changes. Savers are supplying increasing amounts of loanable funds out of their increasing incomes; the business community is demanding increasing amounts of loan-able funds to maintain a growing capital structure and to accommodate future demands for consumer goods that are growing in proportion to current demands. With ongoing shifts in the supply and demand for loanable funds, the equilibrium rate of interest, which also manifests itself as the ongoing rate of return on capital generally, remains constant. Historically, increasing wealth has typically been accompanied by decreasing time preferences. Accordingly, shifts in the supply of loanable funds will likely outpace the shifts in demand, causing the interest rate to fall. Our treatment of secular growth abstracts from this relationship between wealth and time preferences.

The unchanging rate of interest of Figure 3.8 translates into an unchanging slope of the hypotenuse for the successive Hayekian triangles. The interest rate allocates resources among the stages of production so as to change the size but not the intertemporal profile of the capital structure. As the economy grows, more resources are committed to the time-consuming production process, and more consumer goods emerge as output of that process. Over time and with technology and resource availability assumed constant, the increases in both consumption and saving implied by the outward expansion of the PPF are consistent with the conventionally conceived long-run consumption function. That is, consumption rises with rising income, but it rises less rapidly than income since saving, which equals – and enables – investment, rises, too.

The macroeconomics of secular growth provides a more realistic baseline for analyzing particular changes in preferences or policies. In putting the graphics through their paces, however, the secular component of growth will be kept in the background. Changes in intertemporal preferences as well as policy changes will be analyzed on the assumption that we begin with a no-growth economy. With this simplifying assumption, the movement of the macroeconomy from one equilibrium to another will sometimes involve an absolute reduction in some macroeconomic magnitudes. Current consumption, for instance, might decrease while the economy's capacity to satisfy future consumer demands is being increased. In the fuller context of ongoing secular growth, the absolute decrease in consumption would translate into a reduced rate of increase in consumption. More generally, the macroeconomic adjustments required by some particular parametric or policy change are to be superimposed (conceptually if not graphically) onto the dynamics of the ongoing secular growth.

The macroeconomics of secular growth as depicted in Figure 3.8 does not keep track of the relationship between the money supply and the general level of prices. Money and prices can be kept in perspective, however, with the aid of the familiar equation of exchange, $MV = PQ$. For a given money supply (M) and a given velocity of money (V), the increases in both consumption and investment ($C + I = Q$) imply decreases in the general price level (P). That is, secular growth is accompanied by secular price deflation. Unlike the deflationary pressures associated with an increase in the demand for money (or a decrease in the supply of money), growth-induced deflation does not imply monetary disequilibrium. Quite to the contrary, in a growing economy, equilibrium lies in the direction of lower prices and wages. The downward market adjustments in the prices and wages take place in the particular markets where the growth is actually experienced, with the result that the average of prices is reduced. These are the issues dealt with by Selgin (1991), Garrison (1996a), and Horwitz (2000). The consequences of policy-induced changes in the price level will be deferred until the Austrian perspective on Monetarism is set out in Part IV.

The following chapter will deal with technology-induced changes in the economy's growth rate and with changes in the rate of interest and in the shape of the structure of production caused by changes in intertemporal preferences. Identifying the market process at work here is preliminary to the critical distinction between healthy economic growth, which is saving-induced (and hence sustainable), and artificial booms, which are policy-induced (and hence unsustainable).

4 Sustainable and unsustainable growth

Secular growth characterizes a macroeconomy for which the ongoing rate of saving and investment exceeds the rate of capital depreciation. A change in the growth rate – or more generally – in the intertemporal pattern of consumable output may occur as a result of some change in the underlying economic realities. Advances in technology and additions to resource availabilities, as well as preference changes that favor future consumption over present consumption, impinge positively on the economy's growth rate. Such parametric changes have a direct effect in one or more of the panels of our capital-based macroeconomic framework and have indirect effects throughout. These instances of change in the sustainable growth rate are offered as preliminary to our discussion of the unsustainable growth induced by policy actions of the monetary authority.

Changes in technology and resource availabilities

Technological advance has a direct effect on the production possibilities frontier and on the market for loanable funds. Although a typical technological innovation occurs in one or a few markets, it allows, through resource reallocation, for increases in the production possibilities all around. That is, the frontier shifts outward (and possibly experiences a change in shape depending on the specific nature of the change in technology); the demand for loanable funds shifts to the right, as business firms take advantage of the new technological possibilities. The resulting higher incomes cause the supply of loanable funds to shift to the right as well.

The direction of movement of the interest rate is indeterminate, depending, as it does, on the relative magnitudes of the shifts in supply and in demand. This indeterminacy, however, presents us with no fundamental puzzle. It simply derives from the fact that the net gain attributable to the technological advance can be realized in part as greater consumption in current and near-future periods and in part as greater consumption in the more remote periods. Although the specific nature of the change in technology may set limits on the particular way in which the gains can be realized, there remains much scope for trading current consumption and future consumption against one another. The advance in technology, what-ever its particulars in terms of the timing of inputs and outputs, serves, in effect, to increase the potential of investable resources. To use the old Classical terminology, it is *as if* the subsistence fund had increased. There will almost always be ample opportunities to draw down the subsistence fund in ways not directly related to the change in technology (for instance, by decreasing current inventories of consumption goods) so as to take imme-diate advantage of the technological advance. While the rate of interest may rise temporarily while the economy is adjusting to the new technology, it is not necessarily the case – as it is in other macroeconomic constructions – that a (positive) technology shock causes the equilibrium rate of interest to rise.

Figure 4.1 depicts technology-induced growth in an instance where the technological change is interest-rate neutral. Here, we can identify two cases: (1) the technological advance affects all stages of production directly and proportionally, so that no reallocation of resources among the different stages is called for; and (2) scope for resource reallocation allows the imple-mentation of technology that is usable only in one or a few stages to have an immediate or nearly immediate impact on current consumption. In either case, the economy's growth path would be shifted upward but would not otherwise change. The initial and subsequent equilibria are shown by the solid points in Figure 4.1. In the first case, there is no reason to believe that the interest rate would rise even temporarily. Investment, output, income, consumption, and saving would all rise together without putting pressure one way or the other on the rate of interest. In the second case, the demand for loanable funds rises first as producers seek to take advan-tage of new technology that directly affects, say, an early stage of production. The increase in investment is shown in Figure 4.1 by a rightward shift in the demand for loanable funds from D to D$'$. The interest rate rises, as indicated by the hollow point marking the intersection of S and D$'$. (Note also that the adjustment path between the initial PPF (t_0) and the subse-quent PPF (t_i) exhibits an initial investment bias.) Because the technological advance occurred in an early stage, consumable output does not experience an immediate increase. However, the increased interest rate causes resources not directly involved in implementing the new technology to be reallo-cated towards the late and final stages of production, which allows consumption to increase. As incomes increase (due to increased investment spending) and consumption increases (due to resource reallocations), saving also increases. The supply of loanable funds shifts from S to S$'$, and the interest rate is driven back to its initial level.

Apart from its showing the temporary increase in the rate of interest and the correspondingly bowed-out adjustment path between the two PPFs, our Figure 4.1, depicting technology-induced growth, is virtually identical to Figure 3.8, which depicts secular growth. We might as well have simply modified Figure 3.8 (p. 54) to show a discontinuity in consumable output

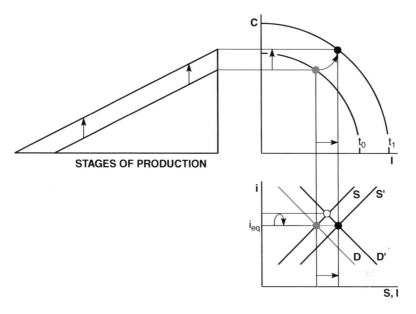

Figure 4.1 Technology-induced growth.

occurring at the time of the change in technology. For instance, the set of curves labeled t_2 (in Fig. 3.8) could be relabeled t_1', indicating that a technological advance that had occurred in period t_1 allowed the economy to experience two years' worth of secular growth in a single year.

The notion that the economy experiences smooth secular growth has always been something of a fiction. By their very nature technological advances occur at irregular intervals and with some advances more dramatic than others. Knut Wicksell ([1898] 1962: 165–77) relied on this irregularity to help reconcile observed movements in the rate of interest and the level of prices and to give plausibility to his rocking-horse theory of the business cycle. Joseph Schumpeter ([1911] 1961: 57–64) featured the irregularity in his theory of economic development. Modern proponents of real business cycle theory (Nelson and Plosser, 1982) point to irregular technological shocks as the source of the variation of output that appears – but only appears – to be cyclical in nature. That is, for real business cycle theorists, what looks like cyclical variation may be nothing but the market's response to changes in technology.

Although a technological change is conceived as being interest-neutral in the comparative-statics sense, it is quite possible for the market process that takes a capital-intensive economy from one equilibrium to another to involve high interest rates for a substantial period. Unlike our second case above involving only a transitory change in the interest rate, the application of new technology may require committing resources to capital-intensive and hence time-consuming production processes in circumstances where the scope for reallocating other resources toward the late stages is limited. In this case, the increased demand for loanable funds may have a dominating effect on the interest rate for some time. Alternatively stated, if the increased supply of loanable funds is not fully accommodating (because higher-priced consumer goods have claimed a larger portion of incomes), the interest rate will rise, serving as a partial brake against fully exploiting the technological advance. The structure of production is being pushed in the direction of increased production time by the technological change itself and pulled in the opposite direction by people's reluctance to forgo current consumption.

It is possible to conceive of a technological change that causes the rate of interest to *fall* during the adjustment process. Imagine the discovery of some simple process that can quickly and almost effortlessly convert kudzu (a worthless vine that blankets the south-eastern United States) into grits and other consumables. The immediate result of the new technology is that income earners are awash in current consumption. With demands for current output more fully satisfied than before, they willingly put more of their incomes at interest. The increase in the supply of loanable funds lowers the rate of interest and channels funds into the implementation of longer-term projects, using technology that, though not new, can only now be prof-itably implemented. The fact that the kudzu-to-grits technology seems a bit contrived gives plausibility to the more common association between technological advance and a (temporarily) higher interest rate.

As suggested by our reference to Figure 3.8, tracking the changes of the macroeconomic magnitudes after a technological innovation requires that these changes be superimposed onto the secular growth that the economy was experiencing even before the innovation. It may well be that the initial increase in the interest rate, which acts as a brake on the rate at which technological advance is exploited, is followed by a decrease in the interest rate, as the accelerated accumulation of wealth (relative to accumulation prior to the innovation) is accompanied by a change in intertemporal con-sumption preferences. Allowing for this effect (from innovation to increased wealth to lower time preferences), we see technological innovation as caus-ing the equilibrium rate of interest to fall even though the adjustment to this new equilibrium may involve a temporarily high interest rate. More impor-tantly for the application of our capital-based macroeconomic framework, the economy's pattern of growth, as boosted by the technological advance, is a sustainable one. That is, the change in the underlying economic realities imply an altered growth path; the market process translates the technological advance into the new preferred growth path; and there is nothing in the nature of this market process that turns the process against itself.

The possible consequences of an increase in resource availabilities are similar to those of technological advance. Discovering new mineral deposits is equivalent in many respects to discovering new and better ways of extracting minerals from old deposits. In either case, the economy's post-discovery growth path is sustainable in the above-mentioned sense. In each instance of increased resource availabilities and technological advance, the specifics of the market process triggered by the parametric change depend on the specifics of the parametric change itself. Apart from our suggested reinterpretation of Figure 3.8 and the incorporation of the wealth effects on intertemporal consumption preferences and hence on the interest rate, the attempt to identify and deal further with some general case is not likely to be worthwhile.

In contrast to changes in technology and resource availabilities, a change in intertemporal consumption preferences has consequences for which the direction of change in the rate of interest and related macroeconomic magnitudes is determinate and for which a general case can be identified. Further, the parallels between the consequences of a change in intertemporal preferences and the consequences of a policy of credit expansion by the monetary authority give special relevance to these preference changes and policy actions.

Changes in intertemporal preferences

Changes in technology and resource availabilities give rise to permanent, or sustainable, changes in the economy's growth path. Sustainable growth can also be set in motion by changes in intertemporal preferences. Our framework is well suited to trace out the consequences of such a preference change. It is convenient simply to hypothesize an autonomous economy-wide change in intertemporal preferences: people become more thrifty, more future oriented in their consumption plans. In reality, of course, inter-temporal preference changes are undoubtedly gradual and most likely related to demographics or cultural changes. For instance, baby boomers enter their high-saving years. Or increasing doubts about the viability of Social Security cause people to save more for their retirement. Or education-conscious parents begin saving more for their children's college years. The essential point is that intertemporal preferences can and do change and that these changes have implications for the intertemporal allocation of resources.

The assumption underlying labor-based macroeconomics is that there is a high degree of complementarity between consuming in one period and consuming in the next. On the basis of this assumption, it is believed, changes in intertemporal preferences can be safely ruled out of consideration. By contrast, capital-based macroeconomics allows for some degree of intertemporal substitutability of consumption. Rejecting the assumption of strict intertemporal complementarity does not imply – as Cowen (1997: 84), for one, suggests that it does – that the actual changes experienced are frequent and dramatic. Quite to the contrary, the claim is that over time even small changes have a significant and cumulative effect on the pattern of resource allocation. More pointedly, capital-based macroeconomics suggests that if the interest rate reports a small change when none actually occurred (or fails to report a small change that actually did occur), the consequences can be cumulative misallocations that eventually lead to a dramatic correction.

In Figure 4.2 an increase in thriftiness – in people's willingness to save – is represented by a rightward shift in the supply of loanable funds. The implied decrease in current consumption is consistent with a change in the intertemporal pattern of consumption demand: people restrict their consumption now in order to be able to consume more in the future. The implication of higher consumption demand in the future was expressed in Chapter 3 as SUFS: saving-up-for-something. This understanding of the nature of saving gives rise to a key macroeconomic question: How does the market process translate changes in intertemporal preferences into the appropriate changes in intertemporal production decisions? To presuppose, following Keynes, that reduced consumption demand in the current period implies proportionally low consumption demands in subsequent periods is wholly unwarranted. It would follow trivially that for an economy in which the expectations of the business community were governed by such a presupposition, the market process would experience systematic coordination failures whenever saving behavior changed. This rather telling aspect of the Keynesian vision begs the question about the viability of a market economy in circumstances where intertemporal preferences can change and raises the more fundamental question of how the current intertemporal pattern of resource allocation ever got to be what it is.

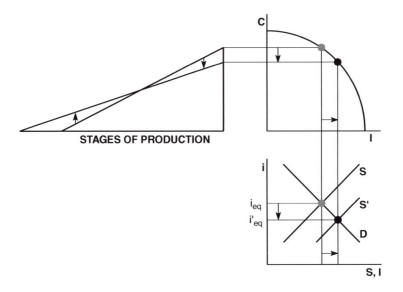

Figure 4.2 Saving-induced capital restructuring.

Straightforwardly, the change in credit-market conditions results in a decrease in the rate of interest and an increase in the amount of funds borrowed by the business community, as depicted by the solid point marking the new equilibrium in the loanable-funds market. The corresponding solid point in the PPF diagram shows that the resources freed up by the reduced consumption can be used instead for investment purposes. Note the consistency in the propositions that (1) there is a movement *along* the PPF rather than *off* the PPF; and (2) there is no significant income effect on the supply of loanable funds. If consumption decreased without there being any offsetting increase in investment, then incomes would decrease as well and so too would saving and hence the supply of loanable funds. The negative income effect on the supply of loanable funds would largely if not wholly negate the effects of the preference change. Keynes's paradox of thrift would be confirmed: increased thriftiness leads not to an increased growth rate but to decreased incomes. Making matters worse, the decreased incomes and hence decreased spending may well induce a pessimism into the business community, which would result in a leftward shift in the demand for loanable funds. These and other perceived perversities will be explored more fully in Chapter 8.

In our capital-based macroeconomics, allowing a shift of the supply of loanable funds to move us along a given demand, allowing a lower interest rate to induce a higher level of investment, and allowing the economy to stay on its production possibilities frontier are just mutually reinforcing ways of acknowledging that markets, even intertemporal markets, need not function perversely. The mutually reinforcing views about the different aspects of the market system is what Keynes had in mind when he indicated at the close of his chapter on the "Postulates of Classical Economics" that those postulates all stand or fall together. Figure 4.2 reflects the view that our postulates stand together. The market works. But just how the intertemporal markets work requires that we shift our attention to the intertemporal structure of production. The altered shape of the Hayekian triangle shows just how the additional investment funds are used. The rate of interest governs the intertemporal pattern of investment as well as the overall level. The lower interest rate, which is reflected in the more shallow slope of the triangle's hypotenuse, favors relatively long-term investments. Resources are bid away from late stages of production, where demand is weak because of the currently low consumption, and into early stages, where demand is strong because of the lower rate of interest. That is, if the marginal increment of investment in early stages was just worthwhile, given the costs of borrowing, then additional increments will be seen as worthwhile, given the new, lower costs of borrowing. While many firms are simply reacting to the spread between their output prices and their input prices in the light of the reduced cost of borrowing, the general pattern of intertemporal restructuring is consistent with an anticipation of a strengthened future demand for consumption goods made possible by the increased saving. It is not actually necessary, of course, for any one entrepreneur – or for entrepreneurs collectively – to explicitly form an expectation about future aggregate consumption demand.

The triangle depicts relative changes in spending patterns attributable to increased savings; it does not show the ultimate increase in output of consumption goods made possible by increased investment. To visualize the intertemporal pattern of consumption that follows an increase in thrift, we must superimpose the relative changes depicted in Figure 4.2 onto the secular growth depicted in Figure 3.8. Figure 4.2 by itself suggests an actual fall in consumption. The two figures taken together suggest a slowing of the growth of consumption while the capital restructuring is being completed followed by an acceleration of the growth rate. The growth rate after the capital restructuring will be higher than it was before the preference change. The rate of increase in consumption may go from 2 percent to 1½ percent to 2½ percent. This pattern of output is consistent with the hypothesized change in intertemporal preferences.

Figure 4.3 differs from Figure 4.2 only by its including some auxiliary diagrams that track the movement of labor during the capital restructuring. The increased saving can be seen as having two separate effects on labor demand. The two concepts at play here, already discussed in the context of the Hayekian triangle itself, are derived demand and time discount. (1) Labor demand is a derived demand. Thus, a reduction in the demand for consumption goods implies a proportionate reduction in the labor that produces those consumption goods. For stages of production sufficiently close to final output, this effect dominates. The demand for retail sales personnel, for instance, falls in virtual lockstep with the demand for the products they sell. (2) Like all factors of production in a time-consuming production process, labor is valued at a discount. The reduction in the interest rate lessens the discount and hence increases the value of labor. In the late stages of production, this effect is negligible; in the earliest stages of production, it dominates. The two effects, then, work in opposite directions – with the magnitude of the time-discount effect increasing with temporal remoteness from the final stage of production. Together, they change the shape of the Hayekian triangle. The intersection of the two hypotenuses (that characterize the capital structure before and after the intertemporal preference change) marks the point where the two effects just offset one another.

The structure of production in Figure 4.3 is cut at three different points to illustrate the workings of labor markets. Labor experiences a net decrease in demand for the stage between the intersection of the hypotenuses and final output; labor experiences a net increase in demand for the stage between the intersection of the hypotenuses and the earliest input. Initially the wage rate falls in the late stage and rises in the early stage. After the pattern of employment fully adjusts itself to the new market conditions (with workers moving from the late stage to the early stage) the wage rate returns to its

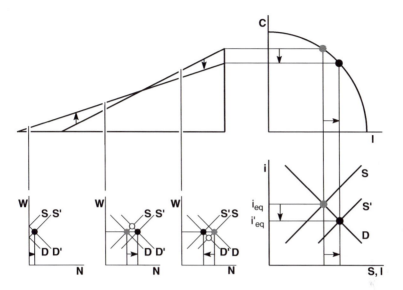

Figure 4.3 Capital restructuring (with auxiliary labor-market adjustments).

initial level. Also shown is the labor market for a stage of production that is newly created as a result of the preference changes. The supply and demand for labor at this stage did not intersect at a positive level of employment before the reduction of the interest rate; after the reduction, some employment is supplied and demanded. The pattern of demand in our stage-specific markets for labor is consistent with that shown by Hayek ([1935] 1967: 80) as a "family of discount curves," with which he tracks the differential changes in labor demand in five separate stages of production.

Labor in this reckoning is treated as a wholly nonspecific factor of production, but one that has to be enticed by higher wage rate to move from one stage to another. That is, the short-run supply curve is upward-sloping, the long-run supply curve is not. This construction requires qualification in two directions. First, skills that make a particular type of labor specific to a particular stage would have to be classified as (human) capital, an integral part of the capital structure itself. Workers with such skills would not move from one stage to another. Instead, they would enjoy a wage-rate increase or suffer a wage-rate decrease, depending upon the particular stage. Second, the auxiliary graphs depicting movements of nonspecific labor could also depict the movements of nonspecific capital. These capital goods will simply move from one stage to another in response to the differential effects of the time discounting. For instance, trucks that had been hauling sawhorses and lawn furniture may start hauling more sawhorses and less lawn furniture. In general and for any given stage of production, the specific factors undergo price adjustments; the nonspecific factors undergo quantity adjustments. This understanding allows full scope, of course, for both price and quantity adjustments for the various degrees of specificity that characterize the different kinds of capital and labor. In putting our capital-based macroeconomic framework through its paces, however, it is often convenient – and is consistent with convention – to think of labor as representing the nonspecific factor of production.

The idea that the wage rate returns to its initial level after all the relative adjustments have been made deserves further comment. In Figure 4.3, the interest rate falls; the wage rate remains unchanged. This pattern of change stands in contrast to the pattern that characterizes the analytics offered, for instance, by Samuelson (1962). The neoclassical construction features a so-called factor-price frontier that depicts a negative relationship between the wage rate and the interest rate. In this reckoning, however, labor is cast in the role of the time-intensive factor of production. Inputs consist of dated labor that matures with time into consumable output. Capital, which is nothing but the not-yet-fully-matured labor input, is by construction closer in time to final output than is labor itself. Hence, a fall in the rate of interest would lead, by virtue of the time-discount effect, to a rise in the wage rate. This relationship has its parallel in our capital-based macroeconomics: a fall in the interest rate leads to a rise in the prices of factors of production that are employed in the early stages. The rise is permanent for the specific factors; temporary for the nonspecific factors.

Our treatment of labor in Figure 4.3 also stands in contrast to certain aspects of classical theory, such as is found in David Ricardo's ([1817] 1911: 263–71) treatment of labor and machinery. In his writing, capital is treated as the long-term, or time-intensive, factor of production and labor is treated as the short-term factor. A reduction in the rate of interest, then, favors the use of machinery over the use of labor. If this were Ricardo's whole story, then interest rates and wage rates would move up and down together. In the final analysis, however, displaced labor is hired to help produce the machines. This is the general thrust of Mill's ([1848] 1895: 65) fourth fundamental proposition respecting capital: "demand for commodities [i.e. consumption goods] is not demand for labor." Though slightly cryptic, this once famous aphorism simply means that the principle of derived demand does not apply to labor as a whole. The time-discount effect is sufficiently offsetting in the earlier stages of production that the net effect on total demand for labor is nil. Ultimately, that is, the change in the interest rate affects the pattern of employment and not the magnitude. This is the message in Hayek's third and final appendix in his *Pure Theory of Capital*, "'Demand for Commodities is Not Demand for Labor' versus the Doctrine of 'Derived Demand.'"

In our capital-based macroeconomics, labor is treated as a nonspecific factor of production that is employed in all stages of production. It is neither so predominantly concentrated in the early stages of production that the wage rate rises when the interest rate falls nor so predominantly concentrated in the late stages that the wage rate falls along with a falling interest rate. Of course, in particular applications, if labor is for some reason believed to be disproportionally concentrated in early stages or in late stages, then Figure 4.3 must be modified to show the corresponding change in the wage rate.

Finally, we can note that the treatment of labor in Figure 4.3 warns against any summary treatment of the labor market. The market's ability to adjust to a change in the interest rate hinges critically on differential effects within the more broadly conceived market for labor. In the late stages of production, wages fall and then rise in response to a reduced interest rate; in the early stages, wages rise and then fall. (The opposing transitional adjustments in wage rates are shown by the hollow points in the auxiliary labor-market diagrams in Figure 4.3.) These are the critical relative wage effects that adjust the intertemporal structure of production to match the new intertemporal preferences.

The macroeconomics of boom and bust

Understanding the market process that translates a change in intertemporal preferences into a reshaping of the economy's intertemporal structure of production is prerequisite to understanding the business cycle, or more narrowly, boom and bust. Capital-based macroeconomics allows for the identification of the essential differences between genuine growth and an artificial boom. The key differences derive from the differing roles played by savers and by the monetary authority.

The intertemporal reallocations brought about by a preference change, as illustrated in Figures 4.2 and 4.3, did not involve the monetary authority in any important respect. The different aspects of the market process that transformed the macroeconomy from one intertemporal configuration to another were mutually compatible, even mutually reinforcing. Equilibrium forces were taken to prevail whether the central bank held the money supply constant, in which case real economic growth would entail a declining price level, or (somehow) increased the money supply so as to maintain a constant price level but without the monetary injections themselves affecting any of the relevant relative prices.

Our understanding of boom and bust requires us to take monetary considerations explicitly into account for two reasons. First, the relative-price changes that initiate the boom are attributable to a monetary injection. The focus, however, is not on the quantity of money created and the consequent (actual or expected) change in the general level of prices. The nearly exclusive attention to this aspect of monetary theory was the target of early criticism by Hayek ([1928] 1975a: 103–9). Rather, following Mises and Hayek, our focus is on the point of entry of the new money and the consequent changes in relative prices that govern the allocation of resources over time. A second reason for featuring money in this context is very much related to the first.

The different aspects of the market process set in motion by a monetary injection, unlike the market process discussed with the aid of Figures 4.2 and 4.3, are *not* mutually compatible. They work at cross-purposes. But money – to use Hayek's imagery – is a loose joint in an otherwise self-equilibrating system. The conflicting aspects of the market process can have their separate real effects before the conflict itself brings the process to an end. The very fact that the separate effects are playing themselves out in intertemporal markets means that time is an important dimension in our understanding of this process.

Dating from the early work of Ragnar Frisch (1933), it has been the practice to categorize business cycle theory in terms of the impulse (which triggers the cycle) and the propagation mechanism (which allows the cycle to play itself out). Describing the Austrian theory of the business cycle as monetary in nature on both counts is largely accurate. Money, or more pointedly, credit expansion, is the triggering device. And although in a strict sense the relative-price changes within the intertemporal structure of production constitute the proximate propagation mechanism, money – because of the looseness that is inherent in the nature of indirect exchange – plays a key enabling role.

Figure 4.4 depicts the macroeconomy's response to credit expansion. Intertemporal preferences are assumed to be unchanging. The money supply is assumed to be under the control of a monetary authority, which we will refer to as the Federal Reserve. The supply of loanable funds includes both saving by income earners and funds made available by the Federal Reserve. The notion that new money enters the economy through credit markets is consistent with both the institutional details of the Federal Reserve and with the history of central banking generally. Students of macroeconomics find themselves learning early on the differences among the three policy tools used by the Federal Reserve to change the money supply: (1) the required reserve ratio set by the Federal Reserve and imposed on commercial banks; (2) the discount rate set by the Federal Reserve and used to govern the level of direct short-term lending to commercial banks; and (3) open market operations through which the Federal Reserve lends to the government by acquiring securities issued by the Treasury. These tools differ from one another in terms of the frequency of use, the intensity of media attention, and the implication about the future course of monetary policy.

Of overriding significance for our application of capital-based macro-economics, however, is the characteristic common to all these tools. The three alternative policy tools are simply three ways of lending money into existence. Reducing the required reserve ratio means that commercial banks have more funds to lend, which means they will have to reduce the interest rate to find additional borrowers. Lowering the discount rate will cause banks to borrow more from the Federal Reserve – with competition among the banks reducing their lending rates as well. Central bank purchases of Treasury securities constitute lending directly to the federal government,

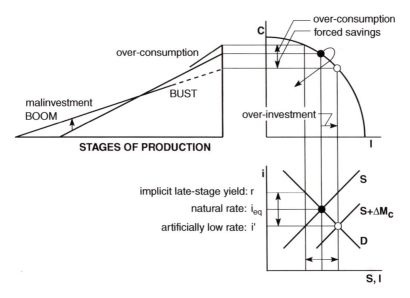

Figure 4.4 Boom and bust (policy-induced intertemporal disequilibrium).

which, like other instances of increased lending, puts downward pressure on the interest rate.

We see the direct effect of lending money into existence, the impulse, on the supply side of the loanable-funds market in Figure 4.4. The extent of the credit expansion (the horizontal displacement of the supply of loanable funds) is set to match the increase in saving shown in Figures 4.2 and 4.3. This construction gives us the sharpest contrast between a preference-induced boom and a policy-induced boom. The new money in the form of additional credit is labeled ΔM_c in recognition that monetary expansion may not translate fully into credit expansion. Some people may choose to increase their holdings, or hoards, of money (by ΔM_h) in response to policy-induced changes in the interest rate. Such changes in the demand for cash balances, while certainly not ruled out of consideration and not without effects of their own, are of secondary importance to our capital-based account of boom and bust.

The initial effect on the rate of interest is much the same for both the preference-induced boom of Figure 4.2 and the policy-induced boom of Figure 4.4. An increased supply of loanable funds causes the interest rate to fall. In application, of course, we must gauge this "fall" relative to the rate that would have prevailed in the absence of credit expansion. What matters is the divergence between the market rate and the natural rate (to use Wicksell's terminology). Suppose, for instance, that there is upward pressure on the natural rate because of technological innovations that directly affect the early stages of production (as depicted in Figure 4.1) but that the Federal Reserve expands credit to keep interest rates from rising. There is no basis for believing that the unchanged rate of interest would allow the market to adjust more quickly or more efficiently to the change in technology. Rather, our analysis of boom and bust would still apply – due allowances being made for the market's simultaneous attempt to adjust for changes in the underlying economic realities.

The telling difference between Figures 4.2 and 4.4 is in terms of the relationship between saving and investment. In Figure 4.2, investment increases to match the increase in saving. But in Figure 4.4, these two magnitudes move in opposite directions. Padding the supply of loanable funds with newly created money drives a wedge between saving and investment. With no change in intertemporal preferences, the actual amount of saving decreases as the interest rate falls, while the amount of investment, financed in part by the newly created funds, increases.

We can trace upward to the PPF to get a second perspective on the conflicting movements in saving and investment. Less saving means more consumption. Market forces reflecting the preferences of income-earners are pulling in the direction of more consumption. Market forces stemming from the effect of the artificially cheap credit are pulling in the direction of more investment. One set of forces is pulling north (parallel to the C axis); the other set pulling east (parallel to the I axis). The two forces resolve themselves into an outward movement – toward the north-east. Increases in the employment of all resources, including labor, beyond the level associated with a fully employed economy cause the economy to produce at a level beyond the PPF.

Is it possible for the economy to produce *beyond* the production possibilities frontier? Yes, the PPF is defined as *sustainable* combinations of consumption and investment. Why is it that the opposing market forces do not simply cancel one another, such that the economy is left sitting at its original location on the PPF? There are two ways to answer this question both of which derive from Hayek's notion of money as a loose joint. First, because of the inherent looseness, the decisions of the income-earner-cum-consumer-saver and the separate (and ultimately conflicting) decisions of the entrepreneur-cum-investor can each be carried out at least in part before the underlying incompatibility of these decisions become apparent. The temporary success of monetary stimulation policies as experienced by all central banks of all Western countries is strong evidence of the scope for real consequences of the sort shown. Second, and equivalently, the movement beyond the PPF is in fact the first part of the market process through which the opposing forces do ultimately cancel one another.

If this temporary movement beyond the frontier were the essence of capital-based account of boom and bust, then our capital-based theory and the widely exposited labor-based theory that involves a play-off between the short-run Phillips curve and the long-run Phillips curve would be very similar. At this point in the analysis, the most salient difference between the two theories stems from the difference in the way money is injected. In our capital-based analysis, money is injected through credit markets and impinges in the first instance on interest rates. In Phillips curve analysis, money is (somehow) injected directly into spending streams of income earners and impinges in due course on (perceived and actual) wage rates. The directness of the capital-based analysis gives it a certain plausibility that is lacking in the labor-based analysis. The labor-based analysis has to incorporate some counterfactual method of injection money – such as Friedman's often invoked supposition that the money is dropped from a helicopter – in order to eliminate injection effects and focus attention on the differential perceptions of employers and employees, which, in turn, affect the supply and demand for labor. A full discussion of this and other relevant aspects of Monetarism is offered in Chapter 10.

Also significant is the fact that the capital-based analysis is more broadly applicable since the market process set in motion by credit expansion does not depend in any essential way on there being a change in the general level of prices. For instance, during the boom of the 1920s, the relatively constant price level was the net result of genuine growth, which put downward pressure on the price level, and credit expansion, which put upward pressure on the price level. The short-run/long-run Phillips curve analysis simply does not apply to this episode since there is no scope for expected inflation lagging behind actual inflation. There was no inflation. Our capital-based analysis, hinging as it does on relative price changes and not on changes in the general level of prices, does apply to the 1920s episode. In other words, the boom and bust of the inter-war years is an exception to the labor-based story but is a primary example of our capital-based story. Still other important differences – pertaining to the two theories' differing implications – will be identified below.

Figure 4.4 shows that the initial phase of the market process triggered by credit expansion is driven by the conflicting behavior of consumers and investors and involves the over-production of both categories of goods. The wedge between saving and investment shown in the loanable-funds market translates to the PPF as a tug-of-war (with a stretchable rope) between consumers and investors. Conflicting market forces are trying to pull the economy in opposite directions. Understanding subsequent phases of this process requires that we assess the relative strengths of the combatants in this tug-of-war. As the rope begins to stretch, the conflict is resolved initially in favor of investment spending – because the investment community has more to pull with, namely, the new money that was lent into existence at an attractive rate of interest. In the Austrian analysis, while an increased labor input – and a general over-production – is undoubtedly part of story, there is also a significant change in the pattern of the capital input. The movement beyond the frontier gives way to a clockwise movement; the unsustainable combination of consumption and investment takes on a distinct investment bias.

We have seen that a change in intertemporal preferences sets in motion a process of capital restructuring, as depicted by the Hayekian triangles of Figure 4.2. Credit expansion sets in motion two conflicting processes of capital restructuring, as depicted in Figure 4.4. The tug-of-war between investors and consumers that sends the economy beyond its PPF pulls the Hayekian triangle in two directions. Having access to investment funds at a lower rate of interest, investors find the longer-term investment projects to be relatively more attractive. A less steeply sloped hypotenuse illustrates the general pattern of reallocation in the early stages of the structure of production. Some resources are bid away from the intermediate and relatively late stages of production and into the early stages. At the same time, income earners, for whom that same lower interest rate discourages saving, spend more on consumption. A more steeply sloped hypotenuse illustrates the general pattern of reallocation in the final and late stages of production. Some resources are bid away from intermediate and relatively early stages into these late and final stages. Mises (1966: 559, 567, and 575) emphasizes the "malinvestment and over-consumption" that are characteristic of the boom. In effect, the Hayekian triangle is being pulled at both ends (by cheap credit and strong consumer demand) at the expense of the middle – a tell-tale sign of the boom's unsustainability. Our two incomplete and differentially sloped hypotenuses bear a distinct relationship to the aggregate supply vector and aggregate demand vector suggested by Mark Skousen (1990: 297) and are consistent with the expositions provided by Lionel Robbins ([1934] 1971: 30–43) and Murray Rothbard ([1963] 1972: 11–39).

In sum, credit expansion sets into motion a process of capital restructuring that is at odds with the unchanged preferences and hence is ultimately ill-fated. The relative changes within the capital structure were appropriately termed malinvestment by Mises. The broken line in the upper reaches of the less steeply sloped hypotenuse indicates that the restructuring cannot actually be completed. The boom is unsustainable; the changes in the intertemporal structure of production are self-defeating. Resource scarcities and a continuing high demand for current consumption eventually turn boom into bust.

At some point in the process beyond what is shown in Figure 4.4, entrepreneurs encounter resource scarcities that are more constraining than was implied by the pattern of wages, prices, and interest rates that characterized the early phase of the boom. Here, changing expectations are clearly endogenous to the process. The bidding for increasingly scarce resources and the accompanying increased demands for credit put upward pressure on the interest rate (not shown in Figure 4.4). The unusually high (real) interest rates on the eve of the bust is accounted for in capital-based macroeconomics in terms of Hayek's ([1937] 1975c) "Investment that Raises the Demand for Capital." The "investment" in the title of this neglected article refers to the allocation of resources to the early stages of production; the "demand for capital" (and hence the demand for loanable funds) refers to *complementary* resources needed in the later stages of production. The inadvisability of theorizing in terms of *the* demand for investment goods – and hence of assuming that the components of investment are related to one another primarily in terms of their substitutability – is the central message of Hayek's article. Though without reference to Hayek or the Austrian School, Milton Friedman coined the term "distress borrowing" (Brimelow, 1982: 6) and linked the high real rates of interest on the eve of the bust to "commitments" made by the business community during the preceding monetary expansion. While Friedman sees the distress borrowing as only incidental to a particular cyclical episode (correspondence), capital-based macroeconomics shows it to be integral to the market process set in motion by credit expansion. These issues are raised again in Chapters 10 and 11.

Inevitably, the unsustainability of the production process manifests itself as the abandonment or curtailment of some production projects. The consequent unemployment of labor and other resources impinge directly and negatively on incomes and expenditures. The period of unsustainably high level of output comes to an end as the economy falls back in the direction of the PPF. Significantly, the economy does not simply retrace its path back to its original location on the frontier. During the period of over-production, investment decisions were biased by an artificially low rate of interest in the direction of long-term undertakings. Hence, the path crosses the frontier at a point that involves more investment and less consumption than the original mix.

Had investors been wholly triumphant in the tug-of-war, the economy would have been pulled clockwise along the frontier to the hollow point, fully reflecting the increase in loanable funds. The vertical component of this movement along the PPF would represent the upper limits of forced saving. That is, contrary to the demands of consumers, resources would be bid away from the late and final stage and reallocated in the earlier stages. The horizontal component of the movement along the PPF represents the over-investment that corresponds to this level of forced saving. (Had consumers been wholly triumphant in the tug-of-war, the economy would have been pulled counter-clockwise along the frontier, fully reflecting the policy-induced decrease in saving. The vertical component of this movement along the PPF represents the upper limits of the corresponding over-consumption.)

Since the counterforces in the form of consumer spending are at work from the beginning of the credit expansion, the actual forced saving and over-investment associated with a credit expansion are considerably less than the genuine saving and sustainable investment associated with a change in intertemporal preferences. (Notice also that the actual forced saving is not inconsistent with the actual over-consumption that characterized an earlier part of the process.) The path of consumption and investment shown in Figure 4.4 has the economy experiencing about half the movement along the PPF as was experienced in the case of an intertemporal preference change. The only substantive claims suggested by our depiction is that the direction of the movement will be the same (in Figure 4.4 as in Figure 4.2) and that the magnitude will be attenuated by the counterforces. Alternatively stated, our construction suggests that the counterforces are at work but do not work so quickly and so completely as to prevent the economy from ever moving away from its original location on the PPF. This is only to say that a market economy, in which the medium of exchange loosens the relationships that must hold in a barter economy, does not and cannot experience instantaneous adjustments.

Although the point at which the adjustment path crosses the PPF is a sustainable level of output, it is not a sustainable mix. Here, capital-based macroeconomics highlights a dimension of the analysis of an unsustainable boom that is simply missing in short-run/long-run Phillips curve analysis. With its exclusive focus on labor markets and its wholesale neglect of injection effects, the economy's return to its natural rate of unemployment leaves the mix of output unaltered. In these circumstances, prospects for a "soft landing" at the natural rate seem good. Considerations of the economy's capital structure, however, cause those prospects to dim. There is no market process that can limit the problem of *mal*investment to the period of *over*-investment. We could not expect – or even quite imagine – that the economy's adjustment path would entail a sharp right turn at the PPF. Almost inevitably, some of the malinvestment in early stages of production would involve capital that is sufficiently durable and sufficiently specific to preclude such a quick resolution. Here, a key difference between the effects of a change in technology and the effects of a cheap-credit policy are worth noting. In the case of technological innovation, we argued that the drawing down of inventories in the late stages can convert some stage-specific change in technology into greater consumption without the particulars of the technological change having a dominating effect on the time pattern of consumption. By contrast, the general reallocation of resources towards long-term projects during a period of decreased saving can result in a structure of production that has limited scope for accommodating current and near-future consumption demands. The specificity and durability of the long-term capital does not allow for a general and timely reversal. The limitations on a timely recovery are stressed by Hayek (1945a) and more recently by McCulloch (1981: 112–14) with specific reference to movements off and along the PPF.

Further, the conventionally understood interaction between incomes and expenditures that initially propelled the economy beyond the PPF and then brought it back to the PPF would still be working in its downward mode as the adjustment path crosses the frontier. There would be nothing to prevent the spiraling downward of both incomes and expenditures from taking the economy well inside its PPF. And leftward shifts in the supply and demand of loanable funds can compound themselves as savers begin to hold their savings liquid and as investors lose confidence in the economy. That is, self-reversing changes in the capital structure give way to a self-aggravating downward spiral in both income and spending. This increase in liquidity preference – or even a seemingly fetishistic attitude toward liquidity – is not to be linked to some deep-seated psychological trait of mankind but rather is to be understood as risk aversion in the face of an economy-wide crisis. The spiraling downward, which is the primary focus of conventionally interpreted Keynesianism, was described by Hayek as the "secondary deflation" – in recognition that the primary problem was something else: the intertemporal misallocation of resources, or, to use Mises's term, malinvestment.

Through relative and absolute adjustments in the prices of final output, labor, and other resources, the economy can eventually recover, but there will be inevitable losses of wealth as a result of the boom–bust episode. A fuller discussion of depression and recovery must await the treatment of labor-based macroeconomics in Part III.

The Austrian theory of the business cycle is sometimes criticized for being too specific, for not applying generally to monetary disturbances whatever their particular nature (Cowen, 1997: 11). We can certainly acknowledge that the bias in the direction of investment is directly related to the particular manner in which the new money is injected. Credit expansion implies an investment bias. Lending money into existence, as we have already noted, accords with much historical experience. We can certainly imagine alternative scenarios. Suppose, for instance the new money makes its initial appearance as transfer payments to consumers. The story of a transfer expansion (Bellante and Garrison, 1988) has a strong family resemblance to the story of a credit expansion, but it differs in many of the particulars.

The output mix during a transfer expansion would exhibit a consumption bias. The initial increase in consumer spending would favor the reallocation of resources from early stages to late stages of production, but considerations of capital specificity would limit the scope for such reallocations. Thus the temporary premium on consumption goods would result in an increase in the demand for investment funds to expand late-stage investment activities. Both consumption and, to a lesser extent, investment would rise. The economy would move beyond its production possibilities frontier, and the rate of interest would be artificially high. Subsequent spending patterns and production decisions would eventually bring the economy back to its frontier. As in the case of credit expansion, the intertemporal discoordination could give way to a spiraling downward into recession. The recovery phase would differ in at least one important respect. Excessive late-stage investments are by their very nature more readily liquidated than excessive early-stage investments. If only for this reason, we would expect a transfer expansion to be less disruptive than a credit expansion.

Figure 4.5, "A generalization of the Austrian theory," shows three possible cases of monetary expansion: credit, credit-and-transfer, and transfer. The

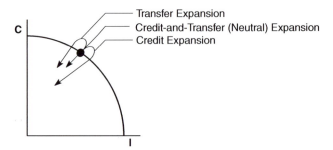

Figure 4.5 A generalization of the Austrian theory.

family of cases exhibits both symmetry and asymmetry. The general adjustment paths of the credit expansion and the transfer expansion are largely
symmetrical about the path of the neutral (credit-and-transfer) expansion.
But the potential for a severe depression as gauged by the kind and extent
of intertemporal discoordination translates into an asymmetry. It is undoubtedly greatest for a credit expansion (because early-stage capital can take
more time to liquidate) and least for a neutral expansion (because there is
no systematic intertemporal discoordination).

The earliest treatment of the intertemporal effects of monetary expansion
(by Mises and Hayek) was offered not as a completely general account but
rather as the most relevant account. The very terminology used here to
make the distinction between the different kinds of monetary expansion –
the relatively familiar "credit expansion" and the relatively unfamiliar
"transfer expansion" – suggest that the former is still the more relevant.
And though specific, the case of credit expansion is readily generalizable in
a way that the alternative theories in which the possibility of a bias favoring
investment or consumption is simply assumed away at the outset are not.

We turn now to retrace some of the key issues about the Austrian theory
of the business cycle in the context of some critical assessments of the
theory.

Elasticity of expectations and lag structure

In the previous section, we tracked the economy through the artificial boom
and subsequent bust without much explicit reference to entrepreneurial
expectations. However, there are strong implications about the consequences
of entrepreneurial behavior in the very notion of a market process: the
market works, but it does not work instantaneously. In the present section,
we make our views on the role of the entrepreneur explicit by focusing on
the issue of expectations in the context of early and ongoing criticism of
the Austrian theory. The focus will be on Hicks (1967), although similar
criticism can be found in Cowen (1997). Our response to Hicks, which

makes use of the boom–bust dynamics depicted in Figure 4.4, is fully consistent with the response offered by Hayek ([1969] 1978).

In Chapter 2 we identified the two assumptions – or more accurately, the two understandings – about expectations that are consistent with the Austrian theory: (1) prices, wages, and interest rates do convey information about underlying economic realities; and (2) market participants do not already have enough information about those realities to make the conveyed information irrelevant. Together, these two propositions leave much scope for the interpretation of the market's reporting on changes in the particular circumstances of time and place. This is only to say that price changes are market signals, not marching orders. Market participants do not react mechanistically to a price change. Their reactions will depend upon their expectations about future changes in this and other prices.

Ludwig Lachmann has taught us that expectations cannot legitimately be included in our list of givens. We must allow for price changes – and changes in market conditions generally – to affect expectations. And in some if not most applications, not even the direction of the effect is determinate. As mentioned in Chapter 2, Keynes was notorious for using this particular indeterminacy as something of a wild card to turn his argument in one direction or the other depending upon where, in his judgment, the argument needed to go. The Austrians use this same indeterminacy to establish the critical importance of the entrepreneur and the market process.

It was John Hicks (1939: 204–6) who provided the terminology for discussing the effect that a change in a price (or in a wage rate or interest rate) has on the expectations about future movements in that price. If the interest rate is forced down (by increased saving or by monetary expansion), will it stay down, fall even further, or rebound towards its previous level? We can ask this same question using Hicks's terminology: Is the elasticity of expectations unity (stay down), greater than unity (fall further), or less than unity (rebound)? The answer hinges critically upon the entrepreneurs' perceptions – or, more generally, the market participants' perceptions – of the nature of the reduced interest rate: Is it widely perceived that the new rate reflects new underlying economic realities? Is it widely perceived that the new rate is a contrivance of the monetary authority? Or, are perceptions mixed and ill-formed?

For the market to be able to accommodate a permanent change in intertemporal preferences, the manifestation of which is a saving-induced increase in loanable funds, the elasticity of expectations with respect to the interest rate has to be much greater than zero. The closer the elasticity of expectations is to unity, the more fully and quickly the market will adjust. (Actually, an elasticity of expectations greater than unity during the period in which the loan market itself is still adjusting to the increased savings would speed up the overall adjustment.)

For the market *not* to be misled at all by a monetary expansion, whose initial manifestation is a bank-induced increase in loanable funds, the elasticity of expectations with respect to the interest rate would have to be zero. An initial rate of, say, 8 percent would be accompanied, even under the downward pressure of monetary expansion by the central bank, by the expectation of an enduring 8 percent (real) interest rate. If the interest were actually to fall as a result of the downward pressure, it would revert to its initial level very quickly as speculators traded on the basis of their inelastic expectations. In the limiting case, in which the market is not misled at all, the lag between the fall and the reversion would itself have to be zero. The downward pressure on the interest rate would be pressure only, the (real) interest rate would remain at 8 percent, and the only effects of credit expansion would be those associated with excessive cash balances: the general price level would rise and the nominal interest rate would include an appropriate inflation premium.

The notion that the central bank cannot, even for a short period, reduce the rate of interest is as implausible as the notion that it can completely fool the economy – permanently – into behaving *as if* market participants were more future-oriented than they actually are. Like back scratchers in a New Classical construction, who cannot determine instantly whether a price change is a local (real) or a global (nominal) phenomenon, market participants in the Austrian construction cannot determine instantly whether a reduction in the interest rate will prove to be a lasting (saving-induced) change or a temporary (money-induced) change. The New Classical/Austrian parallel is stated in terms of a *reduced* rate of interest rather than in terms of (ineffective) downward pressure on the interest rate, implying that the relevant elasticities are greater than zero for both schools. We might even posit a "Hayek Demand Curve" that relates to the markets for inputs in early stages of production in the same way that the "Lucas Supply Curve" relates to the market for output in New Classical constructions.

Market participants can be fooled by the central bank. Expectations about the interest rate are, at best, mixed and ill-formed. The only questions open for discussion, then, are: Just what are they fooled into doing? And to what extent? And for how long?

Expectations here are endogenous in a way the business cycle theorist cannot afford to ignore. That is, expectations about the interest rate, which are mixed and ill-formed at the time that the interest rate falls, will change with the cumulative market experience that flows from the consequences of the lower rate. Changes in the pattern of prices and wages, as well as the more direct interest-related changes in the pattern of capital assets will increasingly favor one interpretation over another. Expectations will change accordingly. The economy will find itself well on its way along a new growth path, or it will find itself dealing with a cyclical downturn. The critical issue can be expressed in terms of lags. How long will it take for the new – or possibly unchanged – economic realities to become fully reflected in expectations? If the lag is sufficiently short, then artificial booms and subsequent crises are of little significance, and all prolonged interest-rate reductions are real and give rise to an increased growth rate. If the lag is sufficiently long, then the distinction between artificial and genuine booms is itself an artificial distinction. The central concern of business cycle theory is one that entails an intermediate lag, one long enough to allow a boom to get under way but short enough to prevent it from maturing into real growth.

In some critical assessments of the Austrian theory of the business cycle, such as in Hicks's telling of "The Hayek Story" (1967), the question "What about expectations?" morphs into the question "What about lags?" And here, as with expectations, the question is typically posed anachronistically. Dating from the Keynesian revolution and the breakaway of macroeconomics (discussed in Chapter 2), lags have been treated as amendments to a theory that is otherwise formulated in terms of contemporaneous macroeconomic magnitudes. Many of the thematic variations of modern labor-based macro-economics derive from the "adding" of some lag structure. Hicks considered alternative lag structures to see if he could save Hayek, who – mysteriously, or so it seemed to Hicks – had failed to specify just what supposedly lags what: Does the inflation premium built into the market rate of interest supposedly lag behind the current rate of inflation? No, Hayek's theory does not hinge in any important way on changes in the general purchasing power of money. Do prices and/or wages supposedly lag behind nominal demands for output and/or labor? No. These features would be distinctly un-Hayekian. In fact, as Hicks recognizes, all such attempts to shore up the Austrian theory by guessing at the supposed lag structure have the effect not of saving Hayek from himself but of making Hayek look like Keynes.

As with expectations, lags are not added to Austrian theory but rather are embedded in it from the outset. Capital-based macroeconomics gives us a lag-infused theory of the business cycle. The means-ends framework of the Austrian School features the time element between the employment of means and the achievement of ends. In Hayek's formulation, as depicted by the Hayekian triangle, the time element manifests itself as the temporal sequence of stages of production. Hicks might have asked: Does the selling of automobiles supposedly lag behind the mining of the iron ore that consti-tutes one of the inputs in the automobile production? Yes, it supposedly does. But it would be misleading simply to answer in the affirmative and declare that we have at long last discovered the Hayekian lag. What we have discovered is the fundamental difference between Keynes-inspired labor-based macroeconomics, which fails to incorporate in any direct way the idea that production takes time, and the capital-based macroeconomics of the Austrian School, for which production time is a central feature.

Hicks actually considers the possibility that Hayek's theory of the business cycle is based on the "production lag (of outputs behind inputs)." He rejects this avenue of interpretation on the grounds that as long as there are no lags in market adjustment, the time-structure of production is irrelevant.

Here, Hicks is implicitly assuming that, in the face of a monetary expansion, an elasticity of expectations of zero applies, if not directly to interest rates, then to each of the individual inputs and outputs that define the temporal sequence of stages of production. Or rather, he is suggesting that if these elasticities of expectations are not all zero, then it is incumbent upon Hayek to explain just why not. The explanation, of course, which typically goes without saying in the Austrian literature, is that market participants do not know, cannot know, and cannot behave as if they know the true nature of a change in market conditions at the moment of change. It is, in fact, the market process itself, as guided by the new market conditions, that reveals the nature of the change. If the process plays itself out as an increased growth rate, then the initiating change was a preference change; if rather than play itself out, the process does itself in, then the initiating change was a policy change.

Superior expectations or good guesses on the part of some will allow them to avoid losses or even to make profits during the time that the process is revealing its true nature. A creative reading of the yield curve (the pattern of interest rates across securities of varying maturities) will provide clues about the market's interest-rate forecasts. But only the attribution of the most extreme and implausibly "rational" expectations to entrepreneurs and to market participants generally would convert this otherwise time-consuming process into an instant revelation about the nature of its results.

The Austrian lag structure, then, mirrors the structure of production. Still, there is some explaining to do to link the cycle-relevant lag with the production-relevant lag. Overly simple expositions of the Austrian business cycle theory tend to play into the hands of critics such as Hicks. Untenable expositions have the economy moving *along* the PPF in the direction of greater investment and then (when?) moving back. Consider the following capsulization of the theory: a policy-induced decrease in the rate of interest causes entrepreneurs to initiate new long-term projects, bidding labor and other resources away from consumer-goods industries and paying for them with the cheap credit. But these workers and resource owners have not changed their attitudes toward thriftiness. They want to spend their incomes in the same pattern as before the interest rate was reduced. Demand in the consumer-goods industries, then, would remain unchanged. Consumer spending will sooner or later (why not immediately?) reverse the process of capital restructuring, turning the artificial boom into a bust.

It would seem (to Hicks and many others) that labor and other resources would be bid back almost immediately, reversing the process or, most likely, preventing the process of capital restructuring from getting under way. Hicks (1967: 208) insists that the spending first by borrowers of the new money and then by the subsequent income earners would be almost instantaneous – within a "Robertsonian week." To believe otherwise would seem to imply that the income earners, inexplicably, are holding unusually large cash balances for a considerable period of time. Was Hicks right after all? Is there some spending lag here that gives duration to the period of malinvestment – some systematic lag between the earning of income made possible by cheap credit and the spending of that income on the economy's output? We think not. But while there is no lag between earning and spending, there is some scope, as we have already depicted in Figure 4.4, for the expansion of output in *all* stages of production. Here, Hayek's concept of money as a loose joint in an otherwise self-equilibrating system is critical. His theory of the business cycle, after all, is a monetary theory. The injection of money through credit markets serves as the trigger, or impulse, that initiates the artificial boom. The use of money throughout the system loosens the otherwise tight joints in the economic process and allows the artificial boom to perpetuate itself well beyond the Robertsonian week.

As indicated in the previous section, the idea that an increased output can be experienced in all stages of production has its counterpart in modern labor-based macroeconomics. Unsustainably high levels of output characterize both the Austrian story and the long-run/short-run Phillips curve story as told by Milton Friedman and Edmund Phelps. In the Friedman–Phelps analysis, however, too much labor and too much output is the whole story. In the Austrian analysis, the (limited) scope for increased output at all stages translates into scope (i.e. time) for misallocations *among* stages. During the upswing, then, the changes in output levels throughout the structure of production have both an absolute and a relative dimension to them. In terms of the PPF in Figure 4.4, the path away from the initial equilibrium goes beyond – rather than along – the frontier.

The Austrian theory has often been described as an over-investment theory of the business cycle. If this were the whole story, Mises–Hayek would simply be a variation of Friedman–Phelps. Defenders of the Austrian theory, including the present writer, have often argued that to categorize the theory as an over-investment theory is to miscategorize it. The Austrian theory is a malinvestment – rather than an over-investment – theory of the business cycle. It is certainly true that policy-induced malinvestment is the unique aspect of the theory. We now see, however, that while malinvestment – the misallocation of resources in the direction of stages remote from consumption – is rightly taken to be the unique and defining aspect of Austrian theory, over-investment is a critical enabling aspect of the theory. Without the over-investment, the malinvestment would be as short-lived as Hicks's critical remarks suggest.

If it is the over-investment that allows the boom to perpetuate itself beyond the Robertsonian week, it is the malinvestment that eventually brings the boom to an end. Here, again, the market process rather than some set of expectations or elasticities that existed at the beginning of the boom is what counts. On the specific issue of intertemporal malinvestments and their eventually being revealed as such, the Hayekian triangle has to be interpreted with great caution. It is all too easy for the Austrian macroeconomist to become a not-so-Austrian geometrician. In response to a policy-induced reduction of the interest rate, one leg of the triangle (measuring the stage dimension of the structure of production) lengthens; the other leg (measuring the final output of the production process) shortens. The forced saving, i.e. the reduced output of consumption goods allows for expansion of the early stages of production. This is the pure malinvestment. In response to Hicks's critical assessment, we must superimpose this relative effect onto the absolute effect in the form of a general expansion of all stages.

It is not implied, however, that this compounding of over-investment with malinvestment applies to each business firm in a way that can be fully anticipated at the outset of the expansion. If this were the implication, then the analysis would, once again, be vulnerable to Hicks's critique. As soon as each entrepreneur learned of the cheap-credit policy, he could correct for the resulting distortions in input prices and output prices associated with his or her firm. For the individual entrepreneur, this correcting for distortions would constitute a hedge against losses in the coming crisis; for entrepreneurs collectively, this systematic correcting would cut the boom short, minimizing the crisis if not avoiding it altogether.

Such correcting for distortions, however, presupposes that each entrepreneur knows precisely where he or she is in the structure of production. In this connection, Hayek's triangle can be more misleading than enlightening. The entrepreneur is not supplied with – and cannot create for himself – a Hayekian triangle complete with a clearly marked sign that reads: YOU ARE HERE. Designed to emphasize the essential time element in the production process, the triangle abstracts from the actual complexities of the economy's capital structure. Feedback loops, multiple alternatives for inputs, and multiple uses of outputs, all of which destroy the strict linearity implied by the triangle, are not the exceptions but the rule. These complexities, emphasized by Lachmann, preclude the hedging against crisis and downturn on a sufficiently widespread basis as to actually nullify the process that would have led to the crisis. The idea that entrepreneurs know enough about their respective positions in the Hayekian triangle to hedge against the central bank is simply not plausible. It all but denies the existence of an economic problem that requires for its solution a market process.

But it is equally implausible that no entrepreneur has any idea where he or she is in the Hayekian triangle – or, more to the point, in the economy's complex structure of production. Entrepreneurs are not in total ignorance about the relationship between their own activities and the rest of the economic system. To claim that they are would be to deny even the possibility of a market solution to the economic problem. Many entrepreneurs can and will make some judgments in this direction and those judgments will be conveyed to others through the price system. Entrepreneurs who perceive their own judgments to be superior ones may even attempt to leverage their gains during the artificial boom before hedging against the inevitable crisis.

The intertemporal allocation of resources, like the allocation of resources even more broadly conceived, requires both (a) the knowledge and hunches of entrepreneurs, including their expectations about future changes in prices, wages, and interest rates, and their understanding of their relationship to the rest of the economy; and (b) the unfolding of the market process, during which price and quantity changes confirm or contradict the entrepreneur's knowledge, hunches, and understanding and provide a continuous basis for adjusting expectations. Accordingly, it is the process itself that translates a change in intertemporal preferences into a new growth rate and that translates a monetary disturbance into a crisis and downturn. The "lag" that Hicks and others have been looking for is nothing but the recognition that this market process takes time.

5 Fiscal and regulatory issues

The contributions of the Austrian School to macroeconomics are commonly seen as being limited to the issues surrounding the business cycle or even more narrowly to the issues pertaining to the upper turning point of the cycle. It is as if mainstream, labor-based macroeconomics is perfectly adequate for all circumstances except those that prevail on the eve of the bust. In those rather special circumstances, the multistage structure of production, the notions of roundaboutness and production time which vary with the interest rate, and all the other thorny issues of capital theory must be ushered in to explain the waning of the boom and the inevitable reversing of the direction of movement of output, income, and expenditures, after which the mainstream macroeconomics again becomes perfectly adequate. This view stands in contrast to the one offered here. While the Austrian theory of the business cycle identifies a special twist in macroeconomic relationships and, for that reason, has become the primary focus of Austrian-oriented macroeconomics and particularly of business cycle theory, the Austrian theory is much more generally applicable than commonly appreciated.

Chapter 3 put forth a full-bodied capital-based macroeconomics; Chapter 4 put the framework through its paces in the contexts of the economics of growth and of cyclical variations. The present chapter considers several loosely related fiscal and regulatory issues (deficit finance, deficit spending, credit controls, and alternative tax bases) to demonstrate the relevance of capital-based macroeconomics beyond its application to the business cycle. Our discussion of fiscal policy in this chapter complements the previous chapter's discussion of monetary policy but not in conventional ways. The focus of mainstream macroeconomics on the circular flow and hence on income and expenditures gives rise to a conception of monetary policy and fiscal policy as alternative and sometimes complementary ways of affecting spending. Our explicit attention to the time dimension of the capital structure precludes any such simple reckoning. As Chapter 4 suggested, monetary expansion – or, more pointedly, injecting new money through credit markets – has the effect of throwing the intertemporal structure of production into disequilibrium. The present chapter will show that fiscal expansion –

borrowing and spending – will move the economy from one equilibrium to another and that the characteristics of the new equilibrium will depend upon the particular nature of the spending. Distinctly different instances of deficit spending can be identified in terms of their differing effect on the intertemporal structure of production as depicted by the Hayekian triangle. The relative political attractiveness of different policies and reforms derive from considerations pertaining to the economy's adjustment path from one equilibrium to the other.

Deficit finance

The graphical framework developed in Chapter 3 can help to shed light on an important and enduring issue of deficit finance: Is government borrowing equivalent to taxing? Or does a policy of deficit finance impose an identifiable burden of its own on future participants in the market process? By featuring the market for loanable funds and the intertemporal capital structure, our graphical construction is particularly helpful in providing answers to these questions.

In Figure 5.1, we consider an economy in which a portion of the public sector that was tax-financed becomes deficit-financed. As indicated in Chapter 3, the PPF can be drawn net of the economy's tax-financed public sector. To focus the analysis on the effects of deficit finance, we hold government's spending – and hence its resource appropriation – constant. And to keep the spending from having systematic effects of its own on the market's intertemporal allocation of resources, we conceive of some kind of spending that is wholly unrelated to the economy's capital structure. That is, at the margin, the government is not spending its tax revenues and/or receipts from the sale of government securities on publicly owned industry or infrastructure but is spending instead on, say, humanitarian foreign aid. The spending on foreign aid does take real resources out of the domestic economy, but that general reduction of resources is already reflected in the PPF, which applies to the resources remaining in the private sector. The question, then, is one of how the domestic economy will be affected – if at all – by financing this foreign aid with debt rather than with tax revenues.

It also must be assumed that a change in the current tax burden does not, by itself, have an effect on the intertemporal allocation of resources. With a simple lump-sum tax or even an income tax, which affects both consumption and investment, this assumption is reasonable. Any change in the intertemporal allocation, then – and, more specifically, any shifting forward of the debt burden – will be attributed to the sale of government securities.

When the government issues additional debt, it increases the demand for loanable funds. This is shown in Figure 5.1 as a rightward shift of demand from D to D'. The consequences for the private sector follow straightforwardly. The higher demand puts upward pressure on the interest rate

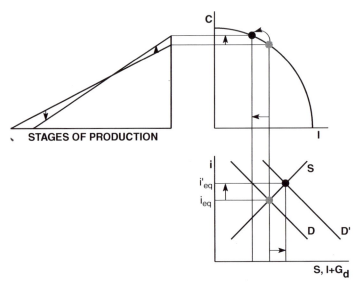

STAGES OF PRODUCTION

Figure 5.1 Deficit finance (shifting the debt burden forward).

and moves savers along their supply curves. We should note here that the interest rate in this figure – and all previous such figures – does not allow for possible differences in the risk premiums for different kinds of securities. To the extent that government securities are considered virtually risk-free, savers may be willing to lend to government at rates that are below the relatively more risky securities in the private sector. The issues concerning risk will be addressed at greater length in the following chapter. For our present purposes, we simply take it that an increased demand for loans results in a higher rate of interest.

We see that at the higher rate of interest, the government's demand for loanable funds, which is measured by the horizontal distance between D and D′, is accommodated in part by an increase in the amount of funds supplied and in part by a reduction in the amount demanded by borrowers in the private sector. At the higher rate of interest, less investment is undertaken. This effect is shown by a counter-clockwise movement along the PPF to a point that entails less investment and more consumption. The result is fully consistent with a common-sense understanding of the change in fiscal policy: the tax cut that accompanied the sale of securities is used in part to take advantage of the higher interest rate and in part to increase consumption.

The economy's capital structure is modified to conform to the new intertemporal pattern of demands. A high interest rate reduces the profitability of long-term projects. Resources are reallocated away from the earlier stages of production and into the late stages where consumption demand is now higher. The Hayekian triangle is reshaped to reflect the bias toward present consumption. This pattern of resource reallocation is what constitutes the temporal shifting of the cost of deficit finance. With more of the economy's output now consumed in the present and with a reduced rate of investment, the economy grows at a slower rate, impinging negatively on the consumable output available in the future. To this extent, the debt burden is shifted forward.

Because of our assumption that the government is sending the borrowed funds abroad, our conclusion about deficit-financed spending is a very one-sided one. If the government spending made possible by the increased indebtedness has benefits in the home country that are reaped largely in the future, then there may be no *net* burden shifted forward. Infrastructure or even a war that safeguards individual liberties may entail a shifting forward of benefits that offsets or possibly more than offsets the shifting forward of the debt burden. By taking government spending to be humanitarian foreign aid (which, presumably, has little or no demonstrable future benefits to the home country), we assure that the shifting forward of the debt burden that constitutes one side of the story of deficit-financed spending is in fact the whole story.

The effects of deficit finance are presented above in comparative-statics terms. The economy is moved from one intertemporal equilibrium to a second intertemporal equilibrium which is more present-oriented than the first. To bring the treatment of deficit finance into conformity with the analysis of boom and bust, as discussed in Chapter 4, we can consider the market process that takes the economy from one equilibrium to the other. Modern debate on deficit finance focuses on the question of whether government debt is perceived to be net wealth. The operative word here is "perceived." By construction, the government is appropriating resources in unchanged amounts, leaving to the private sector the same amount of resources as before the switch from collecting taxes to creating assets. Nonetheless, if the perceived value of the government securities is not fully offset by some perceived costs lying in the future, then the market process will be affected by the net change in perceived wealth. As a result, consumption may rise more quickly than is implied by the shape of the PPF. That is, the economy moves beyond – rather than along – the frontier.

Adding to the perceived-net-wealth effects are some possible distress-borrowing effects similar to those experienced on the eve of a cyclical downturn. That is, firms in the early stages of the structure of production who had not anticipated the change in the government's fiscal strategy may be committed for some time to investment strategies that are no longer viable, given the increased rate of interest. But, in some instances, seeing the projects through to completion involves less of a loss than abandoning the projects. Because of considerations of this sort, total investment for the economy may not fall as quickly as implied by the shape of the PPF. For this reason too, then, the economy moves beyond – rather than along – the frontier.

The economy expands temporarily beyond the PPF – with the increased interest rate giving a consumption bias to the pattern of spending. The unsustainable movement beyond the PPF is shown in Figure 5.1. The market process plays itself out as perceptions come into line with realities and as the intertemporal structure of production comes into conformity with the higher rate of interest. The very nature of the market process – its entailing unsustainably high levels of investing and consuming, of earning and spending, gives deficit finance a political kinship to monetary expansion. Both policies are favored by politicians despite the fact that a strict comparative statics analysis would fail to provide any justification for either.

Although our conclusions about deficit finance follow directly from the application of our capital-based macroeconomics, strong arguments to the contrary can be found in the writings of Ludwig von Mises, whose more general understanding of the relevant macroeconomic relationships underlies our graphical construction. Mises argues that there is no scope for shifting the burden of debt forward. Discussing the costs of war rather than the costs of foreign aid, he rejects the idea that these costs can in any way be shifted forward. Hence, it is "completely wrong" to claim that the debt burden *should* be shifted forward since winning the war benefits future as well as current generations. Mises argues that waging war requires the taking of real resources from the private sector and that the decrease in resources available to the private sector must be fully felt – and can only be felt – as they are taken:

> War can be waged only with present goods. One can fight only with weapons that are already on hand. From an economic point of view, the present generation wages war, and it must also bear all material costs of war. ... Whether the state now finances the war by debts or otherwise can change nothing about this fact.
>
> (Mises, [1919] 1983: 168)

What is advertised here as "an economic point of view" – and repeated in summary form in Mises (1966: 227) – is more accurately described as "a metaphysical point of view." Even though it is true that all "material" costs must be borne in the present, the particular way in which these costs are incurred may affect the allocation of the "materials" *not* used in the war effort, which can shift the *economic* costs of waging war into the future. Lecturing at Auburn University, Leland Yeager, who was the translator of the 1983 English edition of Mises's book, has criticized Mises-the-avowed-subjectivist for not being sufficiently subjectivist in his treatment of deficit finance. Our own application of capital-based macroeconomics reinforces Yeager's assessment by showing just how the burden of debt can be shifted forward.

Mises even goes so far as to assert what has now come to be known as the Ricardian Equivalence theorem. After supposing that the state has to take half of the wealth of the citizenry to pay for the war, he focuses on a representative citizen and asks whether it matters whether the war is tax-financed or deficit-financed. If the state takes half the citizen's wealth:

> it is fundamentally a matter of indifference whether it does so in such a way that it imposes a one-time tax on him of half of his wealth or takes from him every year as a tax the amount that corresponds to interest payments on half of his wealth.
>
> (Mises, [1919] 1983: 168)

The only (less-than-fundamental) difference identified by Mises derives from the circumstance – routinely recognized in modern literature – that some citizens may have to borrow to pay the one-time tax and that they may have to pay a higher interest than the government would have to pay if it did the borrowing. With this conventional qualification, then, Mises has asserted Ricardian Equivalence in its strongest form. There is no perceived change in net wealth because the citizenry perceives the future tax liabilities as clearly as it perceives the government-issued assets. Figure 5.2 shows that if the citizenry increases its saving rate to meet these future tax liabilities, then the supply of loanable funds will shift from S to S', fully matching the rightward shift in the demand for loanable funds. The virtual simultaneous shifting of both curves keeps upward pressure off the interest rate, so that there is no movement – or even any tendency of a movement –

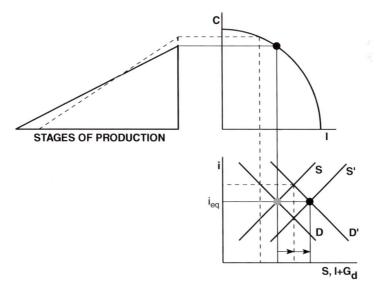

Figure 5.2 Deficit finance (with Ricardian Equivalence).

beyond or along the PPF. Correspondingly, the economy remains at its initial location on the private-sector PPF, and the structure of production remains unaltered. The dotted lines in Figure 5.2 facilitate a comparison between deficit finance both without (dotted) and with (solid) Ricardian Equivalence.

Modern expositions of Ricardian Equivalence (Barro, 1974) identify the circumstances under which the increase in private saving might match the increase in government borrowing. Individuals would have to live infinite lives or, in the context of overlapping generations, all individuals would have to have heirs and would have to care about – or, strictly, behave *as if* they cared about – the heirs as much as they care about their future selves. Critics of Ricardian Equivalence (Buchanan, 1976) have pointed out the implausibility of these circumstances. Defenders of Ricardo (O'Driscoll, 1977a) have shown that the whole point of Ricardo's discussion was to demonstrate the ways in which the two methods of finance are *not* equivalent. A recent quantitative review, or meta-analysis (Stanley, 1998), has shown that the empirical evidence weighs in favor of Ricardo and against Ricardian Equivalence.

The focus of our capital-based macroeconomics on the market process casts doubts on the notion that perceptions at the outset can cut the process short, such that the effects of government borrowing are confined to one axis of one diagram in our macroeconomic construction. Further, the absence of the conditions required for Ricardian Equivalence implies a nontrivial comparative-statics result, entailing a shifting forward of the debt burden. This reckoning could allow for *some* rightward shifting of the supply of loanable funds, though an immediate and wholly offsetting shift would have to be considered an extreme and implausible case. And finally, as emphasized by Buchanan (1976: 341), if the government's shifting from taxing to borrowing actually did stimulate an increase in the supply of loanable funds to match the increase in demand, thus leaving all other real magnitudes unchanged, then it would also leave unexplained the widely known fact that policy-makers tend to favor borrowing over taxing.

Deficit spending

In discussing the possible consequences of deficit finance, as depicted in Figures 5.1 and 5.2, it was assumed that the level of government spending is held constant. In those figures, government borrowing was accompanied by a PPF-neutral reduction in taxes. Dealing in this section with deficit spending, we assume that the level of taxation is held constant and that government borrowing is accompanied by an increase in government spending. We assume further that the government spends borrowed funds on the same kinds of resources ordinarily employed in the private investment sector. Ruled out of consideration, then, are debt-financed transfer payments to consumers. This construction allows us to measure the govern-

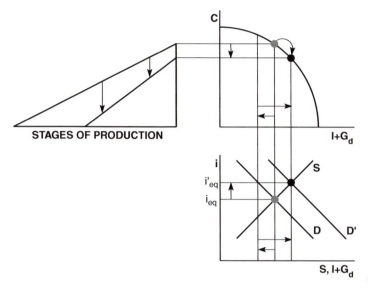

Figure 5.3 Deficit spending (borrowing to finance inert government projects).

ment spending on the horizontal axis of the PPF diagram as the same magnitude of the government borrowing that we measure on the horizontal axis of the loanable-funds diagram. In Figure 5.3, the market for loanable funds and the PPF depict an economy in which the government borrows and bids resources away from the private investment sector. In this application, tax-financed government spending helps establish the shape and position of the PPF itself; deficit-financed government spending – together with private investment spending – are represented explicitly on the horizontal axes. The salient difference between Figure 5.1 and Figure 5.3 is seen in the labeling of the axes. In our analysis of deficit finance, the I was replaced with $I + G_d$ only in the market for loanable funds; in our analysis of deficit spending, the I is replaced with $I + G_d$ in both the loanable-funds diagram and the PPF diagram.

Further specification in terms of the government's use of the resources that it commands with the borrowed funds allows us to draw some conclusions about the macroeconomic effects of deficit spending. Distinguishing among the various uses of public resources is unavoidable, given our attention to the capital structure. Along with Brenner (1994: 130–4) we believe that the absence of these critical distinctions in conventional theorizing about deficit spending accounts for the inclusiveness of the various theories. We can identify and deal with three distinct instances of deficit spending, though we will actually depict only the first one and the third one.

Inert government projects

We begin with the relatively simple instance in which the government is buying resources that would otherwise be bought by the investment community, but it is using these resources in ways that do not interrelate with the resources remaining in the private sector. We might imagine that the government is buying some basic building materials for use in a remote and largely isolated military outpost. Or possibly the government is building monuments to revered political leaders or fallen war heroes. What is essential in this application is that resources are simply withdrawn from the private investment sector. We can refer to this use of borrowed funds as inert government projects.

Including the government among the borrowers in the market for loanable funds is depicted by a shift in the demand for loanable funds from D to D'. Straightforwardly, the interest rate rises to clear the market. The increased demand is accommodated in part by a decrease in the amount of funds borrowed by the private investment sector and in part by an increase in the amount of loanable funds supplied. The increased saving implies decreased consumption, as depicted by a clockwise movement along the PPF. The new equilibrium point is consistent with a decreased level of private investment together with a more than offsetting increase in deficit spending. The resources remaining in the private investment sector are reallocated in accordance with a higher rate of interest, as depicted by a shrunken Hayekian triangle whose hypotenuse has a steeper slope. This result contains no surprises. The private sector's loss of resources takes the form of reduced consumption and reduced investment. The high interest rate encourages a reduction in production time. The economy grows more slowly. This reckoning is net of the inert government spending itself. That is, the remote military operations or war monuments do not themselves count as consumption or investment and do not directly figure into the calculation of the economy's growth rate. Similarly, the production time, e.g. the time involved both in the monument's construction and in its eternal provision of monument services, is similarly excluded from our graphical accounting.

In this instance as in the case of deficit finance the government borrowing may cause people to increase their saving in order to pay higher taxes in the future. The rightward shift of the supply of loanable funds (not shown in Figure 5.3) would move the economy in the direction of Ricardian Equivalence. In the extreme case where the shift in supply matches the shift in demand, private investment remains unchanged and the private sector's loss of resources is incurred exclusively in the form of reduced consumption. Also, as depicted in Figure 5.3, the market process that takes the economy from one point on the PPF to the other involves a movement beyond – rather than along – the frontier. The reasons are similar to those given in the case of deficit finance. The bubbling up gives the policy of deficit spending a strong family resemblance to the policies of deficit finance and credit expansion. And bubbling up always means politically appealing.

Nationalized industries

Our second instance of deficit spending is one that can be discussed more easily than actually depicted. Suppose the borrowed funds are spent domestically on some industrial undertaking. Unlike in the first instance, the government uses the resources in ways that do interrelate with the resources remaining in the private sector. We might imagine that the steel industry has been nationalized and that the government is borrowing to expand its operations. In this application, we must try to say something about the results of a market process where one key participant – namely, the government – is not playing by the rules. It is not responding to price and interest-rate changes in conventional ways. Rather than borrowing more because the interest rate is low, it borrows more, causing the interest rate to be high.

This high rate of interest, as in our first instance of deficit spending, would favor consumption over investment and would cause resources to be bid away from early stages of production and into late stages. But in this instance of deficit spending, we have supposed that the government is bidding resources into the steel industry, which we can safely take to be included among the early stages of production. In effect, the borrowing that sets the market process in one direction is countered by the spending which constitutes a movement in the opposite direction. Resources are being reallocated towards the steel industry but, in general, away from steel-like industries. Expanding operations in the steel industry while the interest is high is likely to involve losses. The essence of this particular instance of deficit spending hinges importantly on the fact that such losses do not necessarily discourage the expansion of the nationalized industry. The government's objectives are something other than making profits or avoiding losses. Its objectives may include, for instance, the provision of employment opportunities, the showcasing of the nation's industrial strength, or increasing the nation's preparedness in face of real or imagined threats from other nations.

The general reallocation away from the early stages will be partially mitigated by considerations of derived demand and capital complementarity. If, despite cumulative losses, the steel is sold at its demand price, the increased supply of publicly produced steel may partially offset the effects of a high interest rate. Some firms will find that remaining in the higher stages of production is relatively profitable despite the increase in the interest rate. Firms for which steel counts importantly among its complement of capital inputs will expand, as will other firms that are producing those inputs that complement steel. Still other firms whose output constitutes an input in the production of steel will expand operations along with the steel industry. There will be some markets, however, in which the effect of a high interest rate and the effect of a loss-incurring nationalized industry are reinforcing rather than counteracting. A firm producing aluminum, for instance, may undergo a dramatic contraction in part because the high interest rate makes resources more valuable in later stages of production and in part because the price of steel, a substitute for aluminum, is low.

Characterizing the general effects of this instance of deficit spending entails some imponderables. Movements tracked by the PPF and the loanable funds market would be in the same general direction as those depicted in Figure 5.3. Production time as represented by the base of the Hayekian triangle would be pulled in both directions, the net effect being indeterminate – hence the omission of a figure depicting the effects of deficit spending on a nationalized industry. However, the imponderables that emerge from mixing market and non-market behavior serve to reinforce our understanding of capital-based macroeconomics and its relationship with other subdisciplines. To the extent that nationalized industries dominate our analysis, our subject matter shifts away from the macroeconomic relationships that govern a market economy to the economics and politics of resource allocation in a non-market setting. The issues of economic growth, business cycles, and deficit spending give way to the issue of economic calculation in a socialist society.

Infrastructure

Our third and final instance of deficit spending allows us to draw insights from the first two. Suppose the government spends its borrowings on infrastructure (highways, waterways, airports, and utilities) or on other programs that may have some public-goods character. We adopt here the conventional understanding of public goods, according to which the market's inability to overcome the free-rider problem cuts the market-process short. In the purest case, the government is not competing at all with the private sector but rather is providing essential infrastructure and the like that otherwise would simply not be provided.

Let us suppose initially that the government (somehow) reallocates resources to the provision of infrastructure in the same way as the market itself would reallocate them if only it could (somehow) overcome the free-rider problem. By its very nature this use of resources adds disproportionately to the early stages of production. Infrastructure is, by and large, early-stage fixed capital. Figure 5.4 depicts the macroeconomic consequences of borrowing to finance infrastructure. Changes in the market for loanable funds in this figure are the same as in Figure 5.3 (borrowing to finance inert government spending); changes in the Hayekian triangle are the same as in Figure 4.2, in which the economy experiences saving-induced growth. Significantly, Figure 5.4 is the rare instance in which the market-clearing rate of interest moves in one direction and the slope of the hypotenuse of the Hayekian triangle rotates in the opposite direction. The economy experiences a higher rate of interest and increased production time.

The apparent contradiction of these anomalous movements can easily be reconciled. Just as in the first two instances of deficit spending, the higher rate of interest discourages undertakings that are relatively time-consuming. Many resources in the private sector are reallocated out of early stages of

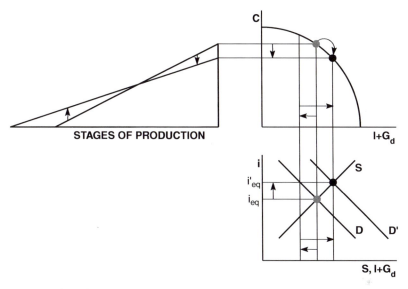

Figure 5.4 Deficit spending (borrowing to finance infrastructure).

production and into late stages. But countering this reallocation is the government's spending on infrastructure. The government, in effect, is going against the market. It is borrowing at a high interest rate and spending on relatively time-consuming projects. Further, some private resources will follow the public resources if considerations of capital complementarity are sufficiently favorable. For instance, a publicly funded rail line into a mineral-rich region may make privately funded mining in that region profitable despite the high interest rates attributable to the government borrowing. Unlike the capital structure depicted in Figure 5.3, the capital structure depicted in Figure 5.4 incorporates the production time associated with the deficit spending on infrastructure. If the effects of over-riding the market process and overcoming the free-rider problem are substantial enough, the (public and private) capital structure will be more time-consuming and the economy will experience an increase in its growth rate.

This conclusion depends critically on the government being able to allocate resources as if it were a market relieved of its free-rider problem. We may conceive of non-market allocation as being relieved of the free-rider problem, but we must recognize that it is also relieved of the guidance that would otherwise be provided by movements in prices, wages and interest rates. Although the government may have a comparative advantage in supplying infrastructure, its ability to allocate resources optimally to the construction of highways, waterways and the like is presumably no better than its ability to allocate resources to a nationalized industry. Deficit spending on infrastructure, then, would take on many of the qualities of the deficit spending on a nationalized steel industry as discussed above. And some further allowance must be made for the misidentification of a public good – as when, for instance, the government spends on a waterway for which there is little or no use. To this extent, what was intended as infrastructure is more accurately described as a monument, and the effects of the deficit spending would be those depicted in Figure 5.3.

The greater point to be made on the basis of understanding of the three instances of deficit spending is that the effects of this fiscal policy cannot be summarily described in terms of the spending alone. Taking into account the higher interest rate still leaves us short of a summary conclusion. Because of the explicit attention to the time element in the economy's structure of production, capital-based macroeconomics must also take into account the intertemporal dimension of the government's spending programs.

Credit control

Capital-based macroeconomics can be applied to an economy subjected to credit control in the form of an interest-rate ceiling. The pay-offs of our particular applications, however, are largely doctrinal and pedagogical. Actual historical episodes of credit control involve selectively imposed interest-rate ceilings. Even seemingly broad-based usury laws, which apply to all categories of loans, must be counted as selective controls in the context of our much more broadly defined market for loanable funds. The supply of loanable funds is made up of saving in all its forms, including, for instance, the purchase of equity shares. The predominant effect of restricting one form of saving would simply be to shift funds into other forms. While this unsurprising consequence is an important and historically relevant one, it is a result that our graphical construction is not well suited to demonstrate. However, our construction is well suited for dealing with one form of credit control that is so narrowly imposed that the control itself makes no direct appearance in our market for loanable funds and a second form of credit control that is so broadly imposed as to have no direct historical relevance. The significance of these two applications are doctrinal in the first case and pedagogical in the second.

Smith's usury laws

Adam Smith, believed by many to be the ultimate defender of the system of natural liberty, recommended an interest-rate ceiling on consumer loans. The intent of this selective prohibition of usury was not to ensure that consumers could borrow at low interest rates but rather to restrict their ability to borrow. The wealth of nations, in Smith's view, would be increased by such a restriction. If the interest-rate ceiling is set just above the rate on secure productive loans, then more of the nation's saving will be channeled into productive undertakings. Smith was in favor of liberty, but he was also in favor of economic growth. At the margin, and taking his cue from the impartial spectator (who is imagined to be more future-oriented than ordinary market participants), he was willing to trade a little bit of liberty for a little more growth.

Whatever modern defenders of the system of natural liberty may think of Smith and his usury laws, our capital-based macroeconomics can show that Smith was on solid ground analytically. Though our concept of loanable funds is a broad one, it does not include consumer loans. The borrowing by consumers is netted out on the supply side of the loanable funds market. Any reduction in consumer loans is represented in our graphical construction as an increase in the supply of loanable funds for other purposes. This interest-rate ceiling, then, manifests itself as a rightward shift in the supply of funds to the business community. If, to overdraw the distinction, the interest rate on all consumer loans is above 6 percent, while the interest rate on all productive loans is below 4 percent, then an interest-rate ceiling of 5 percent would, using Smith's own terminology, shift funds from unproductive purposes to productive purposes.

The macroeconomic effects of Smith's usury laws are those already illustrated in Figure 4.2. In Chapter 4, it was shown that a change in the growth rate would be brought about by a change in intertemporal preferences, which shifts the supply of loanable funds to the right. That same figure applies here with the understanding that now it is a change in the constraints rather than a change in preferences that accounts for the rightward shift. But in both cases, the increased supply of loanable funds (1) decreases the market-clearing rate of interest on funds not directly subject to the ceiling rate; (2) increases the rate of investment; and (3) increases the economy's growth rate. And as long as the preferences stay changed in the first case and as long as the constraints are not circumvented in the second case, the new higher growth rate is sustainable. It is true, of course, that the constraint-induced growth rate is not consistent with the intertemporal preferences of consumers, but it is consistent with the values of the "future-oriented impartial spectator," which is what counted for Smith (Garrison, 1998b).

This reckoning of Smith's usury laws is subject to a major qualification. Not all high-interest rate loans are consumer loans. Lenders who finance risky business undertakings command high interest rates as well. This fact posed no problem for Smith. He wanted to constrain both "prodigals and projectors" (Smith [1776] 1937: 339) because both groups were seen as wasting the funds that they borrow. The prodigals waste them by their spending on present gratification rather than on productive capital; the projectors waste them by their spending on risky business ventures. Smith wanted these funds spent instead on secure business undertakings.

A more modern understanding of the relationship between risk and rate of return calls Smith's pro-growth policy into question. Even the paternalistic moderns, who might be willing to cut consumer borrowing short in order to allow the economy to grow more rapidly, would have to wonder if Smith's interest-rate ceiling is actually conducive to economic growth. High risks may be worth taking – from the point of view of both the individual and society. In fact, there may be some concern that too little of the economy's resources will be devoted to venture capital. That is, an individual may not be willing to take a risk that, in the broader view of the economy or even the business firm, would be very much worth taking. Incorporating this understanding into Smith's thinking would imply the need for a policy to reallocate funds from prodigals to projectors. An interest-rate ceiling set just above the rate on secure productive loans would not do the trick. And any alternative policy that may do the trick is likely to entail – for Smith as well as for the moderns – a little too much interference with the system of natural liberty. The economy may be better off if prodigals, projectors, and risk-averse producers compete for funds on equal terms. *Laissez-faire* turns out to be the obvious policy alternative.

Broad-based usury laws

A wholly different conception of usury laws allows for a more direct application of capital-based macroeconomics. For this application, we have to imagine that an effective interest-rate ceiling could somehow be imposed on our broadly conceived market for loanable funds. As shown in Figure 5.5, the ceiling rate results in a shortage of credit measured by the horizontal distance between the supply and demand curves. At the ceiling rate, many would-be borrowers in the business community can find no funds to borrow; erstwhile savers, constrained by that same ceiling rate, are now more inclined to consume than to save. The ceiling-induced reduction in saving and hence in investment and the corresponding increase in current consumption is shown by the counter-clockwise movement along the PPF. Straightforwardly, the economy grows more slowly.

   With loanable funds in short supply, the value of loanable funds is indicated by the demand price, which must be consistent with the rate of return that can be obtained outside the loanable-funds market. That is, the demand price in the loanable-funds market, labeled "yield on real assets" is the rate of return that governs the capital restructuring. This relatively high yield reallocates resources towards the late stages of production to accommodate the increased demand for current consumption. The Hayekian triangle is reshaped in the direction of shorter production time and increased output of consumption goods. In summary terms, broad-based credit controls create a discrepancy between the interest rate in the market for loanable funds, which is subject to control, and the effective time discount in the intertemporal structure of capital, which is not. Undoubtedly, this discrepancy would give rise to the development of circumventions of the interest-rate ceiling, such as allowing interest payments to masquerade as finance charges or risk premiums. But apart from such circumventions, there is no self-

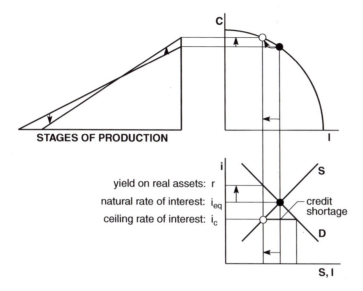

Figure 5.5 Credit control (broad-based interest-rate ceiling).

reversing aspect to this policy of credit control. As long as the interest-rate ceiling is enforced, the structure of production will be biased in favor of consumption, and the economy's growth rate will be diminished.

The pay-off to our depicting the effects of a broad-based interest-rate ceiling comes in our comparing them to the effects of deficit finance and of credit expansion. A comparison of credit control and deficit finance in strict comparative-statics terms reveals some surprising similarities. However, considerations of the differing market processes involved – together with some important qualifications – helps to put the comparative statics into perspective and ultimately to reinforce our understanding of the fundamental relationships that constitute capital-based macroeconomics.

A direct comparison of Figures 5.1 and 5.5 reveals that if we confine our attention to the initial and subsequent equilibria as depicted by the PPF and the Hayekian triangle, the consequences of deficit finance and of a broad-based interest-rate ceiling are identical. Even the market for loanable funds shows the same quantity of loanable funds supplied and demanded and the same demand price of credit. The only difference revealed by the two figures stems from the specific way in which the interest rate is affected. In Figure 5.1, the market-clearing rate is high because of the government's demand for loanable funds; in Figure 5.5, the demand price of credit is high because the interest-rate ceiling has limited the quantity supplied. In both cases, however, conditions in the loanable-funds market lead to an increase in consumption. Further, market reactions to these different policies beyond what is shown in the figures themselves add to the similarities.

To the extent that people increase their savings in anticipation of higher tax burdens in the future, the effects of deficit finance are offset – completely offset in the extreme case of Ricardian Equivalence. Similarly, to the extent that people find ways of circumventing the interest-rate ceiling, the effects of this form of credit control are partially or, in the extreme case, completely offset.

Pointing out two substantive differences may make all these similarities seem less counter-intuitive. First, the interest-rate ceiling is introduced as a wholly gratuitous intervention. It distorts credit markets to no good end. Clearly, the economy would be better off without it. Deficit finance, however, was introduced as an alternative to taxation. By construction government spending was held constant. If we think of deficit finance as distorting credit markets, we must compare this distortion to the distortions associated with the taxes that would otherwise be collected. In order to focus narrowly on the effects of deficit finance, we assumed that the tax-related distortions, whatever their particular nature, are distortions that do not change the shape of the PPF. This (or some similar) assumption is common in macroeconomics. Clearly, actual policy decisions about financing the public sector would have to be based on a comparison between the distortions associated with borrowing and the distortions associated with taxing. And more broadly, the distortions of each would have to be assessed in the light of the benefits, however reckoned, of the corresponding public-sector projects being financed – humanitarian foreign aid in the present discussion.

A second substantive difference between the effects of deficit finance and the effects of a broad-based interest-rate ceiling derives from a closer look at the market process associated with each. As has already been discussed, deficit finance causes the economy to move beyond – rather than along – the frontier. There is a temporary bubble on the PPF that makes the policy of deficit finance a politically popular policy. By contrast, deviation from the PPF in the case of an interest-rate ceiling is in precisely the opposite direction. There is no bubbling up but rather a dipping down. Savers, who begin earning a smaller return because of the interest-rate ceiling, may not start consuming more immediately. Investors in the late stages of production may see no immediate justification for expanding, and when they do see some justification, they may not be able to borrow because of the credit shortage. As indicated in Figure 5.5, the market process that moves the economy to a new equilibrium dips into the interior of the PPF. This aspect of imposing a broad-based interest-rate ceiling helps to explain why such a policy, unlike deficit finance, would not be a politically popular policy.

While our comparison of credit control and deficit finance reveals some surprising similarities (and some essential differences) in terms of the corresponding comparative statics, a comparison between credit control and credit expansion can reveal some enlightening similarities in terms of the corresponding market processes. As we have seen, the element of commonality between Figure 5.5 (credit control) and Figure 5.1 (deficit finance) is the high rate of interest – the demand price of credit – that governs movements depicted by the PPF and the Hayekian triangle. The element of commonality between Figure 5.5 (credit control) and Figure 4.4 (credit expansion) is the low rate of interest associated, respectively, with the interest-rate ceiling and with an increase in the supply of credit. This low rate, together with the differing credit-market conditions associated with it, has important implications about the corresponding market processes.

Consider the ceiling rate in Figure 5.5. The investment community would like to take advantage of this attractive interest rate by increasing investment spending, but savers, constrained by the ceiling, actually decrease the amount of loanable funds available for borrowing. The divergence between actual saving and would-be investment manifests itself as a credit shortage. It is this shortage that, by making itself obvious to frustrated borrowers and other market participants, gives play to the corresponding demand price of credit. Suppose, though, that the government were to accommodate the frustrated borrowers by creating funds and making them available at the ceiling rate. By papering over the credit shortage, the policy-maker would take the high demand price of credit out of play. We would observe, instead, an actual increase in borrowing at the low rate. The added policy of accommodating all borrowers at the ceiling rate sets the market process off on a different course.

But what are the ultimate consequences of this market process? Except for the differing announcement effects, the market process associated with papering over the credit shortage caused by an interest-rate ceiling, and the market process associated with a credit expansion are indistinguishable. Credit creation serves to mask rather than actually eliminate the real shortage in the market for loanable funds. The underlying conflict between savers and investors remains. The problems that would have manifested themselves immediately are allowed to fester as a very different market process begins to unfold. The actual spending of both groups takes the economy in the direction of unsustainable growth. The market process pushes beyond the PPF and gives an edge, by virtue of the low interest rate, to investment spending. It is the story of boom and bust as told in Chapter 4. The only differences in the story lines would have to derive from the differing announcement effects. Imposing an interest-rate ceiling may have a strong announcement effect that warns entrepreneurs not to proceed on a business-as-usual basis. However, if the additional policy of accommodating all borrowers at the ceiling rate is implemented at the outset, then the actual imposition of the ceiling becomes redundant. There need be no announcement of the ceiling – which, of course, would mean no announcement effect. The two policy schemes themselves (credit expansion and credit control with accommodation) become indistinguishable.

As already indicated, the significance of our treatment of credit control is not in its direct application but rather in its contribution to pedagogy. Critics of the Austrian theory of the business cycle often ask: Why, during a credit expansion, are the prices of consumer goods not bid up almost immediately such that the investment boom is very short-lived? They are asking, in effect, why the effects of credit expansion are different from the effects of broad-based credit control. An effective answer emerges from our comparison of Figures 5.5 and 4.3: (1) credit control causes a problem that is immediately apparent – namely, a credit shortage; (2) masking the credit shortage with credit creation does not eliminate the problem but rather allows it to fester; (3) credit expansion initiates the festering without there being even an announcement effect that might mitigate against the market responding on a business-as-usual basis. The market processes associated with (2) and (3), which throw the capital structure into an intertemporal disequilibrium, are turned against themselves when – as the market process unfolds – the relative price of consumers, goods are *eventually* bid up. To argue that credit control and credit expansion are indistinguishable in their effects is to ignore the differences in the corresponding market processes and to leave unexplained the fact that credit expansion has political appeal while broad-based credit control does not.

Tax reform

Neither taxes nor tax-financed government spending make a direct appearance in our framework. Despite this fact, the graphics are well suited for depicting the consequences of some kinds of changes in the tax environment. To isolate tax considerations, we assume in this section that there is no deficit spending. We deal with a mixed economy in which the public-sector budget remains in balance. The PPF, then, depicts the production possibilities faced by the private sector. It traces out the after-tax terms of trade between consumption and investment.

These terms of trade will be affected by the fiscal authority's particular choice of a tax base. More specifically, an income tax, which impinges on both consumption and investment activities, will imply a different private-sector PPF than is implied by a consumption tax, which excludes saving and investment from its tax base. Let us take the PPF of earlier figures to be the one implied by an income tax. Our framework, then, allows us to identify the consequences of replacing the income tax with a consumption tax, as proposed by Hall and Rabushka (1995) and others.

If the alternative consumption tax is to raise the same amount of revenue, the tax rate will have to be higher to offset the effect of adopting a smaller tax base. (In our construction – and in reality – the change in tax rate calculated to achieve revenue neutrality will apply to a particular range of the PPF and will not imply revenue neutrality over all ranges of the frontier.) The replacement of an income tax with a consumption tax differentially affects the intercepts of the private-sector PPF. The consumption intercept will move toward the origin, reflecting reduced after-tax consumption possibilities; the investment intercept will move away from the origin, reflecting

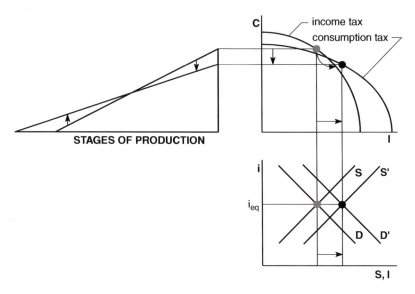

Figure 5.6 Tax reform (from an income tax to a consumption tax).

tax-free investment possibilities. Equivalently, the generally decreased slope of the PPF reflects the fact that tax reform of this sort changes the intertemporal trade-off in favor of investment. Figure 5.6 shows the economy both before and after the transition from an income tax to a revenue-equivalent consumption tax.

The change in the tax base has no first-order effect on the rate of interest. The increase in the amount of saving available and in the amount of investment undertaken is directly driven by tax considerations, not by interest-rate considerations. The actual magnitude of the shift in demand depends upon the technological constraints that affect the terms of trade between consumption and investment; the actual magnitude of the shift in supply depends upon the extent to which income earners are willing to substitute future consumption for current consumption in order to postpone their tax liabilities. Figure 5.6 shows the two curves shifting to the same extent, leaving the rate of interest unchanged. While revenue neutrality does not imply interest-rate neutrality, this depiction serves to emphasize that the primary consequence of the change in the tax base is the alteration of the after-tax PPF, which, despite the unchanged interest rate, results in increased investment and hence an increased rate of economic growth. Of course, if there is reason to believe that the supply of loanable funds would shift, say, more than would demand – possibly because of special features of a particular tax reform package – then the equilibrium interest rate would fall.

However, even with an unchanged rate of interest shown in Figure 5.6, the Hayekian triangle changes in shape. The slope of the hypotenuse is lessened. Here, as in the case of borrowing to finance infrastructure shown in Figure 5.4, the hard link between the interest rate in the loanable-funds market and the slope of the hypotenuse of the Hayekian triangle is broken. This is only to say that with a change in the tax base, any given interest rate will be paired with a different slope of the hypotenuse than before.

Significantly, the increased growth due to tax reform is sustainable growth. The change in the tax base sets in motion a market process that reallocates resources in accordance to the new constraints. There is nothing in the nature of this market process that would turn the increased growth rate into an economy-wide crisis. There is no reason to believe that the adjustment to the tax reform would have a boom–bust character to it. And after the reconfiguration, the Hayekian triangle will once again change in shape in accordance with saving-induced changes in the interest rate as in Figure 4.2.

Our treatment of the consequences of replacing an income tax with a consumption tax provides a useful basis for assessing the merits of tax reform in this direction. The consumption tax is sometimes touted as being pro-growth – as if the higher growth rate is a pure gain to the economy. But prerequisite to the higher growth rate, as our graphical treatment clearly shows, is a reduction in current consumption. That is, it is precisely this reduced current consumption that frees up resources which can then be used to increase the economy's capacity for producing greater levels of output in the future.

Curtailing current consumption permits more rapid economic growth. Decisions about how much to consume now and how much to save for the future are made every day by the millions of market participants whose decisions constitute the market process. Legislating tax reform in the direction of a consumption tax may best be understood as a means of (partially) collectivizing the decision to increase saving. This understanding calls into question the various provisions of proposed reform that affect consumption spending during the transition from the income tax to the consumption tax and even beyond. First, there is the issue of "old wealth." People who have earned income before the reform and have already paid an income tax should not have to pay a consumption tax when they spend their after-tax income. There should be a grandfathering, then, that applies to the spending of pre-reform income. Let us overlook the administrative difficulties of implementing such a provision and look instead at the consequences of exempting this consumption spending from the consumption tax. From a macroeconomic point of view, we see that it is precisely the reduction of consumption that makes a higher growth rate possible. If this grandfathering allows wealth holders to maintain their consumption levels, then to this extent the intended consequences of the reform are directly countered. Or, alternatively, if the full pro-growth effects are to be realized, then the grandfathering will mean that the grandsons (the market participants who finance consumption out of current income) will have to endure a disproportionally large reduction in their consumption during the period of transition

Second, most actual proposals for reform in the direction of a consumption tax allow for very generous personal exemptions. Exemptions as high as $25,000 and $36,000 per household, which add a strong element of progressivity to the tax structure, are thought by many to be essential for the political viability of tax reform. But given the relationship between current consumption and the growth rate, political viability of this sort translates directly into a negation of the hoped-for effect of the reform. To the extent that income earners are allowed to maintain or even increase their consumption by virtue of the exemption, then the economy's resources would be channeled into the provision of consumption goods and not into increased productive capacity. Any net shift in the reallocation of resources away from current consumption would have to derive from a more-than-offsetting increase in saving by individuals whose consumption is actually subject to the consumption tax. Alternatively, with a generous personal exemption, the rightward shift of the supply of loanable funds in Figure 5.6 may be much less than the rightward shift in demand.

Third, there is some concern that the transition from the income tax to the consumption tax may send the economy into recession. That is, the reduction in consumption may precede the increase in investment, as shown in Figure 5.6 by a dipping down rather than a bubbling up as the economy moves from the pre-reform equilibrium to the post-reform equilibrium. But stimulating consumption during the transition by means of, say, a transfer expansion may be counter-productive. Again, if the net effect of the transitional dipping down and of the transfer expansion is actually to leave consumption spending unchanged, then the supposed beneficial effects of more rapid growth would be negated.

Even apart from these political and transitional considerations, there seems to be no clinching argument that allows for an unambiguous preference between a consumption tax and an income tax. Each is deficient when judged by the standard set by the other. If we take consumption as the appropriate base, we would judge the income tax to be too broadly applied – such that some consumption, in effect, gets taxed twice. If we take income as the appropriate base, we would judge the consumption tax to be too narrowly applied – such that some income escapes taxation altogether. Both judgments are question-begging; they follow trivially from the proposition that if we take "X" to be the appropriate tax base, then "Z" is an inappropriate tax base.

Current consumption can be traded for future consumption. Participants in the market process do it by putting their saving at interest in the loanable funds market. Participants in the political process do it, in part, by voting to replace an income tax with a consumption tax. In both cases, the economy experiences a more rapid growth rate to the extent – and only to the extent – that current consumption in reduced.

The substantive issues surrounding the consumption tax – and surrounding deficit finance and credit control – are only touched upon here. The greater goal is to demonstrate that capital-based macroeconomics has applications beyond the business cycle. Issues in fiscal policy, credit control, and tax reform have provided some obvious extensions. Undoubtedly, there are others.

6 Risk, debt, and bubbles

Variation on a theme

Capital-based macroeconomics features the time element in macroeconomic relationships. Time is a fundamental and pervasive dimension in the economics of sustainable and unsustainable growth (Chapter 4) and in several related fiscal and regulatory issues (Chapter 5). The particular treatment of time as one dimension of the Hayekian triangle allows us to incorporate another aspect of the production process. Specifically, the remoteness in time of investment decisions from the eventual availability of consumable goods translates to some extent into riskiness. The more roundabout the production process, the more time for unexpected changes in market conditions to occur. But a fuller understanding of the macroeconomics of risk and uncertainty requires that we look beyond the simple geometry of our capital-based macroeconomic framework.

Time is inherent in a capital-using production process; risks are inherent in all future-oriented undertakings. Considerations of risks willingly borne and of risks not-so-willingly borne can add a new dimension to our theory. Paralleling the contrast in the macroeconomics of intertemporal allocation between preference-based growth and a policy-induced boom is a contrast between preference-based risk-taking and policy-induced risk-bearing. The macroeconomics of risk is not a substitute for the macroeconomics of capital structure (as it is in Cowen, 1997), but it can complement our understanding of the more fundamental intertemporal aspects of the market process.

Integrating considerations of risk can help to increase the relevance and extend the applicability of capital-based macroeconomics. The Hayekian triangle was introduced at a time when Hayek and the rest of the profession were contemplating the dramatic economic boom of the 1920s and the subsequent depression that had yet to find its bottom. The 1990s found the profession in similar circumstances – contemplating America's dramatic bull market of the 1980s and wondering if and how the recession of 1991–2 was related. In a similar time frame, the Asian miracle had somehow turned into the Asian malaise. Do these stories of bulls and bears and of miracle and malaise parallel the older story of boom and bust? It would be a mistake to assume that Hayek's triangulation as applied to the inter-war episode applies in some wholesale fashion to the so-called bubble economies of recent years, but it ,would be a greater mistake to assume that Hayek's insights have no modern application of all.

Hayek's theory of boom and bust can be modified so as to extend its applicability. After making the appropriate conceptual and institutional adjustments, the story of boom and bust can be retold in a way that sheds light on contemporary macroeconomic problems and helps to put in perspective the macroeconomics of the intervening years which grew out of the Keynesian revolution. The rate of interest figures importantly in both early and modern applications. The needed modification requires that we focus attention on a different aspect of the interest rate, namely, the risk premium.

Three components of the interest rate

Production time can put a lag between an intervention in credit markets and the ultimate consequences of the intervention. Of particular concern to Hayek was credit expansion, which affects the capital structure's intertemporal orientation. Cheap credit favors a reallocation of resources among the stages of production that is inconsistent with intertemporal preferences of consumers. More specifically, the artificially low rate of interest causes production plans to become more future-oriented and consumption plans to become less so.

Other sorts of intervention that might have lagged consequences on an economy-wide scale can be identified by taking the interest rate to be the key market signal that translates cause into lagged effect and considering the individual components of the market rate on interest. To this end, it is convenient to conceive of the market rate as consisting of three components: (1) an underlying time discount; (2) an inflation premium; and (3) a risk premium. Hayek's triangulation in the early 1930s – and our development of it in Chapters 4 and 5 – are based squarely on the first component.

By the 1960s the focus of macroeconomists had shifted from the first component to the second. Practiced use of monetary tools as economic stimulants – and repeated experience with the fading of the stimulants' real effects – gave increasing importance to the role of expectations. Scope for a significant discrepancy between expected and actual inflation rates resulted in macroeconomic constructions that featured the inflation premium. Arguably, the most interesting consequences of imperfectly anticipated inflation are those that manifest themselves as the misallocation of capital and labor among the stages of production. But as chronicled in Chapter 2, by the time the problem of inflation had captured the attention of modern macroeconomists, capital theory had been in eclipse for more than two decades.

The Keynesian revolution had so weakened the perceived link between capital and interest that it became commonplace to theorize in terms of the level of employment in the context of a given capital structure. Monetary expansion, which has its most direct effects in credit markets and on interest rates, came to be analyzed in terms of labor markets and wage rates. This shift in focus was seen as a glaring incongruity by economists who learned their macroeconomics from Hayek but was second nature to economists who had long since left capital theory behind.

The nature and significance of the inverse relationship between the inflation rate and the level of employment, as depicted by the Phillips curve, were derived from (1) differences in the abilities of employers and employees in forming relevant expectations; and (2) the experience of market participants, broadly conceived, in adjusting their expectations to realities (Friedman, 1976). The first difference governed the strength of the short-run trade-off between inflation and unemployment; the second difference governed the length of the short run. What came to be the conventional account of the consequences of monetary expansion traces the movement along a short-run Phillips curve, which reflects given expectations about changes in the level of prices, then allows for a shifting of the curve as expectations change. The adjustment process involves a temporary decrease in the unemployment rate as wage-rate adjustments lag behind price adjustments followed by a permanent increase in the inflation rate as the general levels of prices and wages catch up to the expanding money supply.

Except for occasional reference to temporary and wholly incidental effects on the stock-flow relationships in markets for financial and real assets, business-cycle theory based upon short-run/long-run Phillips curve dynamics takes no account of capital misallocation. The critical time element, which was a fundamental aspect of capital-based macroeconomics, was retained in the tenuous form of time-consuming adjustments of perceptions to realities – adjustments that are accomplished differentially by employers and employees.

The general focus of macroeconomic discussion changed dramatically between the 1930s and the 1960s as the focus changed from the time-discount component of the interest rate to the inflation premium and from capital markets to labor markets. In summary terms, Hayek's *Prices and Production* provided a capital-based account of policy-induced distortions in time discounts, while the macroeconomics of the 1960s provided a labor-based account of policy-induced changes in the inflation premium. A further assessment of this particular strand of Monetarism will be offered in Chapter 10. It can be noted here that when Hayek himself (1975e) adopted a labor-market perspective, his account of boom and bust became virtually indistinguishable from that of the Monetarists. The purpose here in contrasting Phillips curves and Hayekian triangles is to set the stage for still another perspective – one that, refocusing attention on capital markets, may prove more applicable to the 1990s and beyond.

The third component of the market rate of interest, the risk premium, has played a significant role neither in Hayekian constructions nor in more modern ones. Typically, risk premiums get mentioned (as they did in Chapter 5) only in introductory throat-clearing paragraphs in which considerations of risks along with administrative charges and other workaday matters are assumed away. At most, the perceived riskiness of holding non-monetary assets helps in some formulations to explain the changing demand for money. But there has been no macroeconomic theory attempting to explain episodes of boom and bust by contrasting the market's allocation of risk-bearing and policy-induced distortions of risk-related market mechanisms. Except for relatively recent experience, such a theoretical formulation would have little if any application. But the macroeconomic experience of the 1980s and 1990s – and possibly beyond – might best be accounted for by just such a theory.

The risk-based formulation parallels Hayek's original triangulation and, to a lesser extent, the more modern theorizing about short-run and long-run Phillips curves. In summary terms, we can say that the market allocates risk-bearing among market participants in accordance with the willingness of each to bear risk. Policies can create a discrepancy between risk willingly taken and risk actually borne. The critical time element embedded in risk-bearing manifests itself as a lag between the risks unknowingly borne and the subsequent increased frequency and severity of losses unexpectedly incurred. Accordingly, such policies have cause-and-effect relationships that manifest themselves macroeconomically as boom and bust.

Risk control and risk externalization

Not all conceivable policies that would interfere with the market's allocation of risk-bearing have consequences of a cyclical nature. Suppose, for example, that the legislature considers all market rates of interest of more than, say, 5 percent above the Treasury-bill rate as constituting excessive riskiness. Accordingly, it simply prohibits the payment for all such risk-bearing. A legislated Treasury-plus-five cap on interest rates would have a direct and immediate effect on credit markets. Entrepreneurs interested in relatively risky undertakings would face a credit shortage. The effects of this partial prohibition against risk-taking would differ little from the effects of a simple interest-rate cap as discussed in Chapter 5. Black and gray credit markets would emerge to partially offset the effects of legislation. And the trade-off between debt and equity financing would be biased in favor of equity, if only because illegal risk-bearing by shareholders would be more difficult to police. Apart from these effects, which are wholly predictable on the basis of conventional microeconomics, there is no basis for predicting that any cyclical movements would follow from such risk-control legislation.

The effects of this hypothetical risk-control legislation are set out here in order to provide a basis for contrasting those distortions of market mechanisms for allocating risk-bearing that do have consequences of a cyclical nature and those that do not. The exposition also allows us to identify links between the economics of risk allocation and the economics of credit allocation. We can anticipate the argument by saying that, in this context, credit control is to risk control what credit expansion is to risk externalization. Unlike a simple interest-rate cap, some legislative actions and policy innovations may allow borrowers to take risks that are systematically out of line with the risks perceived or actually borne by both borrowers and lenders. So long as risk is effectively concealed from borrowers and lenders or actually shifted to others, risk-taking will be excessive. The initial phase of excessive risk-taking will manifest itself as an economic boom, but eventually, when actual losses begin to change the perceptions of borrowers and lenders and begin to impinge upon unsuspecting others, the boom will give way to a bust. Adding substance to this summary account of boom and bust attributable to distortions of the risk premium requires the identification of legislative action and policy innovation that create a discrepancy between actual and perceived risk-bearing.

The single piece of legislation most relevant to risk allocation in the 1980s US boom was the Depository Institutions Deregulation and Monetary Control Act of 1980 (DIDMCA). Intended to help the banking industry survive in an increasingly inflationary environment, this act dramatically changed the banking industry's ability and willingness to finance risky undertakings. Increased competition within the banking industry and from non-bank financial institutions drove commercial banks to alter their lending policy so as to accept greater risks in order to achieve higher yields. The deregulation gave new significance to the Federal Deposit Insurance Corporation (FDIC), which continued to absolve the banks' depositors of all worries about illiquidity and even about bankruptcy, while the Federal Reserve in its long-established capacity of lender of last resort diminished the banks' own concerns about such problems. The risks in the private sector, then, were only partially reflected in higher borrowing costs and lower share prices. In substantial measure, private-sector risks were transformed into risks of inflation in the event of excessive last-resort lending by the Federal Reserve and risks of a large and unbudgeted liability in the event of excessive last-resort closings by the FDIC. But these risks were borne unknowingly and hence unwillingly by market participants and taxpayers throughout the economy. During the 1980s, then, the increased riskiness in the private sector was effectively externalized and diffused so that the private-sector activity, spurred on by correspondingly increased yields, was largely unattenuated by considerations of risk.

Leveraging the significance of DIDMCA was a policy innovation of the same period, namely, the federal government's dramatically increased reliance on deficit finance. The Federal Reserve in its capacity to monetize government debt keeps the default-risk premium off Treasury bills. This is not to say that the risk that would otherwise attach itself to government securities is somehow shunted into the Potomac River or otherwise eliminated. Rather, the burden of bearing risk is shifted from the holders of

Treasury securities to others. Borrowing and investing in the private sector are more risky than they otherwise would be. Holders of private debt and equity shares must concern themselves with all the usual risks and uncertainties of the marketplace plus the risks and uncertainties attributable to potential changes in market conditions – changes directly attributable to the way the federal deficit is accommodated.

The massive selling of debt by the Treasury in foreign credit markets, in domestic credit markets or to the Federal Reserve can have major effects on the strength of export markets, on domestic interest rates, and on the inflation rate. The inability of market participants to anticipate the Treasury's borrowing strategy translates into unanticipated changes in the value of private securities and the real assets they represent. Speculative lending in the private sector, such as for commercial real-estate development or for highly leveraged financial reorganizations are risky in large part because of possible changes in such things as the inflation rate, interest rate, trade flows, and tax rates – the very things that can undergo substantial and unpredictable change when the federal budget is dramatically out of balance. This summary statement of the economics of risk externalization is supported by our discussion below of the fiscal excesses of the 1980s and the corresponding dynamics of deficit accommodation.

Fiscal excesses in perspective

The hardships and inequities in the 1970s that stemmed from double-digit inflation gave way to concerns in the 1980s and 1990s about dozen-digit deficits. The federal government's outstanding debt rose beyond the $5 trillion mark – with two Presidents (Reagan and Bush) virtually quadrupling the net accumulation of more than 200 years. The federal budget deficit was in the dozen-digit range (i.e. over $100 billion) continuously from 1982 through 1996; during the Reagan and Bush administrations from 1981 to 1993, the cumulative debt rose from $0.995 trillion to $4.351 trillion; the 1992 deficit of $290.2 billion amounted to more than three-quarters of a billion dollars of new debt daily. (Figures are from the *Budget of the United States Government: Historical Tables Fiscal Year 1998*: 23–4 and 103–4.)

Modern macroeconomists have not adequately addressed themselves to the consequences of these fiscal excesses. Academic debate has centered on the preliminary and tangential issues of how, precisely, to define the deficit and whether it is large or small relative to the gross national product, to private-sector borrowing, or to the public-sector deficits of other Western countries. A survey of modern debate (Rock, 1991) has professional opinion ranging from the Keynesian view that the deficit stimulates the economy to the classical (Ricardian) view that the deficit is irrelevant. In some quarters, the deficit is thought to be self-financing; in others, a redefining of the deficit (making adjustments for inflation and interest-rate changes) transforms a conventionally defined deficit into a surplus. Robert J. Barro (in Rock, 1991) argues that increased government borrowing leads to increased private saving, as taxpayers prepare themselves to pay higher taxes in the future. Robert Eisner (in Rock, 1991) argues that the Carter administration's $60 billion deficit in 1979 was actually a $10 billion surplus, once the debt-eroding effects of inflation are factored in.

Debating points aside, the chronically large deficits of the last two decades stand in stark contrast to the minor fiscal imbalances of earlier decades. To begin to understand the macroeconomic significance of this change in fiscal posture, we must ask: From whom is the government borrowing and how does the government's heavy involvement in credit markets affect the performance of the rest of the economy? To pose these questions suggests that the relevant measure of the deficit is one that relates the government's demand for loanable funds to the economy's supply of loanable funds, that is, the deficit-to-saving ratio. This recasting of the deficit problem, by virtue of being a pure ratio, automatically adjusts for the changing value of the dollar. Still, it shows the contrast between the recent years of fiscal excess, during which the deficit-to-saving ratio has consistently been in the 15–30 percent range, and the preceding decades, during which this ratio had been held to the 0–5 percent range. Thus, unlike the more conventional deficit-to-GNP ratio, which seems to trivialize the deficit, the deficit-to-saving ratio provides a sound basis for the claim that the deficits in recent years have been "chronically large." That is, the government is seen to be a big player in credit markets. Also, the contrast with earlier years is preserved by the deficit-to-saving ratio in part because saving has not kept pace with GNP. That is, the deficit-to-saving ratio in the 1980s and 1990s reflects both an increasing deficit-to-GNP ratio and a decreasing saving-to-GNP ratio.

Thinking in macroeconomic terms, we can identify a short list of potential lenders and spell out the consequences of a heavy reliance on any one of these lenders or of switching from one category of lender to another.

Domestic savers

First and most straightforwardly, the government can borrow domestically. That is, it can borrow from US citizens. Most of the population own Treasury bills and other government securities – if not directly, then through banks, pension funds, and other savings institutions. But if individuals or their savings institutions have lent money to the federal government, then that money is not available for private enterprise. Business firms, which are subject to the discipline of the market, tend to lose out when competing with the government for loanable funds. High interest rates attributable to the government's excessive demand for funds "crowd out" private investors as well as consumers.

In recent years, the Treasury's high demand for credit has not resulted in a high rate of interest largely because the Treasury is not relying heavily on domestic savers as a primary source of funds. The experience of the mid-to-late 1960s better illustrates the problem of crowding out. During the Vietnam War, and particularly in the early years of the Nixon administration, the economy experienced high interest rates and tight credit markets as the government drew increasingly on domestic savings to finance its military operations. This period of occasional "credit crunches," as they were called, came to an end only with the implementation of a surtax during the Johnson administration, which created the modest budgetary surplus in 1969. The credit crunches also provided an impetus for breaking the link between dollars and gold and hence increasing the access to another source of funds for the Treasury, namely, the Federal Reserve.

The Federal Reserve

Second, the government can borrow from its own bank – the Federal Reserve. When the Federal Reserve buys Treasury bills, it effectively lends new money into existence. Debt monetization keeps the pressure off credit markets. With the printing press running, there is plenty of money to be borrowed by government, business, and consumers. But money creation cannot be a permanent solution to the government's fiscal difficulties. Initially, interest rates remain low, but soon enough the increased borrowing and spending put upward pressure on prices and wages. The inflation that unavoidably follows excessive money creation is accompanied by high nominal interest rates that compensate for the declining value of money. The economy's long and painful adjustment to inflation creates inequities, perversities, and inefficiencies. Retired workers and others on fixed incomes suffer, wages lag behind prices for workers locked into multi-year labor contracts, and the price system in general functions poorly.

It is true, of course, that inflation also reduces the real value of the government's outstanding debt. If we measure the deficit as the change in the real value of outstanding debt, then debt monetization can turn a conventionally measured deficit into a surplus. We should note, however, that the ability of the Federal Reserve actually to reverse the direction of fiscal imbalance depends critically on two circumstances. First, a large portion of the debt must be long-term. Short-term debt would simply be rolled over at inflated interest rates, and the increased costs of servicing the debt would offset the government's gain from debt erosion. Second, the inflation must be largely unanticipated. Anticipated inflation would be already reflected in interest rates, again offsetting the government's gain. With the maturity structure of government debt becoming increasingly short-term and with the financial sector's increasing sensitivity to future inflation, neither of these two critical circumstances are likely to be all that favorable to the government in the foreseeable future. And more fundamentally, this default-as-you-go aspect of debt monetization provides no solution to the deficit problem. It is, rather, a manifestation of the problem. That is, chronically large deficits are a problem in part because the government may resort to debt monetization.

The late 1970s best exemplifies this form of deficit accommodation. The Carter administration was largely successful in shifting the blame for the double-digit inflation to the Middle East and to the efforts of OPEC to exploit its relative monopoly on the world supply of crude oil. But despite its superficial plausibility, the oil-based account of inflation did not stack up well against the money-based account. Why did other economies that were even more dependent on Middle Eastern oil, particularly Japan's, not experience high rates of inflation during this period? And why were the increased expenditures on oil and oil-intensive products in the USA not accompanied by decreased expenditures in other markets? In the absence of money creation, the economy's adjustment to reduced oil supplies would have been largely an adjustment of relative prices and not a dramatically upward adjustment in the price level. By the end of the Carter administration, the economy's "misery index" (the inflation rate plus the unemployment rate) was approaching 0.20. The double-digit inflation and resulting poor performance of the economy, which were, almost by themselves, responsible for the election of Ronald Reagan, are to be attributed not to OPEC but to the federal government's policy of deficit finance and to the accommodating debt monetization. The increasing public awareness of the downside to debt monetization spurred the government to rely more intensely on still another source of funds.

Foreign savers

Third, the government can borrow in world capital markets – from foreign savers and foreign central banks. If our trading partners – Germany, Japan, and others – are willing to lend funds to our government, then both interest rates and inflation can be kept down in the USA. But there is a downside to exporting government debt. Ordinarily, citizens in these foreign countries trade with citizens in the USA on a more conventional basis. They trade goods for goods: cars, cameras, and electronics for heavy machinery, raw lumber, and agriculture products. During the Reagan revolution of the 1980s, however, they began trading goods for Treasury bills and for other earning assets whose yield was propped up by the government's high demand for credit. Ocean-going freighters, in effect, arrived at our shores with real goods in their cargo compartments and departed for home with government securities in their glove compartments. Many US industries suffered from weak export markets, reflected dramatically during the Reagan–Bush presidencies by the so-called twin deficits – in the federal budget and in international trade.

The dynamics of deficit accommodation

We have now exhausted our short list of options. The government can sell its debt domestically and suffer high interest rates, monetize its debt and suffer inflation, or export its debt and suffer an international trade imbalance. It can opt for a combination of these alternatives, but typically – as illustrated above by the Nixon, Carter, Reagan and Bush administrations, the fiscal strategy that characterizes any particular period involves an emphasis on one alternative – an emphasis that, because of cumulative effects, cannot last indefinitely. Considering for a moment the dynamics of deficit accommodation, especially over the past three decades, sheds further light on the nature of the deficit problem.

The straightforward application of economic principles suggests that given three alternative strategies for raising more funds – four, if we include tax increases – the government would not lean too heavily on any one but, instead, would pursue all avenues simultaneously. It would borrow domestically, monetize, and sell debt abroad – and levy taxes – until the last dollar raised by each alternative method is equally burdensome to the voting public. The strategy of equalizing across the alternatives follows straightforwardly from the principles of marginalism, which has served as bedrock for economic theory for well over a hundred years. This basic reckoning of the problem suggests that a balanced budget – like a zero rate of inflation or the elimination of taxes – is not likely to be achieved and maintained over any substantial period of time. We would be surprised if the government were to foreswear completely and permanently the use of any one of its financing alternatives.

What needs further explanation, however, is the fact that, to a significant extent, the government pursues its alternatives sequentially rather than simultaneously. It binges first on one method of finance, then on another and deals, however inadequately, with the crises (high interest rates, inflation, trade deficits, etc.) that provoke a shift from one deficit accommodation strategy to the next. And during each shift, there is a net increase in taxes brought about through tax reform – the raising of tax rates, the expansion of the tax base, and the imposition of new taxes. The Nixon administration borrowed domestically in the early years before turning to the Federal Reserve for help. The Carter administration, following the lead of Nixon and Ford, monetized debt; the Reagan and Bush administrations sold debt abroad. The Clinton administration, which in its early years flirted with the idea of hidden taxes, such as the VAT (value-added tax), opted for a mix of debt export and debt monetization to help accommodate a somewhat smaller federal budget deficit and then resorted to creative accounting (borrowing from the Social Security trust funds) to turn the deficit into a surplus.

Understanding the sequential binge-and-crisis aspect of deficit finance characteristic of the last two decades requires a little institutional history. Except for wartime emergencies, the US dollar has been tied to a monetary metal (silver and/or gold) from its introduction during the final decade of the eighteenth century through the first seven decades of the twentieth century. The last effective institutional constraint in the form of the dollar's official link to gold was severed by Nixon in 1971, thus marking a critical turning point in matters of money creation and debt issue. Since 1971, the much looser constraint – sometimes binding, sometimes not – is the one imposed by public opinion, which by its nature, forms and changes slowly as the otherwise unconstrained Federal Reserve and Treasury attempt to finance increasing levels of government spending.

The "closing of the gold window" in 1971 is the metaphorical expression for the government's reneging on its commitment to foreign central banks to convert dollars into gold at a preset rate. This momentous event marked the beginning of our experiment with a pure paper money. The government continued to print money and to accumulate debt on the basis of the relative costs of these alternative methods of fund raising. But now the politically relevant costs of raising funds are not the cost as measured by international gold flows but rather the costs as perceived by the citizenry and registered in the voting booth. Unlike the textbook applications of marginalism, where the costs are clear and the market equilibrium is a stable one, the application of marginalism to deficit finance involves changing perceptions of the costs and hence a sequence of unstable solutions to the government's fiscal problems. The ability of the citizenry to perceive the costs of some particular method of finance is not constant over time but varies with experience. When accumulated experience allows the costs of domestic borrowing – or of debt monetization or of exporting debt – to become more fully understood, elected officials tend to opt for some other method: one for which there is little recent experience and hence no widespread understanding or concern – or organized opposition.

Even the particular sequence of financing alternatives takes on a certain significance. We can rank the different alternatives in terms of the difficulty of perceiving the true costs. Plausible arguments could be offered that the ranking – from most easily perceived costs to most difficult to perceive costs – would dovetail with the actual chronology, starting in the 1950s when the deficit was nil. The government has gone from taxing directly to borrowing domestically to monetizing debt to exporting debt to hiding debt.

Coping without a crystal ball

Drawing on his experience as a member of the Grace Commission in the mid-1980s, Harry Figgie (1992) created a graphical projection of debt accumulation through the year 2000. He designated his depiction of past and projected indebtedness as "the hockey stick curve" because of its general shape – a relative flatness through most of the country's history punctuated with a tall spike at the end of the twentieth century. Our shift of focus from the accumulation of debt to the dynamics of deficit accommodation suggests a different analogy. We might say that if debt accumulation resembles a hockey stick, the fate of the market participants in a Treasury-dominated credit market resembles that of a hockey puck.

(Figgie's considerable over-estimate of the debt level at the turn of the century strengthens our own concerns about government indebtedness – the uncertainty about just how much the big player will need to borrow and just how the big player will achieve that borrowing.)

There is significance to the fact that we do not know with any confidence the fiscal strategy of the federal government. We need to step back for a moment from the details of the particular methods of deficit finance to assess the broader significance of the deficit, given that we as business people, income earners, savers and investors have no crystal ball that can tell us what, precisely, to expect next. In a period of chronically large deficits, market participants simply do not know in which direction and how hard the stick will hit the puck.

Let us take a hypothetical year during which the government is collecting in taxes about one-and-a-quarter trillion dollars and spending about one-and-a-half trillion. In effect, the government is putting the private sector on notice: "We're taking $1.25 trillion in accordance with the established tax codes. And we're taking another $250 billion as well, but we're not saying just how, just when, or just whose." Taxes, complex and distasteful as they are to both the business community and the consuming public, are a known quantity. We make our plans around them, we pay our accountants to minimize them, and we brace ourselves for them. But the deficit is a different story. There is no deficit code to parallel the tax code. No matter how certain a large deficit may be, there is no effective way for either business people or the rest of us to minimize it, plan around it, or hedge against it. It could hit us with high interest rates, with inflation, with weak export markets, with increased taxes, or with some combination of these eventualities. But until the government's fiscal strategy takes some definite form, the $250 billion of intent to appropriate funds in some yet-to-be-specified way looms large as a cloud of uncertainty over the private sector.

The economy's poor performance in the early 1990s can be attributed in part to the deficit-induced uncertainties that pervaded the private sector. The recession at the end of the Bush administration reflected an unwillingness on the part of business people to commit themselves to capital-intensive or job-creating business ventures. The uncertainty about market conditions over the near and intermediate future cast too much doubt on the ability of the would-be venturers to meet payrolls and maintain lines of credit.

Ironically, the deficit-related waning of the private sector's demand for credit allowed the government to increase its own borrowings without putting much upward pressure on interest rates. That is, the apparent lack of pressure on credit markets during that period suggests that private-sector activity can be crowded out by the uncertainty-creating effects of the deficit rather than by the interest rate itself. This uncertainty-based crowding out, then, can account for the co-existence of large public-sector demands for credit and relatively low market rates of interest. If correct, this explanation implies that during a deficit-ridden recession, a renewed prosperity stemming from some spontaneous revival of business confidence is unlikely. Given the plateau of government borrowing, any significant resurgence of credit demand in the business community would send interest rates up sharply and put strict limits on private-sector expansion. Restoring fiscal integrity in the public sector and thus eliminating the uncertainties created by a large and chronic deficit, then, should be seen as prerequisite to a lasting revival of business activity and hence to sustainable prosperity in the economy.

But movement in the direction of fiscal integrity is not the main story of the 1990s. Instead, the black cloud of debt was countered by monetary ease. In early 1996, when the economy's unemployment rate had fallen to the midpoint of the full-employment range, the Federal Reserve reduced interest rates. The performance of the economy in the mid-to-late decade is best understood in terms of a chronically large budget deficit compounded by the political business cycle. With unemployment eventually driven almost a whole percentage point below the full-employment range, the cyclical surplus in the federal budget almost wholly offset the structural deficit.

Market uncertainties associated with the political business cycle are a problem in their own right. The discussions in the financial press of "interest-rate jitters" are well grounded in our understanding of the conflict between economically sound policy and politically expedient policy. Traders in securities markets have to keep one eye on the Federal Reserve and try to anticipate when policy will turn political and when it will turn back.

In circumstances where considerations of risk figure importantly in accounting for the performance of the economy, capital markets become the natural focus of attention. The focus on capital is what makes the macroeconomics of the 1980s and 1990s more closely related to Hayekian triangulation than to the labor-based short-run/long-run Phillips curve analysis of the 1960s. Long-term, or capital-intensive, undertakings are inherently more risky than short-term undertakings precisely because more time must elapse before such undertakings can prove their profitability — more time that increases the likelihood of some major change in deficit accommodation or some attempt at deficit reduction that can turn expected profits into losses.

The temporal segregation of stages of production that make up the economy's capital structure puts a dimension in the analysis that is absent in labor-based theorizing. There is scope for profit-taking in early stages of production in cases where ultimately the entire project — all stages considered — yields a substantial loss. The possibility for short-term commitments in the early stages of long-term projects coupled with the many imperfections in contingency markets that allow for some hedging against changes in the federal government's fiscal and monetary strategy warn against too literal an application of the so-called efficient-market hypothesis. Ordinarily, markets allocate both capital and labor efficiently – or at least more efficiently that any alternative allocation mechanism. But a market system whose credit markets involve risks that are partially concealed from the lender and partially shifted to others will be biased in the direction of excessive risk-taking. And excessive risks are converted in time into excessive losses.

Frequent but vague references in the financial and popular press to the "excesses of the 1980s" can be taken to mean excess riskiness in comparison to wealth holders' willingness to bear risk. The 1980s may best be understood, then, as a decade in which risk externalization attributable to legislative action and policy innovation gave rise to a substantial but ultimately unsustainable economic boom. This diagnosis of the macroeconomic ills of the early 1990s is more suggestive than conclusive. The purpose here is to demonstrate that versatility of Hayekian theory rather than to render a final verdict on the sustainability of the most recent booms. Hayek gave us a good start on capital-based macroeconomics. The insights wrapped up in those triangles and the prospects for extension and application are yet to be fully developed or fully appreciated.

Booms and busts in the "emerging nations"

It may seem ironic that our risk-based extension of the Austrian theory is applied to the US economy rather than to the Japanese economy and to economies of South East Asia and Latin America. The Bush Recession was a brief and minor downturn in comparison to the enduring and sometimes dramatic crises experienced by the so-called emerging nations. And the term "bubble economy" – particularly if the bubble has already burst – is applied with less controversy to those nations than to the United States.

But as indicated in Chapter 4, the Austrian theory of the business cycle is a theory of the unsustainable boom. It is not a theory of depression *per se*. In particular, it does not account for the severity and possible recalcitrance of the depression that may follow on the heels of the bust. A crisis of confidence can cause an economy to spiral downward to a much greater extent than was made necessary either by artificially cheap credit or by the externalization of risk. And perverse policies pursued by governments can cause the respective economies to linger in depression for a considerable period of time. The story of depression and recovery, which may involve reflation, devaluation, debt restructuring, and/or capital controls, is unique to each individual episode of each economy.

Further, theorizing about the artificial booms experienced by the emerging nations draws more directly from the Austrian theory's immediate predecessor than from the Austrian theory itself. When Mises introduced his theory, he thought of it not as a new theory but as a development of the Circulation Credit Theory of the British Currency School. He saw two shortcomings of the Circulation Credit Theory: (1) undue attention to the international aspects of the market process; and (2) an inappropriate reckoning of volume of circulation credit. Mises's development of the theory (1966: 571) called attention to the internal aspects of the market process and broadened the conception of circulation credit from the issuance of banknotes to the creation of checkable deposits. But now, to understand the bubble economies of the emerging nations, we have to refocus attention on the international aspects of the market process and augment the role of circulation credit to account for modern developments in international finance.

Credit-driven booms contain the seeds of their own undoing, according to the Circulation Credit Theory, but the market process that turns boom into bust, according to this earlier theory, plays itself out as self-reversing movements in the international flow of funds. The arguments of the Currency School could not show how credit expansion in a single isolated economy – or in a fully integrated world economy – would also engender a boom that would eventually end in a bust. Distinctive to Mises's contribution and to Hayek's development of it was the market process that played itself out as the internal dynamics of domestic capital markets (as set out in Chapter 4).

Japan through the end of the 1980s could be offered up as an episode to which the Austrian theory applies – both in its traditional interpretation where monetary policy depresses the rate of interest below the rate that reflects people's actual intertemporal preferences and in the extended interpretation set out in the present chapter where institutional arrangements result in the externalization of risks. Easy credit policies pursued by Japanese banks during the 1980s were the result of the perception that government would guarantee the solvency and liquidity of the banking industry; the willingness of the banks' customers to use borrowed funds to finance high-risk investments reflected substantial doses of the always-worrisome moral hazard: the borrower gains handsomely if the investment succeeds; the bank (and hence government and hence taxpayers) loses dramatically if the investment fails. The fact that banks nonetheless made such loans (and that government allowed the banks to make such loans) is indicative of the extent to which the impersonal forces of the marketplace were conditioned by very personal relationships between regulator and bank and between bank and borrower. These are the relationships that have given rise to the label "crony capitalism."

Similar perversities have characterized the countries of South East Asia, but these countries, such as Thailand and Malaysia, were impacted – more so than was Japan – by the inflow (and then outflow) of foreign investment funds. The dynamics that kindled these booms and then caused the booms to turn to busts are to be explained in terms of currency speculation and the international repercussions. Currency School arguments apply, but what counts as credit expansion has to be broadened to include the effects of international currency speculation orchestrated by the so-called hedge funds. Operating in a small economy that is actually experiencing an expansionary bubble – or even in a small economy that is simply believed to be bubble-prone, the hedge funds can lend money in that country while simultaneously speculating against the country's currency. The eventuality either of high interest rates (in the case that the country successfully maintains the value of its currency) or of devaluation (in the case that it doesn't) translates into profits for the hedge funds. In the meantime, the country experiences a larger bubble, a more dramatic artificial boom, than it otherwise would have.

The market process of boom and bust can play itself out as the inflow of investment funds coupled with lending policies that exploit the moral hazard that is inherent in the lender–borrower relationship and is magnified by the cronyism that characterizes the emerging nations. Unduly risky ventures whose financing traces to the internationally operating hedge funds are not the basis for sustainable growth.

Leijonhufvud (1998) is surely right in suggesting that some of these cyclical fluctuations are "more Hayekian than Keynesian." The purpose here of this brief and broad-brush treatment of bubble economies around the world is not to make sweeping statements about all the episodes experienced by the emerging nations. But dealing on a country-by-country basis with the individual episodes would take our discussion to far afield. Rather, the point is that the stories of boom and bust in these countries, while different in their particulars, bear a strong family resemblance to the Austrian theory of the business cycle.

Part III
Keynes and capitalism

7 Labor-based macroeconomics

Modern macroeconomic pedagogy has evolved into a curious sequence of arguments. In principles-level courses, we teach income-expenditure analysis – the fixed-price circular flow theory, complete with unemployment equilibrium and plenty of scope for policy-makers to take advantage of the spending and taxing multipliers. At the intermediate level, we bring the supply and demand for money into view by teaching ISLM, a model in which the rate of interest and the level of income are determined simultaneously. Then we allow for a binding supply-side constraint and consequent changes in the price level by teaching Aggregate-Supply/Aggregate-Demand. At the graduate level, we explain why these formulations are all wrong – or, at least, overly mechanistic and largely irrelevant. These potted, mechanistic versions of Keynesianism describe neither the actual workings of the economy nor Keynes's understanding of them. After a wholesale rejection of these sorts of models, our focus shifts to rational expectations with possible information lags, optimal speeds of market adjustment to random technology shocks, and price stickiness that itself reflects optimizing behavior. Both Keynes and the economy are left behind as the graduate students learn to appreciate the logical integrity of these and other more modern constructions.

Axel Leijonhufvud (1968) has taught us to distinguish between *Keynesian Economics and the Economics of Keynes*. Yet, there are grounds for dispute even about the distinction itself. Leland Yeager ([1973] 1997b) expresses amazement at how much mechanistic Keynesianism is actually right there in the *General Theory*; George Shackle (1974), echoing Joan Robinson, is dismissive of the mechanistic aspects of Keynes's book and sees the novel treatment of expectations in an uncertain world as the essence of Keynesianism. Robinson (1975), who condemned the mechanistic constructions as "bastardized Keynesianism," seems to be quite sure about what Keynes did *not* mean but confesses that it was sometimes difficult to get Keynes himself to see just what he *did* mean.

Many a student has made the journey from Classicism to Keynesianism to Monetarism to New Classicism to New Keynesianism without ever having any idea about just what Keynes actually wrote or just how the economy might actually work (or might fail to work). Are we not justified in suspecting that something is wrong with a pedagogy that anchors itself in this spiraling sequence of schools of thought?

The reconstruction of labor-based macroeconomics proposed here entails a first-order distinction between competing frameworks both of which were fully in play at the time of the Keynesian Revolution. The capital-based macroeconomics of the Austrian School, as set out in Chapter 3, is to be contrasted with the labor-based macroeconomics of the Keynesian – and most other – schools. The enhancement of our understanding that comes from sharpening the contrast between labor-based and capital-based frameworks – and, more specifically, between Keynes and Hayek – is what justifies the reconstruction.

But sharpening the contrast also requires recognizing the common denominators. One important common denominator is the very conception of a money-using economy and hence of monetary theory. We borrow again at this point from the monetary disequilibrium theory exposited by Warburton (1966) and more recently by Yeager (1997b) and to be discussed in more detail in Chapter 11: money has no market of its own. Nor, as was emphasized in Chapter 3, does it have a quadrant or even an axis of its own. Beyond some pure theory, which serves as a starting point, we emphasize that the whole economy – each quadrant of it, each axis of it – is shot through with monetary considerations. Monetary theory consists, then, of allowing for money in its role as the medium of exchange when considering each relationship that *is* represented in its own quadrant or on its own axis. Like the Austrian economists, Keynes too (1936: 20–1) was dissatisfied with the conventional theorizing that relegated monetary considerations to a separate chapter or volume – as if some monetary theory could be grafted onto an otherwise pure theory of a market economy. Accordingly, there is no single quadrant or axis that keeps track of money in our labor-based framework. True to Keynes, money allows for a particularly troublesome slippage between the decision to save and the decision to put the saving at interest. More generally, it puts slippage in the economic system all around by appearing, if only implicitly, on virtually every axis.

In this regard, the graphical construction (ISLM) that grew out of Hicks's "suggested interpretation" (1937) is doubly unfortunate. First, the separation of the issues into the real sector (IS) and monetary sector (LM) is contrary to the spirit of Keynes's critical remarks about classical monetary theory. The subsequent combining of ISLM with the so-called classical model of aggregate supply compounds the problem. Aggregate-Supply/Aggregate-Demand analysis relegates money to one sector of one side of the macroeconomy. Second, the further dividing of the monetary sector itself into two separate components of the demand for money (speculative demand and transactions demand) serves to highlight what, in Keynes's own formulation, is only an awkward makeshift. The makeshift is certainly right there in the *General Theory*. Keynes (1936: 199) writes the deceivingly simple *pro forma* equation for the demand for money: $M = M_1 + M_2 = L_1(Y) + L_2(r)$ – as if two different reasons for holding money translate into two additive demands for money. A few pages earlier, however, he had warned against just such a construction.

> Money held for each of three purposes [with transactions and precautionary demands to be combined into M_1 and speculative demand to be represented by M_2] forms, nevertheless, a single pool, which the holder is under no necessity to segregate into three water-tight compartments; for they need not be sharply divided even in his own mind, and the same sum can be held primarily for one purpose and secondarily for another. Thus we can – equally well, and, perhaps, better – consider the individual's aggregate demand for money in given circumstances as a single decision, though the composite result of a number of different motives.
>
> (Keynes, 1936: 195)

We are entitled to be puzzled, then, when just four pages later he writes that we can regard the demand for money, written as the simple sum of two components, as a "safe first approximation." Admittedly, Keynes's use of this additive construction (see especially ibid.: 200) lends support to Hicks's suggested interpretation. Is it possible, though, that the approximation may be safe for some purposes (e.g., showing how a dramatic change in expectations that causes people to get out of bonds and into money can disrupt credit markets) but not for others (e.g. accounting for the more general relationship between money supply and money demand)? As an incidental benefit of our reconstruction, the division of money into two components is rendered unnecessary – and hence the question of whether such a division is not a safe approximation is simply avoided.

After suggesting one interpretation in 1937, Hicks suggested another in 1976. His second interpretation was so fundamentally different from his first as to constitute a virtual recantation. Reflecting on the role of time in economics, Hicks (1976: 140) concluded that he had made the wrong first-order distinction. Rather than divide the macroeconomy into the real sector and the monetary sector, he should have divided it into two sectors, one of which is "in time"; the other, "out of time." "In time" means subject to (possibly dramatic but unpredictable) change on the basis of changing perceptions of an uncertain future; "out of time" means more or less mechanistic, the result of well-established habits. We can translate the components of the 1937 Hicksian framework into the 1976 Hicksian framework by recognizing that the "in time" sector consists of one real and one monetary component (the demand for investment funds and the speculative demand for money) while the "out of time" sector consists of the remaining real and monetary components (the saving behavior of income earners and the transactions demand for money.) The derived demand for labor, which makes no explicit appearance in ISLM (but does in our proposed reconstruction) is also included in the "out-of-time" sector.

Our reconstruction is in the spirit of 1976 Hicks. It does not make a first-order distinction between monetary and real sectors. It does provide substantial separation between "in time" and "out of time" aspects of the macroeconomy. And following Coddington (1982), it shows how the pattern of macroeconomic magnitudes reflects the interplay between the "in-time" aspects and the "out of time" aspects. As suggested above, the elimination of the monetary sector (in the sense of a graph or set of graphs that deal explicitly with the supply and demand for money) actually gives increased significance to the medium of exchange. And – again, not to deny the underlying kernel of truth in the quantity theory of money – it gives decreased significance to the summary relationship between the quantity of money and the general level of prices.

Money is represented ubiquitously, if only implicitly, as one side of every exchange. To this extent, the labor-based macroeconomics of the present chapter is brought into line with the capital-based macroeconomics of Chapter 3. Disputes between, say, Keynes and Hayek can be resolved into a dispute about the difference between a moneyless economy, in which "supplying" and "demanding" are always reducible to two aspects of the same activity, and a money-using economy, in which the intermediation made possible by money breaks the tight link between these two activities. Does money constitute a loose link in an otherwise self-equilibrating system, as Hayek (1941: 408) specifically indicated? Or does it constitute, in effect, a broken link, as Keynes's arguments seem to suggest?

The contrast between money-as-a-loose-joint and money-as-a-broken-joint (Garrison, 1984) and the implications of the contrasting views about the market's ability to achieve intertemporal coordination can be depicted straightforwardly. Keynesian and Hayekian movements of the supply and demand for loanable funds can be tracked separately and contrasted in the context of the production possibilities frontier that depicts (present) consumption and (future-oriented) investment as alternative ways of using resources. The loanable-funds market and the PPF, then, become key elements common to both capital-based macroeconomics and labor-based macroeconomics.

The proposed reconstruction turns out to be true to Keynes in ways that other, more conventional constructions are not. Accordingly, it helps us to answer the tag question in the oft-quoted assessment by Hicks about Keynesian and Hayekian macroeconomics:

> When the definitive history of economic analysis during the nineteen-thirties comes to be written, a leading character in the drama (and it was quite a drama) will be Professor Hayek. Hayek's economic . . . writings are almost unknown to the modern student; it is hardly remembered that there was a time when the new theories of Hayek were the

principal rival of the theories of Keynes. Which was right? Keynes or Hayek?

(Hicks, 1967: 203)

At the root of the rivalry was the question about just which market mechanisms (those associated with markets for capital goods or those associated with the market for labor) are the most relevant ones in assessing the market's ability to achieve coordination in the macroeconomic sense.

Finally, despite its mechanistic appearance, the graphical analysis presented below provides a broad common denominator for articulating – and inter-relating – the various renditions of Keynesianism. It can also help to show how Keynesianism and alternative labor-based theories, including Monetarism and certain strands of New Classicism, relate to one another. We will demonstrate in Chapter 10, for instance, that the labor-based theory developed here is adequate for expositing some aspects of the monetary misperception theories of business cycles offered by Friedman and by Lucas. The overarching goal in the present chapter, however, is one of providing a labor-based macroeconomics that best facilitates a comparison with the capital-based macroeconomics of Chapter 3.

A six-panel rendition of Keynesianism

According to Keynes (1936: 28), it is only by "accident or design" that a market economy achieves its potential of full employment. The perversities of capitalism rule out hopes for a market process that simultaneously strikes a balance between supply and demand through changes in prices, wages, and interest rates, *and* exhibits a balance between income and expenditures, which defines equilibrium in the macroeconomic sense. In fact, it is almost inevitable that the adjustments in earning and spending that bring about the income-expenditure equilibrium will dislocate labor markets, product markets, and loanable-funds markets from their supply-and-demand equilibria. For the economy to prosper, the spontaneous, or accidental, forces of the marketplace will have to be supplemented by demand-management policies designed by the fiscal authority and implemented with the cooperation of the monetary authority.

It is a familiar proposition to all who study macroeconomics at any level that the policy tools of the fiscal and monetary authorities are tailor-made to fight cyclical unemployment. But not all who study macroeconomics are sensitized to the fact that according to Keynes, cyclical unemployment is but one of the two components of involuntary unemployment. The other is secular unemployment. To fight this component of unemployment, policy tools will not suffice; social reform is necessary. An understanding of Keynes, then, is best facilitated by a first-order distinction between (1) cyclical unemployment and policy prescription; and (2) secular unemployment and social reform. Accordingly, Chapter 8 deals with cyclical unemployment, providing an alternative to standard textbook treatments; Chapter 9 deals with social reform, providing a treatment of a major aspect of Keynes's vision that is almost universally ignored by the textbooks. The present chapter provides an analytical framework that captures Keynes's vision of macroeconomic relationships that characterize an economy that is suffering from neither cyclical nor secular unemployment.

Our six-panel diagram is constructed so as to allow us to illustrate (in Chapter 8) the Keynesian vision of market malady and fiscal fix – and to put into perspective the limited potential for a purely monetary fix. We can also show the nature and significance of the paradox of thrift. Then, with a substantial change in perspective, these same diagrams will be used (in Chapter 9) to show the effects of Keynes's proposals for social reform – reform aimed at eliminating the continual need for monetary and fiscal fixes.

Figure 7.1 depicts the relevant macroeconomic relationships that facilitate the analysis of some subsequent accidental unemployment. The economy, initially a wholly private one, is in equilibrium in both the Marshallian sense and the Keynesian sense. Each – or at least most – of the individual panels, which are numbered to reflect the most direct connections among them, are readily identifiable. The discussion of each panel below identifies the relationships being represented, indicates how each relates to Keynes's *General Theory* and to more conventional constructions of labor-based macroeconomics. More so than capital-based macroeconomics, labor-based macroeconomics lends itself to numerical illustration. Some readers may find the numerical reckonings that are carried through the present and the following two chapters helpful in anchoring this construction to more conventional ones; other readers will prefer to follow the argument without bothering with the numbers.

The labor market

Panel 1 of Figure 7.1 represents the market for labor. Units of labor input supplied and demanded are treated as homogeneous. Following Keynes, we reduce skilled labor to its unskilled equivalent and assume that the structure of the labor force – the particular mix of skills and their relative values – is fixed. This construction allows us to take all changes in unskilled-equivalent worker-hours, as measured by N along the horizontal axis, to be proportionate to changes in the number of workers employed. It also allows us to think in terms of *a single* wage rate. The market-clearing wage rate of $10/hr, at which 20 unskilled-equivalent worker-hours are supplied and demanded, translates into a total income to labor (WN) of $200. (A scale factor of, say, 10,000,000 can adjust these illustrative figures into orders of magnitude that are more plausibly descriptive of a macroeconomy.) Our labor market in Panel 1 is fully consistent with that of Keynes (1936: 41), who measured unskilled-equivalent worker-hours in "labor-units," and took the price of each labor-unit to be the "wage-unit."

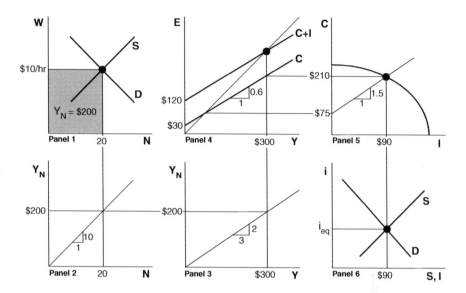

Figure 7.1 Labor-based macroeconomics (full employment by accident).

The 20 worker-hours constitute full-employment. The $10/hr, initially the market-clearing wage rate, is taken to be the "going wage rate" – even if market conditions that gave rise to this wage rate no longer prevail. In Figure 7.1 the market conditions we have assumed to prevail do cause the labor market to clear at the going wage. This coincidence is what justifies our labeling the figure "Full employment by accident." As will be seen in the discussion of Panel 5, however, full-employment need not be *defined* in terms of the wage rate. But a fully employed labor force will, by construction, earn the "going wage."

Our understanding of the nature of the market process, especially as applied to the market for labor, has a first-order effect on our view of the market's equilibrating tendencies and of the need for stabilization policy. Does the wage rate automatically (and expeditiously) adjust to existing supply-and-demand conditions? Or does demand itself, which may reflect perversities in other sectors of the macroeconomy, need to be adjusted to existing supply-and-wage conditions? Keynes, in effect, answered the first question "No" and the second one "Yes." But simply to pit Keynes against his contemporary and modern critics who would answer the first question "Yes" and the second one "No" would be to miss the most insightful messages of both Keynes and Hayek. In a macroeconomic theory, where interdependencies can dominate, neither set of answers can be defended in terms of the relationships in Panel 1 taken by themselves.

As applied broadly to the market for labor, Marshallian partial equilibrium analysis is pushed to the limits and, in the context of Keynes's conception of the circular flow, beyond the limits. Is it permissible to analyze the consequences of, say a shift in the demand for labor (the factor of production that constitutes two-thirds or more of the economy's income-earning potential) while invoking the *ceteris paribus* assumption to preclude having to ask why demand shifted or having to deal with repercussions emanating from the markets for investment goods or consumer goods or with other considerations of general equilibrium? It may be reasonable to lean heavily on Marshall when dealing with the supply and demand for a particular kind of labor but not so reasonable when dealing with the supply and demand for labor in the broadest sense. A more pointed answer to the question of the appropriateness of the *ceteris paribus* assumption in the context of the macroeconomy will emerge naturally from the discussion of the other panels and of the interrelationships among the variables represented in them.

The wage rate

Panel 2 shows the relationship between the level of employment (N) and labor income (Y_N), namely, $Y_N = WN$. While the thrust of Panel 1 is to suggest that it is possible to theorize in terms of unskilled-equivalent worker-hours and *the* wage rate, the key issue in Panel 2 is the behavior of this wage rate. Are wages perfectly flexible, sticky downwards, or rigidly stuck? In the conventional pedagogy, we make the transition from the domain assumptions of textbook Keynesianism, according to which wage rates (and prices) are fixed or at least sticky downward, to the arguments of the New Keynesians, who hold that the downward stickiness of wages (and prices) is a matter not of assumption but of maximizing behavior in the face of costly adjustments.

The *General Theory* begins with Keynes chiding the classical economists for believing that flexibility is a natural characteristic of market wage rates (1936: 12f.) and ends with his advocating that wage-rate *in*flexibility be imposed on labor markets (ibid.: 266). In between the arguments where Keynes laments and then recommends inflexibility, he deals with the perverse consequences of perfect wage-rate and price flexibility (ibid.: 232, 262–5). If wages and prices fall in direct proportion to one another, then it follows that even a dramatic deflation will leave the real wage unchanged. The direct proportionality guarantees that, in the face of an unduly high real wage rate, a labor market out of equilibrium will remain out of equilibrium, while the deflation of the nominal magnitudes induces perverse changes elsewhere in the economy, such as in the real value of outstanding debt and hence in wealth-based spending propensies.

The combined thrust of Keynes's arguments is that rigidity or stickiness is to be imputed to the *real* wage rate – whether because the nominal wage rate and the price level are separately sticky downwards or because the nominal wage rate and the price level always move together. But given a choice between these two alternative circumstances each of which results in real wage stickiness, the preference should be, as Keynes makes clear, nominal inflexibility.

If the bad news is that the real wage rate is stuck, the good news is that it is stuck at the right level – as depicted in Panel 1. There is a critical initial condition in Keynesian economics here that is rarely given due emphasis. The "going wage rate" is the market-clearing wage rate that prevails before the problem of a demand deficiency materializes. Hence, it turns out to be the wage rate that again clears the labor market once the demand deficiency has been remedied. Just how the going wage rate got going, however, is no part of Keynes's theory. We must presume that (1) there was enough flexibility in the real wage rate for it to become adjusted to the supply and demand conditions in the market for labor; and (2) the demand for labor (the supply is not in question) was not infected by perversities elsewhere in the macroeconomy.

In putting labor-based models through their paces, perfect nominal-wage flexibility is almost always ruled out. We will be able to show, however, that even under conditions of perfect nominal-wage flexibility, there still would be market malady and fiscal fix – although the malady as measured by changes in N would be less severe than in circumstances of nominal-wage stickiness. Apart from secondary considerations, however, the particular treatment of the wage rate is largely a matter of analytical convenience. That is, we can get at the problem of involuntary unemployment by taking the nominal wage rate and the price level to be separately inflexible. Or, dividing both Y_N and W by P (and making the appropriate adjustments in other panels), we can take the real wage rate to be inflexible even though the nominal wage rate and the price level are separately flexible. Keynes makes both arguments. In general, Keynes presented his arguments on the assumption of fixed prices and wages, and then (after his stocktaking in Chapter 18) he offered qualification that derived from the fact that, to some extent, prices and wages can and do change.

Reflecting a recurring assumption in the *General Theory*, Panel 2 is set up to feature nominal wage-rate inflexibility, which can be seen, alternatively, as an understandable characteristic of the pricing process, as the New Keynesians argue, or as a consequence of a fixed-wage policy, which Keynes recommended. The going wage rate of $10/hr, measured on the vertical axis in Panel 1, translates as the slope in the relationship shown in Panel 2; total labor income ($Y_N = \$200$), represented by an area in Panel 1, is represented in Panel 2 as the vertical axis.

The structure of industry

Panel 3 shows the relationship between labor income and total income, $Y_N = 2/3Y$. Although it is clear – both empirically and from reading Keynes – that labor income is the majority of total income, the particular fraction chosen here, 2/3, is otherwise arbitrary. The greater point is that incomes of the various factors of production are assumed to move together, and so (except in the face of crises, fundamental social reform, or other unusual circumstances) the fraction does not change. Keynes's assumption, sometimes explicit, sometimes implicit, that "factor cost bears a constant ratio to wage cost" (1936: 55, n. 2) gets translated in Panel 3 to the assumption that income to all factors bears a constant ratio to income to labor. Much of the discussion in the first few chapters of the *General Theory*, particularly in Chapters 2, 4, and 6 is aimed at justifying this construction and contrasting it with the conception of economics that Keynes identifies with David Ricardo.

The classical vision of economics is doubly rejected. Ricardo insists that we cannot say just where the economy will find itself along the income axis of Panel 3, but we can say something about the slope of the line, which depicts the division of that income between labor and other factors. In Ricardo's own words (as quoted by Keynes, 1936: 4, n. 1), "No law can be laid down respecting quantity [output as measured by income], but a tolerably correct one can be laid down respecting proportions [between labor income and income to other factors]."

Keynes, in effect, is saying that we are entitled to assume unchanging proportions in order to facilitate the laying down of laws respecting changes in quantity. To a large extent, macroeconomics has come to be defined in terms of its focus on "changes in quantity," i.e. on variations in the level of income and related macroeconomic magnitudes – to the near-exclusion of "proportions," i.e. the relative prices and corresponding allocations within the income (and output) magnitudes. The reversing of the Ricardian conception of economics, which entails the assumption of a fixed structure of industry, allows Keynes to argue indiscriminately in terms of the total income and income to labor. By construction, then, non-labor income is constrained to move in proportion to labor income. With an assumed ratio of 2/3, labor income of $200, as shown on the vertical axis of Panel 3 corresponds to a total income of $300, as shown on the horizontal axis.

As an alternative construction, Panels 2 and 3 could be eliminated and Panel 1 reinterpreted. The supply and demand in Panel 1 could be taken to represent labor plus the labor equivalent of all other factors of production. In this construction, N would be 30 and WN would be $300. It is as if all income is labor income. Packing all the assumptions that underlie Panels 1, 2, and 3 into this newly interpreted Panel 1 – and more pointedly, into the construction of the Keyensian Cross – is what allows textbook authors to make their arguments in terms of income (Y) to *all* factors while drawing their conclusions in terms of the quantity (N) of *one* factor. This is to say that our multi-panel construction or its degenerate one-panel alternative is implicit in the conventional teaching of basic income-expenditure analysis.

The relationship in Panel 3 is given prominence in our exposition of labor-based macroeconomics because it contrasts so sharply and importantly with the corresponding relationships in capital-based macroeconomics. If the fixed structure of industry entails a fixed intertemporal structure of production, as represented in Chapter 3 by the Hayekian triangle, then the market mechanisms featured in the Austrian theory are simply ruled out by assumption. The triangle can change in size but not in shape. But, of course, changes in the "proportions," i.e. reallocations within the structure of production, as represented by changes in the triangle's shape, were shown to be central to the Austrian theory.

The Hayekian "proportions" are not the same as the Ricardian "proportions," but they move in sympathy with one another to the extent that labor in Ricardo's theory can be considered the "short factor" and capital the "long factor." Hayek, though, was not simply embracing the Ricardian view. Rather, he was insisting that we must feature changes in "proportions" in our explanation of changes in "quantity." In more modern terminology, we need suitable microeconomic foundations, including the intertemporal price and quantity movements, for our macroeconomics. Further, Hayek's criticism of Keynesianism is illustrated by the contrast between the constant slope associated with Keynes's structure of industry and the variable slope of Hayek's structure of production, which is featured in capital-based macroeconomics: "Mr. Keynes's aggregates conceal the most fundamental mechanisms of change" (Hayek, 1931: 277).

Income and expenditures

The relationships most closely associated with principles-level macroeconomics are shown in Panel 4. The Keynesian Cross shows expenditures (E = C + I) rising as income (Y) rises and identifies a single level of income for which income and expenditures are equal. Autonomous consumption of $30 and a marginal propensity to consume of 0.6, together with investment expenditures of $90, imply an equilibrium level of income (and expenditures) of $300. Consumption spending alone is $210. (Although the near-equality here between labor income and consumption spending is coincidental, Keynes's frequent lapses into the classical mode of thought, in which economic functions are closely associated with economic classes, suggest that these two magnitudes will not differ greatly: workers tend not to save much of their incomes; capitalists tend not to consume much of theirs.) The two spending magnitudes whose sum is measured on the vertical axis are dimensionally conformable. That is, consumption (C = $210) and investment (I = $90) are additive components of total spending (E = $300). The time dimension inherent in investment gets no direct representation.

The two components differ in terms of their stability properties and their relationship to income. Specifically, consumption is stable and directly related to current income: C = a + bY, where "a" is autonomous consumption and "b" is the marginal propensity to consume. Investment, which is unstable and not related to current income, changes with changing profit expectations, which, in turn, depend critically upon expectations about the future state of demand. The key difference between the two components of aggregate spending is captured by Hicks's contrasting phrases: "out of time" (consumption) and "in time" (investment).

The production possibilities frontier

Panel 5 gives play to the production possibilities frontier and hence will give us a direct point of comparison between labor-based macroeconomics and capital-based macroeconomics. The PPF highlights the constraints imposed by the underlying economic realities – whether the focus is supply and demand or income and expenditures. The frontier itself represents maximum sustainable levels of output. In this panel consumption and invest-ment, measured orthogonal to one another, are featured as alternative components of output; when scarcity is a binding constraint, more of one implies less of the other. The levels of these magnitudes shown in Panel 5 (C = \$210, I = \$90, a point lying on the PPF) accord with the equilib-rium levels shown in Panel 4 and the assumption of full employment. And we can recognize that, analogous to the dynamics of Figure 3.8, as long as (net) investment is a positive magnitude, the frontier itself (together with related curves in other panels) shifts outward from period to period – the greater the investment magnitude, the more rapid the rate of expansion.

Also depicted in Panel 5 is a linear upward-sloping relationship between consumption and investment. Points along this line are possible combina-tions of the C and I consistent with the income-expenditure equilibrium featured in Panel 4. Conventionally, we take the equilibrium condition (Y = C + I), represented graphically by the 45° line, together with the consumption equation (C = a + bY), and solve for the equilibrium level of income. In Panel 5 we have used those same two equations to solve for the relationship between levels of I and the corresponding equilibrium levels of C. Using our assumed parametric values we determine that C = 75 + 1.5I. Note that (I = 0; C = \$75) in Panel 4 aligns with (Y = C = \$75) in Panel 4. More generally, we can write

$$C = \frac{a}{1-b} + \frac{b}{1-b} I$$

which expresses the Keynesian demand-side relationship between the two spending magnitudes. Accordingly, we refer to this positive relationship between C and I as the Keynesian demand constraint.

Although explicit use of the demand constraint is uncommon, it was clearly in Keynes's mind when he wrote his 1937 restatement of his *General Theory*. Keynes (1937: 220) recaps his "psychological law" (i.e. 0 < b < 1) governing the relationship between income and consumption and then sets out in a sample calculation the implied relationship between investment and consumption. Ignoring for the sake of simplicity the intercept term in the consumption equation, Keynes writes:

> If, for example, the public are in the habit of spending nine-tenths of their income on consumption goods [i.e. a = 0; b = 0.9], it follows that if entrepreneurs were to produce consumption goods at a cost more than nine times [i.e. b/(1 − b) = 9] the cost of the investment goods they are producing, some part of their output could not be sold at a price which would cover its cost of production. . . . The formula is not, of course, quite so simple as in this illustration [i.e. a > 0]. . . . But there is always a formula, more or less of this kind, relating the output of consumption goods which it pays to produce to the output of invest-ment goods. . . . This conclusion appears to me to be quite beyond dispute. Yet the consequences which follow from it are at the same time unfamiliar and of the greatest possible importance.
>
> (Keynes, 1937: 220–1)

If we conceive of total expenditures as the product of the price level and the output quantity, that is, $E = PQ$, we can distinguish between move-ments of E inside the frontier and movements of E beyond the frontier. Consistent with the essential meaning of the PPF and the notion that prices (and wages) are sticky downwards, changes in E inside the frontier consist entirely of changes in Q; changes in E beyond the frontier consist entirely of changes in P. A parallel statement can be made about the movements of N inside the frontier and of W beyond the frontier. These hard-drawn distinctions between real and nominal movements must be softened with two qualifications for levels of output close to the frontier. First, as the level of output approaches the frontier from the inside, "bottlenecks" can develop. Keynes (1936: 300f.) used this term to mean unsystematic struc-tural imbalances; he allowed for the fact that not all sectors, or industries, will achieve full employment at the same time. Scarcity may make itself felt in textiles before it is felt in steel. If so, textile prices will begin to rise before the steel industry has become fully mobilized. Second, it is possible for the economy to experience unsustainable – and hence tempo-rary – levels of real income and real output beyond the PPF. However, any movements beyond the frontier that, in the short run, take the form of changes in real magnitudes will resolve themselves, in the long run, into changes in nominal magnitudes. (This second qualification is what gives play to particular strands of Monetarism and New Classicism – namely, the monetary misperception theory of the business cycle.)

Note that it is the PPF (rather than the supply and demand for labor) that defines full employment – the level of employment consistent with the maximum sustainable level of output. If the economy is in equilibrium in the Marshallian sense as well as in the Keynesian sense, then full employ-ment will entail not only a combination of consumption and investment that lies on the frontier, as shown in Panel 5, but also a wage rate that clears the market for labor, as shown in Panel 1. This formulation is compatible with Keynes's own, where full employment simply means the absence of "involuntary unemployment," which, in turn, is defined, though cryptically, in terms of Panel 5 rather than Panel 1. What Keynes calls his "definition" of involuntary unemployment is more accurately described as a test for the existence of involuntary unemployment:

> Men are involuntarily unemployed if, in the event of a small rise in the price of wage-goods relative to the money-wage, both the aggregate supply of labour willing to work for the current money-wage and the aggregate demand for it at that wage would be greater than the existing volume of employment.
>
> (Keynes, 1936: 15)

That is, if there can be sustainable upward adjustments in the real magnitudes – of labor and of output, then the supply constraint is not binding, the extent of adjustment reflecting the extent to which unemployment is in the involuntary category. In the presence of involuntary unemployment, then, there is scope for the economy to move outward along the demand constraint in Panel 5. Once we reach the PPF, there is no further scope for such movement. We could repeat Keynes's definition, inserting a "not" before the "involuntary unemployment" and a "no" before the "greater." Keynes himself expressed this negation by considering:

> an expansion of employment up to the point at which the supply of output as a whole ceases to be elastic, i.e., where further increase in the value of effective demand will no longer be accompanied by any increase in output. Evidently this amounts to the same thing as full employment. In the previous chapter [i.e. the first-quoted passage above] we have given a definition of full employment in terms of the behavior of labour. An alternative, though equivalent, criterion is that at which we have now arrived, namely a situation in which aggregate employment is inelastic in response to an increase in the effective demand for its output.
>
> (Keynes, 1936: 26)

That is, once the supply constraint – the PPF – becomes binding, increases in effective aggregate demand impinge only on prices and wages and not on output and employment. Movements beyond the PPF translate into upward shifts of both the supply and demand for labor – the intersection tracing out the vertical portion of the so-called L-shaped supply curve.

The relationship between Panels 1 and 5 serves to highlight the essential initial condition in the Keynesian vision of market malady and fiscal fix. The wage rate that prevails on the eve of a demand failure – and that prevails still (or again) after the fiscal authority has made good where the market failed – is the equilibrium wage rate. The wage rate itself is never the root problem. It's never stuck too high; it's always stuck just right. The involuntariness of the unemployment derives from some failure of the market system that has the economy performing inside the PPF.

Anticipating the centrality of Panel 5 in resolving some of the conflicting interpretations of Keynes's *General Theory*, we can raise a critical question about the frontier itself, which was described above as reflecting the "underlying economic realities." Just what all is this facile phrase intended to include? We can think beyond tastes, technology, and resource availabilities and ask if the uncertainties that are inherent in future-oriented decentralized decision making are included. In other words, does the output, especially of investment goods, incorporate allowances for the inevitable losses suffered along the way as the different plans of different entrepreneurs are revealed to be (at least partially) in conflict with one another? What about the perceptions of those uncertainties – if we are allowed to distinguish between the perceptions and the uncertainties themselves? Can the perceptions, like tastes, change (possibly dramatically) even though there is no basis for our thinking that the actual uncertainties have changed at all? And finally, what about the uncertainties that are attributable to the very fact that, in a market economy, decision making is decentralized? Can the case be made that characteristic features of the market system, namely, the uncertainties attributable to the absence of central direction, limit the production possibilities?

Our answers to these and related questions will affect the significance we attach to price and wage inflexibility and to decision making in the face of uncertainty in understanding Keynes's vision of the market economy. More generally, the scope for interpreting the PPF allows for significant departures from the conventional treatments of Keynesian macroeconomics and for a natural segue between the issues of stabilization policy as treated in Chapter 8 and the issues of social reform as treated in Chapter 9.

The market for loanable funds

In comparing capital-based and labor-based macroeconomics, Panel 6 helps to illustrate both commonality and contrast by keeping track of the supply and demand for loanable funds. Championed by Dennis Robertson, the loanable-funds theory of interest stands in contrast to Keynes's own liquidity preference theory. Yet, whether we abstract from considerations of liquidity preference or let changes in liquidity preference – or even the "fetish of liquidity" – play the perverse role that Keynes assigned to it, we can express the Keynesian relationships with the help of these supply and demand curves. This graph, with the axes reversed and the curves drawn for different levels of income, is the sole graph to appear in the pages of Keynes's *General Theory* (1936: 180). Keynes's purpose for presenting it, of course, was to show why he rejected the loanable-funds theory of interest. Abstracting from possible changes in liquidity preference, Keynes argued that a reduction of the demand for investment funds would, by reducing income and hence saving, be accompanied by a reduction in the supply of loanable funds. Supply and demand, then, would both shift leftward to the same extent, leaving the rate of interest unchanged. The intersection of the two curves moves horizontally at a level given by the prevailing rate of interest – a rate which, itself, according to Keynes, has to be explained by other considerations. Whatever restrictions might be imposed on the movements of these two curves, the initial market conditions that define our "full employment by accident" imply an interest rate that clears the market for loanable funds and a corresponding investment magnitude of $90.

The Keynesian flavour of Figure 7.1 derives from the direct relationship (or lack of one) between Panels 4 and 6 – more precisely, between consumption demand and the supply of loanable funds. In the classical view, in which there is no speculative demand for money, all shifts of the consumption equation must be mirrored by opposing shifts in the supply of loanable funds. That is, saving and the supply of loanable funds are simply two names for the same thing. In the Keynesian view, saving and the supply of loanable funds are only loosely linked – in the extreme case, not at all. And it is money, of course, that loosens the link. Individuals can save funds without at the same time supplying them in the loanable-funds market. They can hoard money. An autonomous leftward shift in the supply of loanable funds, then, need not be accompanied by a corresponding upward shift in the consumption function. A decreased supply of loanable funds may be mirrored instead by an increased demand for money.

In accordance with the Keynesian vision, then, we can imagine the consumption equation of Panel 4 not shifting at all while both the supply and demand of loanable funds shift (leftward or rightward) together. Observing the relationship between Panel 6 (the loanable-funds market) and Panel 5 (the PPF), we see that Keynes's reasoning is, to some extent, question-begging. If consumption and investment always move together, along the positively sloped demand constraint in Panel 5, then the implied changes in output (and income) do suggest a dominating income effect. Accordingly, the supply of loanable funds follows the demand. However, if it is possible in a market economy for consumption and investment to move *against* one another along the PPF, then the accompanying income effect would be nil. Accordingly, a shift of one curve in Panel 6 would result in a movement along the other. The interest rate would change in precisely the manner that the loanable-funds doctrine (and Marshallian theory in general) suggest.

We have illustrated two critical aspects of the Keynesian vision: (1) deviating from the general thrust of pre-Keynesian loanable-funds theory, we allow for the building up or drawing down of cash hoards to weaken the link between saving and the supply of loanable funds; and (2) in circumstances of a change in the demand for loanable funds, we allow for a dominant income effect on the supply of loanable funds. In application, the two critical aspects appear together. That is, if a decrease in investment spending is accompanied by hoarding, then, as the demand for loanable funds shifts leftward, the supply shifts even further leftward. The income effect on the supply of loanable funds is compounded by the liquidity-preference effect, causing the rate of interest to rise and causing investment spending, and hence income, to fall dramatically. The demand for labor will fall as well – with the extent of the reduction in employment depending on the flexibility of the wage rate. This summary of interactions among the Panels that make up Figure 7.1 is offered here in anticipation of a fuller, more systematic working out of these relationships in the following chapter.

Contrasting visions

The contrast between Keynes and the Classics is readily apparent in terms of the interrelationships among the panels of Figure 7.1. Consider the initial Marshallian/Keynesian equilibrium as described in terms of (W and N), (E and Y), (C and I), and (i and I). Full-employment equilibrium is clearly marked as the relevant intersection points in Panels 1, 4, 5, and 6. The supposed lockstep movements of the supply and demand for loanable funds (assuming away for the moment all complications stemming from changes in liquidity preference) was described above as "question-begging" – as following trivially from the supposed movements of consumption and investment – along the demand constraint rather than along the PPF. If consumption and investment fall together away from the frontier (and with them, income), then the income effect on savings will cause the supply of loanable funds to keep in step with demand. A similar charge of begging the question can be made with respect to the market for labor in the light of the production possibility frontier and demand constraint. If consumption and investment fall together away from the frontier, then output and the derived demand for labor (and for other factors) will fall as well. And if wages are sticky downwards, then the entire adjustment will be in terms of reduced employment.

While these aspects of the construction that might appear to be question-begging when viewed on a piecemeal basis, they may be more revealingly described as vision-reinforcing. Two alternative visions (depicted in Figures 7.2 and 7.3) can be defined by the envisioned pattern of movements of these magnitudes away from the initial position. In the Keynesian vision, the pattern in Panel 6 of Figure 7.2 is traced out by rightward and leftward movements along the horizontal; the corresponding patterns in Panels 4 and 5 are traced out by outward and inward movements along the diagonal and along the demand constraint, respectively. With the economy initially at full-employment, important qualifications have to be made for the rightward and outward movements. When scarcity is actually a binding

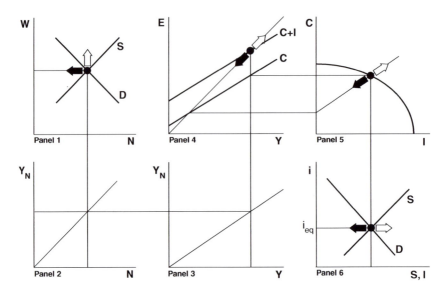

Figure 7.2 Labor-based macroeconomics (with Keynesian adjustment potentials).

constraint, these movements represent changing prices and wages rather than changing output levels and employment. That is, for a given PPF, movements beyond the frontier, as well as corresponding movements in other panels, are nominal movements only. The nominal movements are identified with hollow arrows in Figure 7.2. For Panels 4, 5, and 6, the pattern of possible movements shown applies without these nominal/real qualifications to an economy experiencing economy-wide unemployment, a condition that, in Keynes's vision, generally prevails. The potential movements in Panel 1 depend critically on the initial state of employment. Starting from full-employment the pattern that accords with Keynes's vision is traced out by leftward (solid arrow) and upward (hollow arrow) movements. This pattern of changes in W and N squares with the conventional L-shaped supply curve commonly featured in textbooks.

To Keynes, the classical vision seemed to involve some question-begging of its own. If markets work, there need be no lapse from full employment and hence no dominating income effect. And there need be no lapse from full employment because markets work. As depicted in Figure 7.3, movements from the initial equilibrium in Panel 5 are along the frontier, not away from it. Consumption and investment move in opposition to one another. Accordingly, the change in the *mix* of investment and consumption demand implies no first-order changes in the level of expenditures and no first-order shifts in the demand for labor *per se*. The supply of loanable funds in Panel 6, then, is not dominated by an income effect. Hence, a movement along the PPF is consistent with a loanable-funds market in

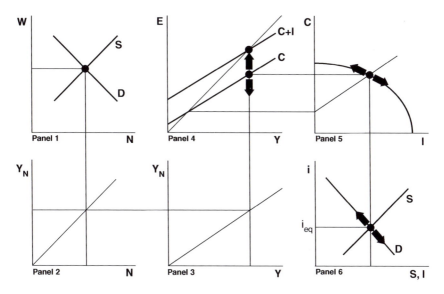

Figure 7.3 Labor-based macroeconomics (with Austrian adjustment potentials).

which one of the curves shifts and moves the economy along the other. In sum, the classical vision allows for changes in the mix of output between consumption and investment, entailing no net changes at all (or only second-order changes) in the level of total expenditures or in the supply and demand for labor. In the classical vision as depicted in Figure 7.3, movements in Panel 5 are confined to the frontier itself. These movements correspond to movements in Panel 6 along the demand for loanable funds. The income-expenditure equilibrium in Panel 4 is maintained, with changes in invest-ment being wholly or largely offset by opposing changes in consumption. And although workers may be moving about to reflect the new pattern of demand, the wage rate and employment levels are maintained.

Keynes (1936: 23) clearly saw that these movements are mutually depen-dent. Focusing more narrowly on the labor market, he closed his second chapter with the observation that the [three] assumptions [of classical economics] "all amount to the same thing in the sense that they all stand and fall together, each of them logically involving the other two." This is only to say, however, that the possible pattern of movements we associate with classical economics are mutually reinforcing. And as we have shown, the same can be said of the possible pattern of movements we associate with Keynesian economics. In fact, these contrasting patterns are consis-tent with – and virtually define – the respective visions of the macroeconomy.

After articulating in his third chapter the principle of effective demand (and the centrality of the dominating income effect in his own macro-economic theorizing), Keynes (1936: 34) offers his own contrast between the classical and the Keynesian vision: "It may well be that the classical theory represents the way in which we should like our Economy to behave. But to assume that it actually does so is to assume our difficulties away." Our own attention to the pattern of movements in Figure 7.3 does not involve assuming our difficulties away but rather heeding the methodological norm identified by Hayek. We must first understand how things could go right before considering how they might go wrong. By contrast, we see that Keynes elevated the difficulties of an economy-gone-wrong to the status of a general theory. In the following chapter, we trace out those difficulties with the aid of our own labor-based macroeconomic framework, and in Chapter 9 we show how Keynes was led to recommend radical economic reform – reform aimed not at making a market economy go right but at severely reducing the scope for market activity.

8 Cyclical unemployment and policy prescription

From accident to design

Beginning with "Full employment by accident," depicted in Figure 7.1, and ending with "Full employment by design," depicted in Figure 8.4, we deal with the issues of market malady and fiscal fix in terms of the phases (peak-to-peak) of the business cycle. The sequence of cause and consequence is tailored to Keynes's treatment of business cycles in Chapter 22 of the *General Theory* (1936, especially pp. 315ff.), and is offered as being true to Keynes except in one respect. Following modern convention, "cyclical unemployment" and "involuntary unemployment" are treated – for the time being – as synonymous. As already noted, Keynes's involuntary unemployment consists of both a cyclical and a secular component. And it is the latter component, according to him, that has an overriding claim on our attention. Secular unemployment is a social tragedy; cyclical unemployment is a complication of secondary importance. Keynes's mid-course summing-up chapter (Chapter 18, "The General Theory of Employment Re-stated"), puts the two components in perspective: consistent with

> the outstanding features of our actual experience, . . . we oscillate, avoiding the gravest extremes of fluctuations in employment and in prices in both directions, round an intermediate position appreciably below full employment and appreciably above the minimum employment a decline below which would endanger life.
>
> (ibid.: 254)

The centrality of secular unemployment (associated with the "intermediate position") as compared to cyclical unemployment (associated with the oscillations) is evidenced by the fact that his discussion of cyclical variation is relegated to Book IV of the *General Theory*, titled "Short Notes Suggested by the General Theory," and, more specifically, to a chapter entitled "Notes on the Trade Cycle."

Allowing cyclical unemployment to be the whole story as told with the aid of Figures 7.1 through 8.4 is strictly a matter of heuristics. After we have turned from the issues of cyclical unemployment and stabilization policy to the issues of secular unemployment and social reform, we can easily transplant our entire discussion of business cycles into the context of an economy that is suffering from ongoing secular unemployment.

True to Keynes, we tell our story peak to peak. Unlike the boom-begets-bust story that emerges from the capital-based macroeconomics of Chapter 4, the story told by Keynes opens with the bust. The onset of the crisis takes the form of a "sudden collapse in the marginal efficiency of capital" – the suddenness being attributable to the nature of the uncertainties that attach to long-term investment decisions in a market economy. The crisis is illustrated in Figure 8.1. The collapse is shown in Panel 6 as a leftward shift (from D to D′) in the demand for investment funds. The initial decrease in investment demand is not offset by a corresponding increase in consumption demand. That is, there is no movement along the PPF in Panel 5. Rather, as reduced investment impinges upon employment and hence income consumption demand decreases, too. The sudden collapse envisioned by Keynes takes the economy off its PPF. The decreases in investment and consumption reinforce one another in multiple rounds, eventually resulting in the income-expenditure equilibrium shown in Panel 4. This decreased income is accompanied with correspondingly decreased saving, as depicted by the leftward shift (from S to S′) in the supply of loanable funds.

The consequences of the sudden collapse, as envisioned by Keynes, square with simple income-expenditure theory, which gives play to Richard Kahn's multiplier as spelled out by Keynes in his Chapter 10 (1936: 114–22). In Panel 6 investment is shown to decrease from $90 to $60. With a marginal propensity to consume of 0.6 and hence a spending multiplier of 2.5, this decrease in investment spending of $30 causes income and expenditures to spiral down by $75 (from $300 to $225), as shown in Panel 4. Panel 5 shows, if somewhat redundantly, that the decrease in income and expenditures takes the form of a decrease in investment of $30 and a decrease in consumption of $45. All these aspects of the new "equilibrium" are marked by a hollow point (in Panel 5) and two solid points (in Panels 4 and 6). The hollow point in Panel 5 (C = $165; I = $60) is better described as a point of classical disequilibrium. Both investment and consumption fall short of the supply-side constraint imposed by the underlying economic realities. The solid point in Panel 4 (Y = E = $225) marks an equality of income and expenditures that, in Keynesian theory, defines macroeconomic equilibrium. The solid point in Panel 6 (S = $60; I = $60 at an unchanged interest rate) is an equilibrium in a limited sense. Given the less-than-full-employment level of income and expenditures, the old rate of interest still clears the market for loanable funds. Note here that the applicability of the simple multiplier relationships does not depend upon the particular elasticities – or inelasticies – that characterize the supply and demand curves in Panel 6. Rather, it depends upon the multiplier process shifting the supply curve to match the shift in the demand curve, such that the rate of

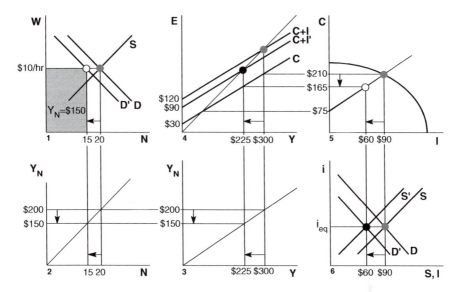

Figure 8.1 Market malady (a collapse in investment demand).

interest remains unchanged. Anticipating this result we did not bother to distinguish between a "decrease in investment" and a "leftward shift in investment demand." The dominant income effect shows itself on the supply side of the market for loanable funds, effectively robbing the interest rate of its classical role. That is, a movement along the new demand curve that would partially offset the initial reduction of investment is cut short by a shifting of the supply curve.

With reductions in both components of output (consumption and investment), the derived demands for labor and for all other inputs fall in strict proportion to one another. Panel 3 shows that the share of income accruing to labor is two-thirds both before the sudden collapse and subsequently. As total income falls from $300 to $225, labor income falls from $200 to $150. Panel 1 shows the corresponding leftward shift (from D to D′) of the demand for labor. If the wage rate is sticky downward (as depicted by the unchanged slope in the income-employment relationship in Panel 2), the entire adjustment in income will be made, at least initially, by a proportional adjustment in employment – from 20 to 15. The change in N shown in Panel 1 constitutes cyclical unemployment, which, in this construction, is identical to involuntary unemployment. The hollow point in Panel 1 indicates that the going wage is no longer a market-clearing wage.

Figure 8.1, then, identifies the initial consequences of a collapse in investment demand. We have a (Keynesian) income-expenditure equilibrium in Panel 4, market clearing in panel 6, and (classical) disequilibria in

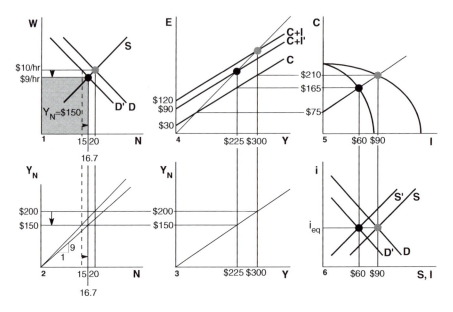

Figure 8.2 Locking in the malady (with a flexible wage rate).

Panels 1 and 5. Note that these movements away from the initial full-employment position are fully consistent with the Keynesian vision as depicted in Figure 7.2.

Figure 8.2 helps to put the issue of wage-rate stickiness into perspective. Are sticky wage rates critical to our understanding of Keynes's cyclical unemployment? It may seem that any answer to this question gets us into trouble. If we say "Yes," then the unemployment follows trivially. Our understanding of it does not require any special Keynesian insights. The classical economists knew all too well that if the wage rate does not adjust to a reduced demand for labor, there will be unemployment. If, allowing for flexible wage rates in both nominal and real terms, we say "No," then there would seem to be no unemployment – cyclical or other-wise – to be understood. Keynes was insistent, however, that the problem was not a wage rate that was too high but an aggregate demand that was too low. Still, we are entitled to ask, "Wouldn't a reduction in the wage rate be a solution to the problem, even if an excessive wage rate was not, in some larger sense, *the* problem?"

The interplay among the Panels of Figure 8.2 suggests how this ques-tion might be answered in Keynes's favor: if a reduction in the wage rate is a solution, it is not a very good solution. A wage-rate reduction would lock in rather than truly solve the problem. Panel 1 shows the wage rate falling (from $10/hr to $9/hr) to its market-clearing level; Panel 2 shows the same wage-rate reduction by a downward rotation; the slope of the income–employment relationship is now 9 instead of 10. For the convenience of exposition, the demand for labor is taken to be unit elastic over the relevant range, such that N increased from 15 to 16.7 and labor income remains unchanged (at $Y_N = \$150$). To the extent that the elasticity actually deviates from unity, second-order adjustments, reflecting the difference between WN and W'N', would have to be made in Panels 4, 5, and 6. But whatever the elasticity of labor demand (and assuming that labor supply is not perfectly *in*elastic), the market-clearing wage rate does not restore the full employment depicted in Figure 7.1. The problem of a collapsed investment demand remains, as shown in Panel 6, and the economy is still performing inside the initial PPF, as shown in Panel 5.

The stickiness or flexibility of the wage rate, then, is not at all essential to our understanding of the problem identified by Keynes. The behavior of the wage rate has implications only for the particular way that the problem manifests itself – as a very dramatic increase in unemployment at the going wage (in the case of a sticky wage rate) or as a less dramatic increase in unemployment, coupled by a reduction in the wage rate (in the case of flexible wage rate). As a theoretical matter, then, the extent of the wage rate's flexibility is very much a subsidiary issue. As an empirical matter, the extent of wage-rate flexibility in the 1930s was hardly an issue at all. The massive unemployment actually experienced during the Great Depression did not inspire Keynes to make a fine distinction between dramatic and not-quite-so-dramatic levels of unemployment. As a policy matter, the sticky wage rate, according to Keynes (1936: 265–6), is to be preferred. It puts the economy one step away (the restoration of aggregate demand) rather than two steps away (the restoration of aggregate demand plus an upward adjustment in the wage rate) from a satisfactory solution to the problem of a collapse in investment demand. In the spirit of Keynes, we are ruling out the possibility of a sufficiently dramatic overall price-and-wage deflation and corresponding real-cash-balance effect as a solution to the unemployment problem. Consistent with the Keynesian vision, this supposed cure would only worsen the disease – by adding to the uncertainty that caused the initial collapse in investment demand.

It could be argued that in Panel 1 of Figure 8.2, we are not two steps away from (the old) full employment, but rather we are no steps away from (a new) full employment. If, as Keynes argues, the sudden collapse in the marginal efficiency of capital is due to changed profit expectations in the face of the uncertainties that attach to investment decisions in a market economy, there is some justification in drawing a new PPF that incorporates those changed perceptions. This aspect of our construction is consistent with the commonly understood difference, in application, between Keynes's marginal efficiency of capital and Fisher's rate of return on capital: Fisher abstracts from the consequences of an uncertain future; Keynes (1936: 140–3) factors them in.

The inward shift of the PPF shown in Panel 5 is proportionate to the investment magnitude. An economy that produces only consumption goods involves little uncertainty of the sort that was of concern to Keynes. Perceptions and expectations apart from those involving long-term investment are well behaved and not subject to sudden and radical change. This is the contrast we get by comparing Keynes's Chapter 5, "Expectation as Determining Output and Employment," with his Chapter 12, "The State of Long-Run Expectation" (see Leijonhufvud, 1984).

The horizontal dimension associated with each point on the PPF, we could argue, should incorporate the implications of uncertainty. The "possibilities" for producing investment goods that will have some particular expected value are limited by the capital losses and other setbacks that the time-consuming process of investment necessarily entails. Increased allowance for such losses should be represented by this inward shift of the PPF.

We now see that the equilibrium shown in Figure 8.2 with the solid points in Panels 1, 4, 5, and 6 is qualitatively indistinguishable from the initial equilibrium of Figure 7.1. If we could take the full employment in Figure 7.1 as, in some sense, the "true" full employment, then we could say that the wage-rate adjustment shown in Figure 8.2 has, unfortunately, locked-in the market malady. But there seems to be no clear justification for the distinction here between a true and a false full employment. What was seen in Figure 8.1 as a market malady, dislocating the economy from its full-employment equilibrium, has been incorporated, in Figure 8.2, into the underlying economic realities that define a new full-employment equilibrium. Any qualitative distinction would have to rest on a comparison for each possible PPF between the perceptions of the uncertainties and the actual uncertainties being perceived. Passing over the difficulties of distinguishing between perceived and actual uncertainties, we might suggest that "true" full employment is depicted by a PPF drawn on the assumption that perceptions and realities coincide. Does Figure 7.1 involve some unperceived or less-than-fully-perceived uncertainties? Or does Figure 8.2 involve some perceived or imagined uncertainties that are no part of the underlying economic realities? A discussion of Keynes's implicit answer to these questions will have to await our treatment of secular unemployment and social reform. For now, we continue to regard Figure 7.1 as representing, if only by construction, the true full-employment equilibrium. Accordingly, we see that a flexible wage rate will only partially eliminate the immediate problem of unemployment while contributing nothing to – and even forestalling – a solution to the root problem, the collapse in investment demand.

Liquidity preference, which is sometimes seen as the *sine qua non* of Keynesianism, plays a secondary role – in terms of both causation and chronology – in Keynes's account of the business cycle. As already indicated, changes in money holdings loosen the link between saving and the supply of loanable funds. Keynes (1936: 166) explained this loosening by identifying what he saw as a critical two-stage decision sequence. First, we decide how much of our incomes to spend and how much to save; then, the amount of saving having been determined, we decide how much of it to put at interest and how much to hold liquid. Keynes's two stages, here, need not be taken literally. He would have done just as well for himself to insist that people are equalizing on three margins instead of just two. In connection with the business cycle, he saw the decision to increase the portion of saving held liquid as an aggravating factor, not an initiating factor. "Liquidity-preference, except those manifestations of it which are associated with increasing trade and speculation [by which he means the transactions demand for money], does not increase until *after* the collapse in the marginal efficiency of capital" (ibid.: 316, emphasis original). Interpreters of the *General Theory* who take an increase in the demand for money as the cause of the cyclical downturn (e.g., Krugman, 1994: 26–8) must base their interpretation on Keynes's qualifying statements rather than on his primary claim to the contrary. The relevant paragraph, quoted here in full, comes early in his chapter on the business cycle.

> Now, we have been accustomed in explaining the "crisis" to lay stress on the rising tendency of the rate of interest under the influence of the increased demand for money both for trade and speculative purposes. At times this factor may certainly play an aggravating and, occasionally perhaps, an initiating part. But I suggest that a more typical, and often the predominant, explanation of the crisis is, not primarily a rise in the rate of interest, but a sudden collapse in the marginal efficiency of capital.
>
> (Keynes, 1936: 315)

Figure 8.3 illustrates the secondary role of a change in liquidity preference. Panel 6 of Figure 8.3 shows the supply of loanable funds shifting sharply leftward, while the consumption schedule in Panel 4, and hence the implied saving schedule, remains unchanged. Income earners intend to save as much (and to consume as much) as before, but they are much less willing to commit those savings to interest-earning assets. The increased liquidity preference that follows on the heels of a collapse in investment demand is certainly an aggravating development. The supply of loanable funds, which had already been shifted leftward by the income effect of the collapse in demand, is now shifted further leftward (from S' to S'') by the liquidity-preference effect. The dominating income effect has already nullified the downward pressure on the interest rate that would otherwise have cushioned the fall in investment (and, according to the classical economists, stimulated consumption), and now, perversely, the liquidity-preference effect puts strong upward pressure on the interest rate, causing it to move dramatically in the wrong direction. The increase in the interest rate causes investment to decrease from $60 to $30.

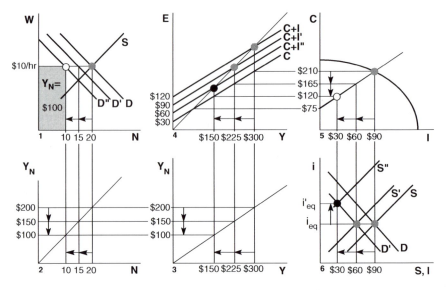

Figure 8.3 Compounding the market malady (with a scramble for liquidity).

The consequent movements in Panels 5, 4, and 1, however, are dictated by this further reduction in investment demand – and not at all by the fact that this reduction, in contrast to the one associated with the initial collapse in demand, is accompanied by a sharp rise in the rate of interest. (The only direct consequence of this sharp rise in the interest rate is to bring into balance the increased demand for money with the unchanged monetary stock.) The economy sinks further along the demand constraint into the interior of the PPF. The new levels of consumption and investment (C = $120; I = $30) are indicated in Panel 5. The new income-expenditure equilibrium (Y = E = $150) is shown in Panel 4 by a shift in the expenditure schedule (from C + I′ to C + I″). The reduction in income causes the rate of saving to fall to the level of investment (S = I = $30).

It may be that an unchanged wage rate and a sharply increased interest rate will have a second-order effect on the relationship between labor income and total income, as represented in Panel 3. But for expository convenience, we can assume that the relevant elasticities are such as to leave this ratio unchanged. Derived demand for labor, then, shifts leftward (from D′ to D″), with N falling in proportion to both labor income and total income (from 15 to 10). Following Keynes, we show the entire adjustment in the labor market in terms of reduced employment – with workers who manage to retain their jobs receiving the still-going wage rate of $10/hr.

Again, as in Figure 8.2, we could (but do not) show the consequences of a flexible wage rate. A full adjustment in the labor market to existing market conditions (given by S and D″) would reduce the extent of unemployment and establish a new going wage rate. The PPF would have to be shifted even further inward to accord with income earners' increased unwillingness to part with liquidity. And again, as in Figure 8.2, we would not be able to distinguish qualitatively between the new equilibrium, as would be defined in terms of Panels 1, 4, 5, and 6, and the initial equilibrium of Figure 7.1. For the same reasons offered earlier, Keynes clearly preferred that the wage rate not adjust. If we take Figure 7.1 as representing the economy's true potential, we can understand Keynes's preference. It is clear from Figure 8.3 that despite the market clearing in Panel 6 and the absence of market clearing in Panel 1, it is the interest rate and not the wage rate that needs the policy-maker's attention.

To put it in Swedish terms (Leijonhufvud, 1981b), the interest rate is out of whack; the wage rate is *in* whack. We can note here, in fact, that our rendition of Keynes is consistent with both the letter and spirit of Leijonhufvud's understanding:

> Keynes's *fundamental contention* that a competitive, private enterprise market economy (with all its prices "flexible") may fail to home in automatically on its equilibrium time-path stems from the contemplation of states like the one just sketched [and the one depicted in Figure 8.3]: the interest rate is wrong, but that market "clears" (without "punishment," so to speak, of those responsible); the money wage is right, but large-scale unemployment prevails and persists and even the willingness of labor to reduce the money wage will not help. The system's "automatic" adjustment tendencies presumed in pre-Keynesian analysis to be self-regulatory, are working to change prices that are right and leaving those we need to have changed alone ...
>
> (Leijonhufvud, 1981b: 167)

Again, as in connection with Figure 8.2, we rule out the possibility of an overall price-and-wage deflation as a viable mechanism for accommodating the increased demand for real cash balances. Instead, we consider counter-cyclical policies that are aimed at recreating the happy conditions of Figure 7.1. The opportunity for implementing these policies, however, is a fleeting one. Following Keynes, we can indicate the expected course of events that would likely unfold in the absence of a timely fix. Almost inevitably, the decidedly unhappy conditions depicted in Figure 8.3 will get even worse. In the face of a slack economy and high interest rates, there will likely be a further waning of the "animal spirits." A complete collapse of investment demand will send the economy into deep depression with its characteristic low interest rate and low marginal efficiency of capital. From this point, conditions will eventually improve on their own, but only after durable assets begin wearing out. In Keynes's (1936: 317) judgment, the beginning of a recovery does not come within a year but can be expected to come in less than ten years. Owing to the average durability of capital equipment, recovery begins in three to five years. We note, then, that although the relationships among macroeconomic magnitudes at any point in time are closely geared to the employment of labor, the (peak-to-peak) length of the business cycle, assuming that no counter-cyclical policies are implemented, is actually governed by considerations of capital.

Before conditions have deteriorated beyond those shown in Figure 8.3, there is an opportunity to re-establish economic prosperity – to return to the conditions shown in Figure 7.1 – by judicious and timely use of both monetary and fiscal policy, as shown in Figure 8.4. The monetary policy is best suited to undo the damage caused by the scramble for liquidity. The ΔM_c (additional money made available in credit markets) shown in Panel 6, shifts the supply of loanable funds from S'' to $S'' + \Delta M_c$ (where $S'' + \Delta M_c$ is the former S') and increases investment from \$30 to \$60. This money-induced increase in investment offsets the effects of the increased liquidity preferences and restores the economy to its position depicted in Figure 8.1. The ΔM_c, however, represents only a part of the total change in the money supply – that part actually made available in the loan market. The rest of the increase is simply added to money hoards (ΔM_h). The limits to the effectiveness of monetary policy, made clear by Keynes, are almost too well known to mention: first, as the interest rate is brought down, an increasing proportion of the increase in the money supply goes into hoards – up to 100 percent if Keynes's remarks about liquidity preference becoming "absolute" are to be given serious consideration. Second, even if a portion of the increases in the money supply finds its way into the loan market,

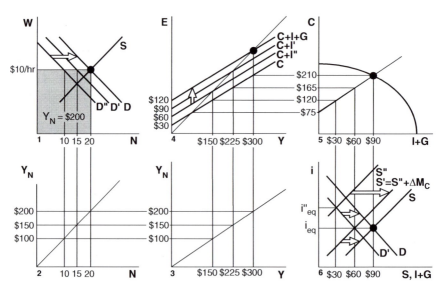

Figure 8.4 Full employment by design (through monetary and fiscal policies).

the interest rate would have to be reduced well below the level that prevailed before the collapse in the marginal efficiency of capital. And the demand for loanable funds (aka the MEC) may be inelastic, such that even the lowest rate of interest achievable by monetary policy alone may not result in a substantial enough increase in investment. Full employment, then, in all likelihood, cannot be re-established by monetary policy alone.

In Chapter 19 of the *General Theory*, "Changes in Money-Wages," Keynes, (1936: 267) clearly recognized that the increase in the real money supply could have been accomplished by wage (and price) reductions rather than by monetary expansion. "[W]hile a flexible wage policy and a flexible money policy come, analytically, to the same thing, inasmuch as they are alternative means of changing the quantity of money in terms of wage-units, in other respects there is, of course, a world of difference." Keynes went on to brand anyone who would prefer wage and price reduction to monetary expansion as a "foolish person" (we have a central monetary authority but no central labor authority), "an unjust person" (differentially flexible factor prices would result in social inequities) and/or an "inexperienced person" (wage and price reductions increase debt burdens). None of this world of difference makes any direct appearance in any of the panels of Figure 8.4. Further, any real-balance effect in commodity markets, whether brought about by increased nominal money or decreased prices and wages, is not in play here. In the Keynesian vision, a real-balance effect works exclusively through the interest rates and is too weak to have any claim on our attention, except in circumstances in which there is a catastrophic spiraling downward of wages and prices – which are precisely the circumstances that policy aims to preclude. Besides, the effects of an appropriately designed policy, as compared to the weak and problematic effects of deflation, can be tailored to fit the actual market malady.

While monetary policy is the best solution to a secondary problem, fiscal policy is the second-best solution to the primary problem. The primary problem, which has manifested itself as a collapse in investment demand, is business pessimism. Individuals who make up the business community have become reflective about the precarious nature of their profit expectations. The problem traces to their thinking, first individually and then (through contagion) collectively, of all the unknowns and unknowables that could interfere with a favorable outcome of current investment decisions. Importantly, the unknowns and unknowables include for each entrepreneur the future actions of other entrepreneurs. The first-best solution would be one that simply turns business pessimism to business optimism – one that recreates the "underlying economics realities" depicted in Figure 7.1. The regained optimism, which would be self-reinforcing, would send the economy spiraling upwards to a level of aggregate demand that would validate the going wage rate. The worst solution is *laissez-faire*, which would allow the wage rate to adapt to the deteriorated conditions and make the economy wait for capital depreciation to initiate an upward spiral.

Recreating the business conditions that underlie the relationships in Figure 7.1 – including the entrepreneurs' expectations about the actions of one another – is simply beyond the scope of policy. It is, in fact, in the province of social reform, which is the subject of the following chapter. Constrained to adopt a second-best solution, then, policy-makers aim at recreating the level of spending that corresponds to those bygone conditions in which optimism prevailed. Public investment demand substitutes for the deficient private investment demand. The fiscal authority engages in just enough deficit spending to produce a rightward shift (from D' to D) in the demand for loanable funds. The resulting upward spiral of incomes and consumption spending, so emphasized in elementary texts, produces a validating rightward shift (from S' to S) in the supply of loanable funds. The increase in investment from $60 to $90, as shown in Panel 6, is accompanied by corresponding changes in all other macroeconomic magnitudes, such that the economy is returned to the initial conditions depicted in Figure 7.1.

In sum, then, the accidental full employment of Figure 7.1 is replaced with the full employment by design, as shown in Figure 8.4. While the labeling of the axes in Panels 5 and 6 (and the expenditure schedule in Panel 4) have been altered to incorporate the deficit spending by the fiscal authority (each instance of I has been replaced by I + G), the resulting pattern of equilibria, as depicted in Panels 1, 4, 5 and 6, is indistinguishable (both qualitatively and quantitatively) from that of Figure 7.1.

So, does design equal accident? Are the economies of Figures 7.1 and 8.4 identical in all relevant macroeconomic respects? We can address these questions in terms of Panel 5. Both figures show economies at the same point on their respective PPFs. However, the rates of economic growth (the rapidity with which the frontier expands outward), are likely to be different. The PPF expands outward on the basis of investment, which adds to the capital base, permitting, in future periods, higher levels of both consumption and investment. Because the private investment (I) in Figure 7.1 has been partially replaced, in Figure 8.4, by public investment (G), the economy with designed full employment will grow at a different rate. Will the rate be higher or lower? The answer to this question is very much vision-dependent. Hayek ([1933] 1975b), following the lead of Mises ([1922] 1951), pointed to fundamental problems in allocating resources in the public sector. The state cannot calculate costs and benefits like the market can. Hayek, then, would expect the economy with designed full employment to grow more slowly. Keynes (1936: 164), who sees the state as being "in a position to calculate the marginal efficiency of capital-goods on long views and on the basis of the general social advantage," would expect the economy with designed full employment to grow faster. We will return to the issues of growth and the related issues of economic reform in Chapter 9.

In the long run, however, the performance of the economy may be affected by the very nature of the fiscal fix. The public investment is deficit financed.

A sequence of such fiscal fixes results in an accumulation of debt that hangs like a black cloud over the private sector. The capital-based macroeconomics of debt-induced growth was the focus of Chapter 6. Changes in the government's strategy in accommodating a chronically large deficit can have dramatic effects on market conditions – on interest rates, inflation rates, and exchange rates. These are the critical market conditions to which entrepreneurs in the private sector must adapt. Having to guess what particular strategy – or what combination of them – will actually be adopted adds to the "unknowns and unknowables" and has its own effect on the business community. With uncertain prospects of rising interest rates, worsening inflation, and weakened export markets, businesspeople in the private sector may be hesitant to commit themselves to investment projects. Business pessimism may be more likely to develop in the circumstances depicted in Figure 8.4 than in those depicted in Figure 7.1. In fact, even if Keynes's belief that investment spending is inherently unstable and that full employment happens only by accident is without foundation, the implementation of Keynesian stabilization policy – the fiscal fix and attending debt and debt-related uncertainties – may well make the economy exhibit the instability and sluggishness characteristic of the Keynesian vision.

Prospects for a spontaneous order

The tracing out of the economy's path from "accident to design" helps to put into perspective Keynes's perception of the problem of cyclical unemployment and of the appropriate policy prescription. It is more revealing, however, to consider just what the phrase "accident or design" excludes. Here, we have to draw on classical or Austrian economics in their broadest senses. Between accident and design is the spontaneous order that, according to Hayek (1955: 39), constitutes the subject matter of economics. How does the spontaneous order work? What might go wrong? In the specific context of market malady and fiscal fix, we can ask: What self-corrective qualities would that spontaneous order have to exhibit for there to be no role for a monetary or fiscal fix? To ask this question is to heed that key Hayekian methodological maxim: before we can even ask how things might go wrong, we must understand how things could ever go right. Given the Keynesian, labor-based vision of the macroeconomy, how could the spontaneous order conceivably adjust to an increased aversion to the uncertainties inherent in investment decisions? This is a question that Keynes neither answered nor even asked – obviously because to him the question itself had no merit. There *are* no such self-correcting tendencies; it is only by accident or design . . .

Figure 8.5 is constructed to show just how the economy would work if it were equipped with the requisite self-correcting tendencies. We treat the initial leftward shift (from D to D′) of the demand for investment funds as a shift attributable to increased uncertainty aversion, a parametric change similar to a change in tastes. The future is uncertain. This inherent uncertainty manifests itself in the economy's investment sector, which is unavoidably future-oriented. If the loanable-funds market functions in accordance with the classical vision, the interest rate is bid down (from i_{eq} to i'_{eq}). As shown in Panel 6, the effects of the increased uncertainty aversion (the extent of the horizontal shift of the demand for loanable funds) are partially offset by the effects of the reduced costs of borrowing (the movement along the shifted demand curve). For the economy to avoid falling into the interior of the PPF, the funds released from the investment-goods sector would have to be absorbed in the economy's consumer-goods sector. This reallocation of resources, however, is already implicit in the movement along the unshifted supply of loanable funds: less saving; more consumption. The new equilibrium in Panel 6 implies an counter-clockwise movement along the PPF in Panel 5 and an upward shift in the consumption equation in Panel 4. The equilibrium in Panel 5, as defined by the PPF and a shifted demand constraint, is consistent with a spontaneous order accommodating itself to increased uncertainty aversion. In effect, the economy moves along the frontier in the direction away from the uncertainty-wracked investment sector until the remaining uncertainty is willingly borne by the business community.

The changes in the pattern of equilibria, however, are not confined to those represented in Panels 4, 5, and 6. The changes summarized by these three panels imply a change in the structure of the economy. We cannot finesse an unchanged structure in Panel 3 – as we have in other applications by assuming that some demand curve (for loanable funds or for labor) is sufficiently close to having unit elasticity as to reduce any change in the corresponding income magnitude to the status of a second-order consideration. In Panel 6, a movement along the *supply* curve reduces both the level of investment and the rate of interest. Non-labor income must fall relative to labor income. This is shown in Panel 3 by a counter-clockwise rotation. The ratio of labor income to total income is now greater than 2/3. This change is consistent with the initiating increase in uncertainty aversion together with the consequences already noted. The unchanged total income shown in Panel 4 is now derived less from time-consuming and hence uncertainty-wracked processes and more from the direct use of labor services. The demand for labor has shifted rightward (from D to D′), increasing both the level of employment and the wage rate. The directions of change in Panels 1, 2, and 3 are determinate, though (without additional information about supply elasticities of labor and capital) the actual magnitudes are not. With a spontaneous order in play, the new pattern of equilibria entails changes in Panels 1, 5, and 6 but entails no first-order change in total income and in total expenditures, as shown in Panel 4.

Three observations about Figure 8.5 are worth making. First, and most important for the issues at hand, the spontaneous order that, at least conceivably, could adjust for changes in uncertainty aversion is at odds with Keynes's

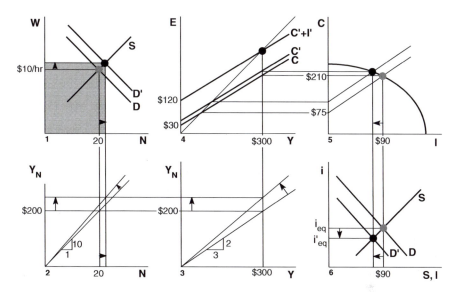

Figure 8.5 The Keynesian vision plus self-correcting tendencies.

assumption of structural fixity. That is, unless the assumption of a fixed relationship between labor income and total income is relaxed, the spontaneous order, whose very existence is – or ought to be – at issue, is precluded by construction. Hayek's methodological maxim (we should first determine how things could go right) is simply flouted. Keynes might like to respond, of course, by pointing out that if, as he believes to be true, the income effect of a reduced investment demand dominates, then the spontaneous order envisioned here – or any other – is cut short, and the assumed structural fixity holds good.

Second, the full employment in Panel 1 of Figure 8.5 is a little fuller than the full employment in Figure 7.1. Both employment and the wage rate are higher. With an unchanged total income, the non-labor component is correspondingly less. In terms of the distribution of income, then, this is the kind of change that Keynes found attractive. As will be seen in the following chapter, Keynes aimed at reform that would have this result – not, though, by allowing the market to move along the *supply* of loanable funds, but by engineering a movement along the *demand* for loanable funds until capital ceases to be scarce.

Third, the Austrians would argue that *marginal* changes in risk aversion on the part of the business community give rise to market forces that edge the economy away from investment and toward consumption. They would not dispute that a *sudden and violent* change in risk aversion – or in perceptions of the riskiness inherent in investment undertakings – is likely to cause the economy to plunge into recession. What they would dispute is that such changes in risk aversion or in perceptions tend to happen spontaneously. They are much more likely to occur during a period in which the counter-movements of a boom–bust cycle have already begun to make themselves felt.

The paradox of thrift

In the Hayekian vision, the spontaneous order trades off consumption against investment largely in response to people's preferences as between consuming now and consuming later, that is, their intertemporal preferences. In the Keynesian vision, the spontaneous order, if one existed, would have to trade off consumption against investment largely in response to businesspeople's aversion to the uncertainties that are inherent in investment and in response to the liquidity preferences of savers. But neither this spontaneous order, nor – as his chiding of the classical economists makes clear – the spontaneous order envisioned by Hayek is believed to be characteristic of the market economy. The classical economists, according to Keynes (1936: 21), "are fallaciously supposing that there is a nexus which unites decisions to abstain from present consumption with decisions to provide for future consumption." Keynes would consider it equally fallacious, if not even more so, to suppose that there is a nexus which unites decisions to abstain from investment (due to increased uncertainty aversion) with decisions to engage in additional present consumption. There is no such nexus; it is only by accident or design. . . .

We get the clearest contrast between the Keynesian and the Hayekian visions when we compare them on the basis of the envisioned market reaction to an increase in saving. The so-called "paradox of thrift" that once dominated discussion in macroeconomic texts has a firm enough basis in the *General Theory*. By trying to save more out of a given income, we find ourselves earning less income out of which to save. In Keynes's (1936: 83) own words "Every . . . attempt to save more by reducing consumption will so affect incomes that the attempt necessarily defeats itself." Note that the unduly strong language here ("necessarily") gives the impression that Keynes is stating some fundamental macroeconomic principle – rather than indicating just how completely in his vision the market's malfunctioning is expected to be. The common view among modern macroeconomists that the paradox of thrift has been overemphasized does not entail a denial that, according to Keynes, an increase in saving has a perverse effect. What is denied is that there is any tendency of the saving schedule to shift. Consumer spending has a stable relationship with income; saving, which is simply income not spent, is similarly stable. A change in saving, that is, a shift of the saving equation, is never – or is rarely – the problem. As illustrated in the discussion of Figure 8.1, it is under-investment, and not over-saving, that sends the economy into a downward spiral. Still, dealing with the possibility of an increase in saving allows us to identify the nature of the

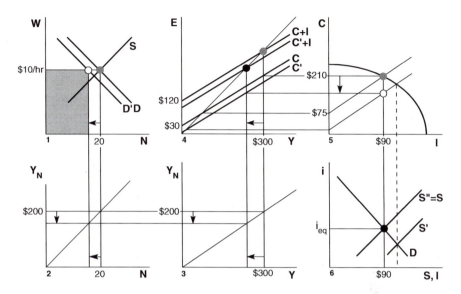

Figure 8.6 The paradox of thrift (saving more means earning less).

market failure, as seen by Keynes, and the workings of the intertemporal market mechanisms, as seen by Hayek.

In Figure 8.6 we start with the initial conditions of Figure 7.1 and allow for an increase in saving, which is to say, a decrease in consumption. Assuming no change in liquidity preferences, the supply of loanable funds in Panel 6 shifts rightward (from S to S′); the consumption function in Panel 4 shifts downward (from C to C′); the demand constraint in Panel 5 shifts downward to reflect the reduced demand for consumption goods. What is needed, of course, is a movement along the PPF to its intersection with the new demand constraint. This intersection represents the allocation of resources between consumption and investment consistent with the hypothesized change in saving preferences. But no such movement occurs. (There is no nexus . . .)

Less money is being spent on consumer goods, and yet, by assumption, people do not desire to hold higher levels of money balances. Saving, then, implies that more money should be spent (by the borrowers of the saved funds) on the only other category of goods, namely, investment goods. However, market signals are, at best, pushing the business community in two different directions. On the one hand, any actual reduction in the interest rate brought about by an increase in saving encourages the business community to borrow and spend on investment goods. On the other hand, the increased inventories of consumption goods associated with the currently weakened consumption demand discourages the business community from expanding even further its capacity to produce consumption goods. In the Keynesian vision, the discouragement wins out and in the process nullifies the encouragement. Actual cash holdings relative to incomes rise despite the absence of any increase in liquidity preferences.

If investment spending remains constant, as shown in Panel 6, the reduction in consumption entails a movement off the PPF. Total output (C + I) and hence total income fall. The negative and dominating income effect on saving fully offsets the initiating rightward shift. The supply for loanable funds shifts leftward (from S′ to S″) such that S″ coincides with the initial S. The initial interest rate is, once again, the market-clearing rate. With the assumption of structural fixity and a sticky wage rate, the reduction in income has its negative effect on labor income as shown in Panel 1. The pattern of equilibria in Figure 8.6 is similar to the pattern in Figure 8.1. If this saving-induced spiraling downward causes a loss of business confidence, as would be represented by a leftward shift of the demand for loanable funds, and causes an increase in liquidity preferences, as would be represented by a leftward shift of the supply of loanable funds, then the economy would spiral downward along the new demand constraint.

We can translate this Keynesian story into a Hayekian setting simply by converting from labor-based macroeconomics to capital-based macroeconomics. In Figure 8.7, we have dropped Panels 1 and 2 which track the consequences of the change in saving in terms of the wage rate that tends to be sticky. As will be seen, it is not just the wage-rate stickiness that has to go but rather the notion that a single labor market can track the consequences of a change in intertemporal preferences. Panel 4, which portrays income and expenditure in terms of the circular-flow framework, is replaced by the time-consuming structure of production, which portrays production and consumption in terms of the means-ends framework developed in Chapter 3. We retain, in Figure 8.7, the Keynesian vision: we have dropped Panel 3, although we have not yet relaxed the assumption of structural fixity. This translation simply shows the uniformity with which the spiraling downward of income and expenditures makes itself felt. The reduction in consumption propagates itself in accordance with the doctrine of derived demand through each of the stages of production. Corresponding reductions in each stage reduce production activities all around while leaving the relative dimensions of the structure unchanged. With Mill's Fourth Fundamental Proposition regarding capital not in play, the Hayekian triangle changes in size but not in shape. Notice that the unchanged slope of the hypotenuse, which reflects the discount from stage to stage, is in accord with the unchanged rate of interest in Panel 6.

We now relax the assumption of structural fixity so that the Hayekian story can be told. In Figure 8.8, we duplicate the relationships of Figure 8.7, and add three auxiliary diagrams to show representative segments of the market for nonspecific labor: one shows the market for labor in stages of production relatively close to the final stage, one shows the market for

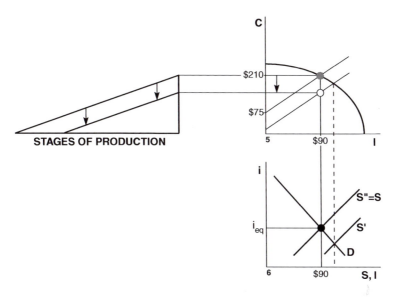

Figure 8.7 The paradox of thrift (the Keynesian vision in the Hayekian framework).

labor in the stages of production relatively remote from the final stage, and
one shows the market for labor in a stage so remote that it didn't even
exist before the preference change. The same diagrams would apply equally
to non-specific capital goods. With these changes, we have abandoned the
Keynesian vision. Now, there *is* a nexus . . . As spelled out in Chapter 4
(compare Figure 8.8 with Figure 4.2), the increased saving reduces the rate
of interest; the lower rate of interest favors long-term production; labor is
bid away from the late stages of production, where demand has fallen, and
into the early stages; the net increase in investment is concentrated in the
early stages. Because we have focused, in Figure 8.8, on non-specific labor,
we show a process that begins and ends with a single wage rate prevailing.
But note that during the transition, the movements in wage rates are stage
specific. In the representative late stage, the wage rate falls and then rises;
in the representative early stage, the wage rate rises and then falls. These
kinds of relative movements, as spelled out by Mill in his Fourth
Fundamental Proposition, that are essential for adjusting the economy to
an intertemporal preference change are hopelessly obscured by the use of a
single market for labor. Of course, the existence of labor and capital goods
that are specific to a particular stage changes the calculus substantially. If
some kinds of labor and other resources cannot move, their corresponding
wage rates and prices change permanently. The intertemporal restructuring
takes on a character that is shaped by the pattern of specificities in the
structure of production.

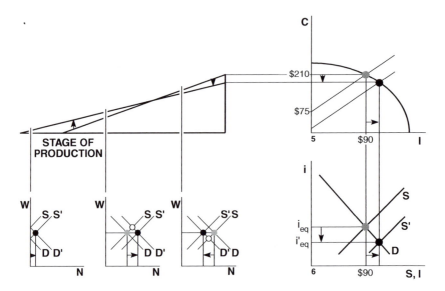

Figure 8.8 Resolving the paradox of thrift (with intertemporal restructuring).

With the intertemporal restructuring, the economy moves along the PPF in Panel 5; current income changes little if at all (unless factor specificities dominate the structure of production), which means there is no dominating income effect in the loanable-funds markets. With a higher portion of the economy's output in the form of investment, the economy will grow faster (the PPF will expand more rapidly), such that in the future, greater levels of consumption are possible. Presumably, it was the anticipation of this greater consumption in the future that inspired the increased saving.

Keynes (1936: 359) was fully aware of – but did not share in – his critics' regard for Mill's Fourth Fundamental Proposition in the context of the paradox of thrift. He quoted from Leslie Stephen's entry in the *Dictionary of National Biography*: "[Mandeville's] doctrine that prosperity was increased by expenditure rather than by saving fell in with many current economic fallacies not yet extinct." Continuing in a footnote and quoting from Stephen's *History of English Thought in the Eighteenth Century*, "the complete confutation of [this fallacy] lies in the doctrine – so rarely understood that its complete apprehension is, perhaps, the best test of an economist – that demand for commodities is not demand for labour."

Keynes and Hayek: head to head

Capital-based macroeconomics identifies aspects of the spontaneous order that allow an economy to adapt to changes in saving preferences or to

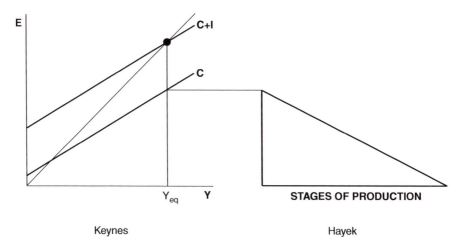

Figure 8.9 Keynes and Hayek (head to head).

changes in risk aversion. Any preference change that changes the preferred mix as between consumption and investment can be accommodated only by a change in the structure of production – by relative changes within the aggregates that form the basis for Keynes's theorizing. Figure 8.9 and Figure 8.10 reveal the essence of the difference between capital-based and labor-based macroeconomics. Consumption is the common element in the two panels of Figure 8.9. For Keynes, consumption is one of the two components of expenditures that characterize a wholly private economy. For Hayek, consumption is the final stage of a time-consuming production process.

In Figure 8.10, we consider the possibility of a shift of resources away from investment and towards consumption. For our current purpose, which is simply to contrast the two visions in the light of Hayek's methodological maxim, it does not matter whether the shift is driven by a change in time preferences (away from future consumption and towards present consumption) or by a increase in uncertainty aversion (which causes the business community to engage in less investment activity). The top two panels of Figure 8.10 show the consequences of the market's failed attempt to make the shift. With Keynes driving and Hayek tracking in accordance with the Keynesian vision, income and expenditures, as well as activity in each of the stages of production, spiral down until the level of saving is brought into line with the new lower level of investment. The bottom two panels of Figure 8.10 show the possibility of the market's success. With Hayek driving and Keynes tracking in accordance with the Hayekian vision, resources freed up in the relatively remote stages of production are absorbed in the late and final stages so as to accommodate increased consumption in the present and near future. To the extent that the shifting within the

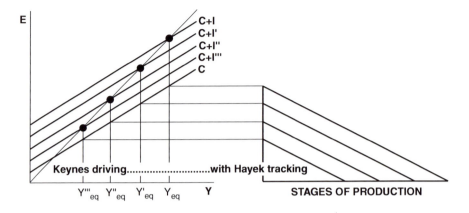

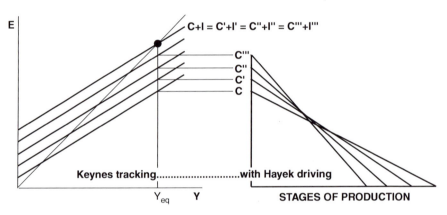

Figure 8.10 A contrast of visions (Keynes and Hayek).

triangle is successful the spiraling downward of all stages is precluded. Both income and expenditures maintain their initial levels.

The point of the contrast between the two visions here is a limited one. There is no claim that the market process *always* or *necessarily* works as the Hayekian vision suggests. But the mere possibility of it working that way negates Keynes's claim that the attempt to save more "necessarily defeats itself." Further, the understanding of just how a market economy would have to work to keep all attempts to increase saving from being self-defeating puts us in a good position to ask about just what can go wrong.

The differences between the Keynesian and the Hayekian visions of the macroeconomy can be summarized in terms of their judgments about the existence – or non-existence – of the relevant spontaneous order. Is it possible for a market economy to accommodate the trade-off between consumption and investment – where the needed changes in the trade-off are attributable to changes in intertemporal preferences (Hayek) or to changes in uncertainty aversion (Keynes)? As demonstrated in Chapter 3, Hayek's intertemporal structure of production, which was inspired by his vision of a spontaneous order at work in this respect, allows us to show just how it works. As this chapter has demonstrated, the absence of a structure of production in Keynes's labor-based macroeconomics, the assumed fixity of the structure of industry, the belief that there is in no relevant spontaneous order at work, and the assumed dominance of the income effect leave us with a macroeconomics of market failure.

9 Secular unemployment and social reform

In the absence of stabilization policy, the economy oscillates with a rhythm that reflects the durability of capital goods. Fortunately, the timely implementation of well-designed monetary and fiscal policy can dampen if not wholly eliminate these irksome oscillations. The tendency to oscillate, then, is not what condemns the capitalist system in Keynes's view.

The background against which it oscillates, however, is another matter. Considerations of money and of decentralized decision making form a constellation of interacting relationships that make the system fundamentally objectionable. According to Keynes (1936: 372), "The outstanding faults of the economic society in which we live are its failure to provide for full employment and its arbitrary and inequitable distribution of wealth and incomes." The previous chapter dealt with only one aspect of the first-mentioned fault (cyclical unemployment) by taking full employment to be identified with a particular pattern of equilibria that define the initial conditions – the conditions that prevail on the eve of a bust.

The present chapter deals with the other, more significant aspect of this fault (secular unemployment) together with the second-mentioned fault, the arbitrariness and inequity that characterize the distribution of income (between labor and other factors of production). The adjectives Keynes uses here (arbitrary and inequitable) are well-chosen ones, designed to bring together in his final chapter the most damning claims advanced in the book. The perceived faults of capitalism beyond its tendency to oscillate are not fixable with monetary and fiscal policy tools. These faults are so embedded in the capitalist system as to require fundamental, though preferably gradual, social reform. Stabilization policy serves primarily to keep the capitalist system propped up long enough for more meaningful measures to be implemented.

The shift in focus from cyclical to secular aspects of the macroeconomy does not require us to abandon our six-panel framework, but it does require a reconsideration of the relationships depicted in almost all the panels. Reform of the underlying economic institutions can affect the meaning and potential movements of the various curves and can even require a radical redefinition of key terms, such as full employment and involuntary unemployment, and the use of an almost universally neglected term introduced by Keynes, full investment. The failure on the part of both Keynes and his interpreters to distinguish clearly between the meanings of such terms in the context of stabilization policy and their meanings in the context of social reform has long been a source of confusion and misinterpretation and implicit grounds for a selective reading of the *General Theory*.

The fetish of liquidity and secular unemployment

Unlike the classical economists, Keynes saw no tendency in a market economy for the rate of interest to decline. Instead, he saw psychological forces leveraging the perversities inherent in the convention that we call the interest rate. People generally want more liquidity than can actually be made available to the economy as a whole. For Keynes, this "fetish of liquidity" is something different from the scramble for liquidity that is associated with a particular phase of the business cycle. The fetish is ongoing, ingrained. It can cause the rate of interest to be chronically too high. The striving for something that cannot be had (liquidity for the economy as a whole) can cut short the striving for something else that could have been had (higher levels of employment and output). Keynes (1936: 155), the critic of capitalism and the advocate of fundamental social reform, identified the "fetish of liquidity" as the most "anti-social maxim of orthodox finance."

According to Keynes (ibid.: 203–4), the rate of interest will rise if money demand is increasing faster than money supply. More significantly, the interest rate "may fluctuate for decades about a level which is chronically too high for full employment." The previous chapter was concerned with the fluctuations; the present chapter is concerned with the level about which those fluctuations occur. Figure 9.1 depicts an economy constrained by a strong preference for liquidity, i.e. for money. The assumed structural fixity is reflected in the unchanged ratio of labor income to total income in Panel 3. We should note that under reasonable assumptions about the elasticity of the demand for investment funds and the size of the existing capital stock, this assumption is simply at odds with fetish-related difference in other panels. Nonetheless, maintaining the assumption helps to highlight some fundamental differences between secular and cyclical aspects of the unemployment problem as seen by Keynes. Relaxing the assumption of structural fixity will then allow us to identify still more differences.

Saving preferences are the same in Figure 9.1 as in Figure 7.1, "Full employment by accident" and Figure 8.4, "Full employment by design." With second-order qualifications to be mentioned later, the consumption equation in Panel 4 and the corresponding saving equation are as applicable in our treatment of the economy's secular problems as they were in our treatment of its cyclical problems. A secular problem derives, according to Keynes, from the circumstance that savers may choose to keep much of

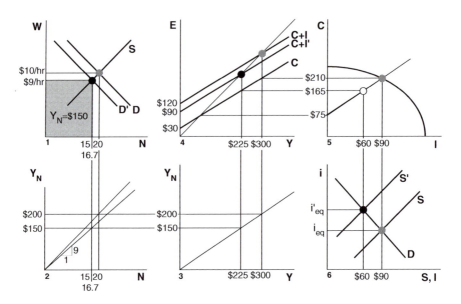

Figure 9.1 Fetish of liquidity (with assumed structural fixity).

their savings in the form of money. If a large part of savings is held liquid, the supply of loanable funds, S′ in Panel 6, lies dramatically to the left of where it would lie but for the fetish of liquidity.

Here, as elsewhere, liquidity preference makes itself felt only in the loanable-funds market and on the interest rate and not (directly) on consumption and investment. This treatment, which embodies what ultimately must be regarded as a fatal error in Keynes's thinking, stems from his two-step construction: first, income earners decide how much of their income to save; second, they decide how much of their saving to hold liquid. Having already been made, then, the decision about how much income to consume cannot be affected by the decision about how much saving to hoard. While this two-step construction may be largely unobjectionable – though wholly unnecessary – in the context of cyclical fluctuations, it is simply indefensible in the context of the economy's real or imagined secular problems. Surely, income earners who are faced repeatedly with saving and hoarding decisions will let one period's hoarding decision affect the next period's saving decision. Over a period of years or decades, which clearly is Keynes's focus here, these decisions about consuming, putting savings at interest, and hoarding would entail simultaneous adjustments at all margins.

To appreciate the nature of the secular problem perceived by Keynes, we continue at this point to ignore the direct interconnectedness between the demand for liquidity and the demands for consumption goods and investment goods. We ignore as well the implied downward pressures on the prices of both consumption goods and investment goods that would accompany a high demand for liquidity. And in recognition of the problem's secular nature, we discuss the interest rate, the wage rate, and the corresponding macroeconomic magnitudes in terms of the location of the various curves (relative to their location in Figure 7.1) rather than in terms of the curves actually shifting in one direction or another.

With a given demand for loanable funds, the fetish-constrained supply keeps the rate of interest high and keeps investment at a low level – $60 rather than $90, as shown in Panel 6 of Figure 9.1. The lower level of investment implies low levels of income ($225 rather than $300) and consumption ($165 rather than $210). Hence, the economy is located inside its PPF at the corresponding point on the demand constraint shown in Panel 5 – namely at C = $165; I = $60. This combination of consumption and investment squares with the simple income-expenditure relationship (Y = C + I' = $225) shown in Panel 4.

Finally, Panel 1 shows that the derived demand for labor lies to the left (D') of where it would lie (D) but for the fetish of liquidity. The very notion that the interest rate may be high for decades rules out the possibility of a non-market-clearing wage rate. In this context, the question is not whether the wage rate is sticky. The question is whether or not the wage rate can adjust over a period of decades to the conditions created by a chronically high rate of interest. Presumably, even for Keynes, it can. Otherwise, we would never be justified in taking as our initial conditions an economy in which there is market clearing for both loanable funds and labor, and hence in taking the wage rate – in the context of cyclical problems – to be the *right* wage rate. Borrowing the illustrative numbers from Figure 8.2, then, Panel 1 shows that the fetish-based deficiency of aggregate demand translates into a labor market that clears at a low wage rate ($9/hr) and a low level of employment (16.7).

At this point we can hardly fail to note the connection between Keynes's diagnosis of this chronic problem of capitalism and the trilogy of concerns advertized in the title of his book: *Employment* is low because *Interest* is kept high because *Money* is the object of a fetish.

Apart from the market for loanable funds, the implications of the fetish of liquidity, as depicted in Figure 9.1, are much the same as the implications of a collapse in investment demand under conditions of wage-rate flexibility, as depicted in Figure 8.2. The primary differences are the obvious ones in Panel 6: in Figure 8.2, the *demand* for loanable funds shifted leftward pulling the supply with it such that the rate of interest did not change; in Figure 9.1, the demand for loanable funds is not the issue; the *supply* of loanable funds lies dramatically to the left, constraining the interest rate to a high level.

Other similarities, differences, and points of comparison of Figures 9.1 and 8.2 are worth noting. First, the fact that Panels 1 through 5 of the two figures are identical reinforces the idea that Keynes believed the interest rate to be largely if not purely a monetary phenomenon. That is, his argument traces cause-and-effect from money to interest and then to the macroeconomic magnitudes. Until we take explicit account of the implications of the fetish of liquidity for the distribution of income, the differing interest rates imply no first-order differences in any of the other five panels. The mix of consumption and investment associated with full-employment equilibrium, for instance, is unaffected. We can conceptualize the monetary nature of the phenomenon of interest by taking the total quantity of money to be the same for the two figures. If people are not fetishistic in their attitudes toward money, they will be content to hold this total quantity even though the rate of interest (which can be earned on savings *not* held liquid) is relatively low. If, however, people are fetishistic in their attitudes toward money, they will be content with this quantity of money only if the rate of interest is relatively high.

Second, Keynes's focus on decades during which the interest rate is chronically too high makes it clear that he is not suggesting a fetish-induced cyclical downturn. Rather, the fetish establishes the generally high *level* around which fluctuations occur. Interpreters who take Keynes as pioneering a monetary disequilibrium theory of business cycles simply have him wrong. When he deals with cyclical unemployment, the high demand for money is a secondary phenomenon; the primary problem is a collapsed marginal efficiency of capital. When he deals with high money demand as a primary problem, he links it to secular and not cyclical unemployment.

Third, what counts as involuntary secular unemployment is certainly not unemployment in the sense of Marshallian partial equilibrium analysis. The labor market clears. The market-clearing combination of wages and employment (W = $9/hr; N = 16.7) associated with a fetish of liquidity is simply different from the combination (W = $10/hr; N = 20) associated with the absence of such a fetish. The difference between the two employment levels is more accurately described as a comparative-statics employment differential. But for the fetishistic attitude toward money, the equilibrium level of employment would be higher. The differential – Keynes's secular unemployment – is involuntary in that the market itself provides no effective mechanism through which individuals, acting separately or in concert, can eliminate the fetish or its consequences.

Finally, we must recognize that Keynes's conclusion that a high demand for money has a negative impact even in the long run on output and employment derives critically from his neglect of the effect of money demand on the prices of both consumer goods and investment goods, that is, from the absence in his theory of a real-cash-balance effect. Accordingly, the unemployment (of both labor and other resources) is more directly registered in Panel 5, which shows the economy's output level lying below the PPF, than in Panel 1, which shows a (Marshallian) equilibrium in the market for labor. Countering Keynes here does not require that we take overall price and wage adjustments to be instantaneous – or even to be fairly quick and smooth. We need only claim that over a period of years or decades, prices of both consumer goods and investment goods along with wages will accommodate themselves to the existing money supply and velocity of circulation. With a real-cash-balance effect in play, long-run levels of consumption and investment would be represented by a point on the economy's PPF.

Thus, even the most sluggish adjustments will allow for a full accommodation of a given monetary demand, fetishistic or otherwise. In the long run, a strong preference for liquidity, that is, a high demand for money, can be expected to have no first-order effects on the demand for output or, derivatively, for labor demand. Depicting the short-run and long-run effects of a change in liquidity preferences or a change in the money supply is best postponed to the following chapter, which deals with Monetarism in the contexts of our alternative (capital-based and labor-based) macroeconomic frameworks.

Keynes (1936: 231–4) offers reasons for us not to expect a decline in prices to accommodate the high demand for money and allow for full employment. But even then he argues as if the only possible effect of the price-level decline is on the supply of loanable funds and hence on the interest rate. It is as if higher real cash balances increase the demand for bonds and other earning assets but not the demand for consumer goods. Elsewhere he simply argues as if there is no downward pressure on prices to be discussed. The supposed absence or total irrelevance of this aspect of the market's pricing mechanism is implicit in his use of comparative-static statements of the problem of insufficient aggregate demand: a poor community may be better off than a rich one (ibid.: 31); Ancient Egypt is more fortunate than modern England (ibid.: 131, 220).

Even if it could be argued that prices do not readily fall, are not we entitled to wonder how they ever got so high? Did they get set several decades ago when the fetish was somehow in remission? Though no satisfying answers suggest themselves, the idea that the price level corresponds to fetish-free conditions while the supply of investment funds and hence the demand for labor are fetish-infected is built into Keynes's thinking. This feature of his vision coupled with his ruling out the possibility of equilibrating changes in the general level of prices is what allows us to omit the price level from the six-panel figures and remain true to Keynes's vision of the macroeconomy.

The unemployment caused by a high demand for money can be fixed only by a correspondingly high supply of money. This is the message in Chapter 17 of the *General Theory* on "The Essential Properties of Interest and Money." Here Keynes writes:

> Unemployment develops, that is to say, because people want the moon;
> – men cannot be employed when the object of their desire [is money].
> There is no remedy but to persuade the public that green cheese is

practically the same thing and to have a green cheese factory (i.e., a central bank) under public control.

(Keynes, 1936: 235)

When Keynes turns his attention from interest and money to prices and wages in his Chapter 19 on "Changes in Money-Wages," he does seem to acknowledge an alternative remedy.

> We can, . . . theoretically at least, produce precisely the same effects on the rate of interest by reducing wages [and prices], whilst leaving the quantity of money unchanged, that we can produce by increasing the quantity of money whilst leaving the level of wages [and prices] unchanged.
>
> (ibid.: 266)

That is, recognizing that the real money supply can be written as M/P, we see that it can be increased either by increasing M or decreasing P [and W]. Here again, as in his Chapter 17, downward price and wage adjustments have their effect only through the rate of interest. There still is no direct effect in markets for consumer and investment goods. Either remedy entails the accommodating of the fetishistic demand for money (through increased M or decreased W and P) so that the supply of loanable funds is once again S and not S'.

Distribution of income and secular unemployment

The two outstanding faults of capitalism (unemployment and the distribution of income) are actually intertwined in Keynes's vision of the macroeconomy. The distribution of income (between labor and other factors of production) has direct implications for the demand for labor. The demand for output and hence for labor is further affected by the difference in spending propensities of workers and capitalists.

In order to exploit the similarities between Figures 9.1 and 8.2, we have maintained the assumption of structural fixity and hence an unchanged distribution of income, as shown in Panel 3. However, if we are dealing with an interest rate that is chronically and dramatically high relative to the rate on which we based our initial construction of the six-panel figures, then the structural characteristics of the economy as reflected by Y_N/Y in Panel 3 must be adjusted accordingly. We cannot dismiss the needed structural adjustment as a second-order consideration. Nor can we finesse the issue on the basis of elasticities. Labor income is lower in comparison to pre-fetish conditions in terms of both the wage rate and the level of employment. Interest income on current investment is higher if the demand for investment funds is interest inelastic, as Keynes believed it to be, and, in any case, interest income on the whole of the capital stock is higher than

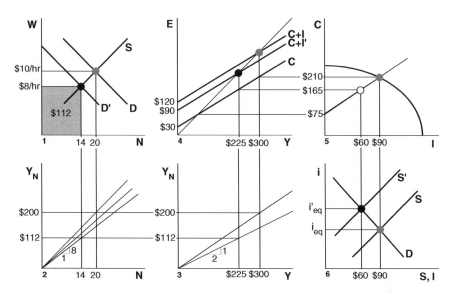

Figure 9.2 Fetish of liquidity (with the implied structural adjustments).

in pre-fetish conditions (though the present value of the stock itself is lower).

With the fetish of liquidity in play, the ratio of Y_N/Y may be, say, one-half instead of two-thirds. With capital and other non-labor resources claiming so large a share, the demand for labor is impacted negatively. As shown in Panel 3 of Figure 9.2, labor receives only half, or $112, of the economy's total income of $225. As shown in Panel 1, in which D' now represents the structurally adjusted demand for labor, the reduced income derives partly from a lower wage and partly from a lower level of employment. Incorporating these direct structural adjustments, we show a macroeconomic equilibrium with a wage rate of $8 and an employment level of 14. The precise solution, which would have to account for interest income on the entire capital stock and would depend upon the precise supply and demand elasticities (of labor and loanable funds, respectively), is not fully determinate on the basis of our illustrative data.

Due to the fetish, the interest rate is too high; the wage rate is too low. However, neither the market for loanable funds nor the market for labor fails to clear. Keynes, though, would identify the difference between the no-fetish employment level of 20 and the fetish-diminished level of employment of 14 as involuntary unemployment. With structural adjustments taken into account, this secular component of involuntary unemployment, better described as a comparative-statics employment differential, stands at 6.

Even the dismal picture of unemployment equilibrium shown in Figure 9.2 does not fully reflect the anti-social nature of the fetish of liquidity as perceived by Keynes. In both Figures 9.1 and 9.2, we show consumption spending in Panel 4 to depend strictly on the total income earned and not at all on the distribution of that income between labor and other factors of production. However, to the extent that workers are spenders while capitalists and resource owners are savers, the full effect of the fetish must incorporate the differential behavior among these income groups. With relatively more income accruing to capitalists and relatively less to workers, the consumption equation would lie below the one shown in Panel 4 and most likely would be less steeply sloped. This adjustment, of course, would require corresponding adjustments in all the other panels. No separate figure to incorporate these considerations of income distribution is provided here. However, such a figure could be straightforwardly produced by starting with Figure 9.2 and adding the shifts shown in Figure 8.6, which in that figure illustrate the paradox of thrift.

A working out of all the implications of the distribution of income has been adopted as the major research agenda by modern-day post-Keynesians. This aspect of Keynes's vision, which gets repeated mention in various contexts in the *General Theory*, is downplayed in our six-panel rendition for several reasons. First, considerations of income distribution do not change qualitatively the implications of the fetish of liquidity. They only make the anti-social behavior of hoarding money even more anti-social. Second, in the decades since Keynes wrote, the identification of types of income with classes of people has lost much of its justification. Although the notion that workers-as-a-class spend and capitalists-as-a-class save permeated the writings of both Ricardo and Keynes, it does not carry over well into a macroeconomic setting in which many income earners derive their incomes partly in the form of wages and partly in the form of interest. That is, functional distribution and personal distribution are only loosely related. And third, since neither capital-based macroeconomics nor non-Keynesian renditions of labor-based macroeconomics emphasize these particular distribution effects, our noting but not emphasizing these effects seems appropriate in a study aimed at sharpening the comparison between capital-based and labor-based macroeconomics.

At this point we are still not yet in a position to offer a comprehensive account of the involuntary unemployment associated with the capitalist system. But we can combine our understanding of cyclical unemployment, which was our primary focus in Chapter 8, and (an important part of) the secular unemployment, which is our present focus. We can simply take the unemployment equilibrium of Figure 9.2 (with further adjustments for income distribution) as our starting point for the analysis of cyclical variation of output and employment. The story that was initially told with the aid of Figure 7.1 "Full employment by accident" through Figure 8.4 "Full employment by design" is simply retold against a background of ongoing secular unemployment associated with the fetish of liquidity. This nesting of cyclical relationships within secular relationships captures an important feature of the structure of Keynes's *General Theory*, one described by Victoria Chick (in Snowden *et al.*, 1994: 399) as a "wheels-within-wheels arrangement with several different time horizons."

With the fetish in play, what counts as full employment is not the level of employment associated with market clearing in the labor market, but some level much higher – the level of employment marked by the intersection of the demand constraint with the PPF. The "initial" wage rate would be the "right" wage only in the sense of being consistent with the excessively high rate of interest. And "accidental full employment" would be accidental indeed. It would result from the coincidence of a cyclical upswing just strong enough to offset, if only fleetingly, the comparative-statics differential attributable to the fetish of liquidity. The demand for investment funds, aka the MEC, would have to be bolstered by undue optimism rather than constrained by undue pessimism. More generally, the oscillations of the economy play themselves out inside the PPF. The potential movements of equilibria depicted in Panels 1, 4, 5, and 6 of Figure 7.2 are largely if not wholly confined to less-than-full-employment equilibria.

Lenders' risk and decentralized decision-making

To focus our attention on another fundamental aspect of the faults of capitalism, let us return to Figure 7.1, where the fetish of liquidity is not in play. Alternatively, we could modify Figure 9.1 by allowing the central bank to create enough liquidity to satisfy those whose demands for it are fetishistic. If psychological considerations make people want to hold money, then let them hold money created for that very purpose, and let the rest of the economy function as if those demands did not exist. With full accommodation of the fetish, the supply of loanable funds is once again S and not S'; the economy is able to stay on its PPF; the demand for labor (D rather than D') is consistent with full employment as defined by the PPF; and the going-cum-market-clearing wage rate is $10/hr.

Still – if Keynes's final chapter and related material in earlier chapters are to be taken seriously – the economy is not realizing its fullest potential. What passes as full employment in the context of a cyclical variation or even in the context of the secular problems rooted in the fetish of liquidity is not as full as it could be. More deeply rooted shortfalls from potential derive from the general nature of interest, from the fragmentation of the saving-investment decision, and from the decentralization of the investment sector.

All fetishes aside, the interest rate is still ultimately attributable to considerations of psychology (1936: 202) and/or convention (ibid.: 203). Accordingly, the demand for liquidity – and hence the interest rate that is determined by supply and demand – is not grounded in any fundamental fact of scarcity. This notion is reaffirmed in Keynes's final chapter: "Interest

Today Rewards no Genuine Sacrifice" (ibid.: 376). His summary judgment is consistent with his earlier claim that *"Any* rate of interest which is accepted as *likely* to be durable *will* be durable" (ibid.: 203, emphasis original). While the rate of interest in Figure 7.1 is less objectionable than the rate of interest in Figure 9.1, it is nonetheless still objectionable. The distribution of income in a capitalist economy is determined by a fundamentally baseless convention that we call the interest rate.

Taking the rate of interest to be a convention rather than an economic necessity, Keynes sees it as being unnecessarily high largely because of an institutional consideration unique to the capitalist system. More specifically, savers and investors in a decentralized system are two different groups of people, a fact that gets reported repeatedly in the *General Theory*. This fragmentation of the economy's saving-investment decisions gives rise to a lender's risk that could be avoided by the appropriate institutional reform.

The focus here is on the riskiness of lending over and above the riskiness of the projects undertaken by the borrowers. In a market economy, saving must wend its way to investment through financial markets. And while the saver-lender and borrower-investor must share in the project's yield, they must cope with a compounding of risk. That is, the so-called lender's risk rides piggyback on the project risk borne by the borrower. The borrower forms a risky expectation about the net yield of the investment project; the lender forms a risky expectation about the borrower's ability to form reasonable expectations. Keynes identifies lender's risk in connection with his discussion of the marginal efficiency of capital (1936: 144) and later includes the difficulties associated with this category of risks in his list of reasons that the monetary authority may face limits on how low the interest rate can be driven in a market economy (ibid.: 208). Alan Meltzer (1988) features lender's risk in his "different interpretation" of Keynes.

According to Keynes (1936: 219), the "costs of bringing borrowers and lenders together and uncertainty as to the future of the rate of interest" may set a lower limit on the long-term rate of 2 or 2½ per cent. In his view, the costs associated with lender's risk are not "real" costs in any fundamental sense. They derive from the fact that we have saddled ourselves with the institutions of capitalism. Although Keynes hints in several passages at the general drift of his argument, he saves his ultimate pronouncement for his final chapter. While voluntary saving under *laissez-faire* may be held in check by the necessity of paying interest, it is "possible for communal saving through the agency of the State to be maintained at a level which will allow the growth of capital up to the point where it ceases to be scarce" (ibid.: 376). In other words, if the decision to save can be centralized, the (implicit) interest rate can be pushed below the floor created in large part by the piggybacking aspect of the saving-investment decisions.

Illustrating the consequences of centralization with the aid of our six-panel framework strains the very meaning of most to the individual panels. What is the meaning, for instance, of the supply and demand for loanable funds if one side or the other – or both sides – of this market is replaced by decisions of a central authority? But using this framework to understand how Keynes could advocate such reforms allows us to remain true to Keynes because he seemed to argue as if socialism is simply capitalism minus capitalism's most objectionable features. In the Keynesian vision, communal saving-cum-investment could be undertaken with the objective of exploiting all investment opportunities whose yield is above zero. It is as if reform that removes the saving-investment decision from the environment of *laissez-faire* simply shifts the supply of loanable funds rightward so as to intersect the demand at a zero or near-zero rate of interest.

Centralizing the economy's saving decisions and increasing the supply of loanable funds has the effect of moving the economy down a given demand for loanable funds. The full consequences of this reform are leveraged by a related reform that has a direct effect on the economy's production possibilities and hence on the demand for loanable funds. The centralization of investment decisions requires a redrawing of the frontier itself. Any point on the pre-reform PPF that involves a positive level of investment also involves uncertainty about the viability and profitability of the individual investment projects. What attitude toward – and response to – this uncertainty is required for the various points on the frontier actually to represent production possibilities? In Chapter 7 (p. 139), we suggested that the relevant PPF might be the one for which perceived uncertainties are consistent with the underlying economic realities. In other words, perceptions – and economic decisions based on those perceptions – are fully warranted by realities – where "realities" are understood to include the institutional arrangements (i.e. capitalism) in which decisions are made.

But in his Chapter 12, "The State of Long-Run Expectations," Keynes makes clear that simply avoiding a misperception of the realities is not good enough. Beyond the routine hedging against risks about which reasonable calculations can be made, the market economy can fully realize its potential only if the business community behaves as if the remaining uncertainties are worthy of little or no attention either collectively or individually. This view is most clear in Keynes's page-and-a-half section (1936: 161–3) in which the term "animal spirits" appears three times. According to Keynes, "individual initiative will only be adequate when reasonable calculation is supplemented and supported by animal spirits, so that the thought of ultimate loss which often overtakes pioneers, as experience tells us and them, is put aside as a healthy man puts aside the expectation of death" (ibid.: 162). Just as living individuals must keep on living, businesspeople must keep on doing business – uncertainties notwithstanding – if the economy is to achieve its potential and stay on its (true, institutions-independent) PPF. G. L. S. Shackle (1967: 6) offers a similar view: "Keynes himself declared in the *QJE* that the *General Theory* was concerned with our mode of coping with, or of *concealing from our conscious selves*, our ignorance of the future" (emphasis mine).

While Keynes sees changes in perceived uncertainty in the business community as being relevant to our understanding of cyclical unemployment, he sees the very existence of market-related uncertainties as critical to the issue of secular unemployment. Writing about speculation in the face of market uncertainties, Keynes claims that "There is no clear evidence from experience that the investment policy which is socially advantageous coincides with that which is most profitable" (1936: 157). In a market economy, "prosperity is excessively dependent on a political and social atmosphere which is congenial to the average business man" (ibid.: 162). It is "excessively dependent" because decision making is decentralized. That is, in addition to the irreducible uncertainty about the future "state of nature," each businessperson has to cope with the uncertainty about what other businesspeople will do. And in a capitalist setting each businessperson is driven by consideration of private costs and benefits rather than social costs and benefits. By itself, this added layer of uncertainty restricts the economy to a level of performance that Keynes finds wanting. Making matters worse, the attitudes of individual businesspeople, not being well anchored in the underlying economic realities in any case, are highly contagious. The dynamics of "mass psychology" give play to "waves of optimistic and pessimistic sentiment" (ibid.: 154).

These are the considerations that led Keynes to doubt, at the end of his chapter on long-term expectations, that counter-cyclical policies narrowly conceived can save the market economy. Its flaws are too deeply rooted for that. The decentralized decision making, which is heart and soul of the market economy, must be eliminated or at least severely restricted. "I expect to see the State, which is in a position to calculate the marginal efficiency of capital-goods on long views and on the basis of the general social advantage, taking an ever greater responsibility for directly organizing investment" (ibid.: 164). Keynes reiterates this judgment in his final chapter: "I conceive, therefore, that a somewhat comprehensive socialization of investment will prove the only means of securing an approximation to full employment" (ibid.: 378).

As with almost every other aspect of Keynes's writing, the phrase "socialization of investment" has been subject to much interpretation. What did Keynes have in mind? While few believe that he was thinking about the outright state ownership of the means of production, other plausible interpretations give rise to further questions that neither Keynes nor modern Keynesians have adequately addressed. It is clear in his discussion following the call for socialized investment that Keynes is concerned with the "volume" and not the "direction" of employment.

> To put the point concretely, I see no reason to suppose that the existing system seriously misdeploys the factors of production which are in use. . . . It is in determining the volume, not the direction, of actual employment that the existing system has broken down.
>
> (ibid.: 379)

Keynes argues as if the government – or cryptically, "forces outside the classical scheme of thought" (ibid.: 378) – could control the volume without affecting any other aspect of the market economy. There is room for belief that his "forces outside the classical scheme" are not to be exerted by the state *per se* but rather by semi-public bodies. Keynes seems to have envisioned large, privately owned firms with public-spirited managers. What sort of powers would government or large public-spirited firms have to wield to be able to exert such forces? And how would the quality of entrepreneurial decisions be affected if entrepreneurs had to anticipate the use – and possible misuse – of such powers? There are no answers to these questions that put socialization in a favorable light. The simple fact is that the conceptually distinct aspects of "volume" and "direction" as applied to employment or output are governed by a single set of market forces. Joan Robinson (1975), who recognized the actual unity of these market forces but favored a more wholesale form of socialization, chided Keynes for even wanting to control volume without controlling direction. Direction, in her view, needed some controlling, too.

Full employment through centralization

Literally to socialize the economy's investment sector would render irrelevant the market relationships that appear in our six-panel framework. But again, we remain true to Keynes if we take the post-reform production possibilities to be the pre-reform production possibilities adjusted for the elimination of the uncertainties associated with decentralized decision making. We can also better capture Keynes's vision by making the demand for loanable funds sharply inelastic. As depicted in Panels 5 and 6 of Figure 9.3, the post-reform PPF lies beyond the pre-reform PPF; and, correspondingly, the post-reform demand for loanable funds (D°) lies to the right of the pre-reform demand (D). The one point the two frontiers have in common is their vertical intercepts: with no investment, the uncertainties at issue here are simply absent. Actual uncertainties and hence the gains from centralization increase with increasing investment. The divergence between the pre-reform PPF and the post-reform PPF, then, is greater the greater the level of investment.

Although Keynes writes repeatedly about driving the marginal efficiency to zero, he does allow a small rate of return to compensate for the residual risks. Reform in the direction of centralization eliminates only those risks associated with decentralized decision making. Keynes explicitly allows for some risks to survive reform by distinguishing between the pure rate of interest and the compensation for residual risks: "There would still be room . . . for enterprise and skill in the estimation of prospective yields about which opinions could differ" (1936: 221). This yield , which is not shared with the (centralized) lender, is reflected by a post-reform PPF that slopes gently downward (and a post-reform demand for loanable funds that, though inelastic, is less inelastic than the pre-reform demand).

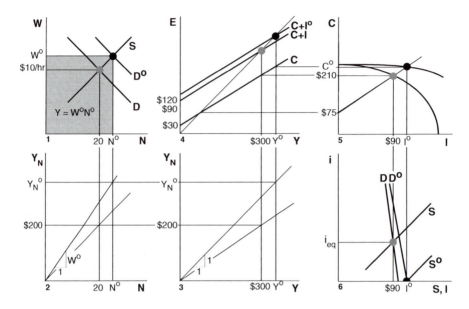

Figure 9.3 Full investment (with zero interest and no scarcity value of capital).

To take the yield literally to be zero would require the frontier to be horizontal and the demand for loanable funds to be perfectly elastic. Capital would be non-scarce, yet the price of capital goods would reflect the undiscounted value of their contribution to the production of (future) consumption goods. By allowing for a small yield, conundrums and contradictions of this sort were avoided by Keynes and will similarly be avoided in our six-panel rendition of his ideas. Both our analytics and the vision that inspired them have a strong grounding in the *General Theory*. In the concluding section of his chapter on the nature of capital, Keynes offers a prognosis:

> I should guess that a properly run community . . . ought to be able to bring down the marginal efficiency of capital in equilibrium approximately to zero within a single generation; so that we should attain the conditions of a quasi-stationary community where change and progress would result only from changes in technique, tastes, population, and institutions, with the products of capital selling at a price proportioned to the labor, etc., embodied in them on just the same principles as govern the prices of consumption-goods into which capital-charges enter in an insignificant degree.
>
> If I am right in supposing it to be comparatively easy to make capital-goods so abundant that the marginal efficiency of capital is zero, this may be the most sensible way of gradually getting rid of many of the objectionable features of capitalism.
>
> (Keynes, 1936: 220–1)

In his final chapter, where "zero" becomes "a very low figure," Keynes reveals his link to Marx in both positive and normative terms:

> I feel sure that . . . it would not be difficult to increase the stock of capital up to a point where its marginal efficiency had fallen to a very low figure. This would not mean that the use of capital instruments would cost almost nothing, but only that the return from them would have to cover little more than their exhaustion by wastage and obsolescence together with some margin to cover risk and the exercise of skill and judgment. In short, the aggregate return from durable goods in the course of their life would, as in the case of short-lived goods, just cover their labor-costs of production plus an allowance for risk and the costs of skill and supervision.
>
> Now, though this state of affairs would be quite compatible with some measure of individualism, yet it would mean the euthanasia of the rentier, and, consequently, the euthanasia of the cumulative oppressive power of the capitalists to exploit the scarcity-value of capital.
>
> (ibid.: 375–6)

In Figure 9.3, the pre-reform supply of loanable funds is represented by S; the post-reform supply, which provides enough additional saving to move the economy all the way down the shifted demand (D°), is represented by S°. In Keynes's final chapter, the post-reform level of investment is referred to as "full investment" (ibid.: 377). In an earlier chapter, Keynes identifies full investment as the result of a number of years (twenty-five years or less) of full employment. Consistent with the notions of a zero rate of interest and non-scarce capital, a properly managed economy may achieve "full investment in the sense that an aggregate gross yield in excess of replacement cost could no longer be expected on a reasonable calculation from a further increment of durable goods of any type whatever" (ibid.: 324).

In addition to increasing investment and hence output and income, reform of this sort has a dramatic and, in Keynes's view, very desirable effect on the distribution of income. Workers no longer get only one half of the economy's total income, as they might have gotten if the investment sector was decentralized and the demand for money was fetishistic, or only two-thirds, as they might have gotten in the absence of the fetish. In the post-reform era, workers get it all. Panel 3 of Figure 9.3 depicts the structure of the economy as a 45° line; the ratio of labor income to total income (Y_N/Y) is equal to unity. With the rate of interest nil, savers-cum-lenders have little or no claim on the economy's output. The small claim on the economy's output made by the borrowers-cum-investors can be squared in several ways with labor's claim of 100 percent. First, as Keynes makes clear, the remaining yield implicit in the post-reform PPF is a very small yield, possibly a negligible one in the context of the distribution of income. Second, that yield is conceived as payment for "skill in the estimation of prospective yields" (ibid.: 221), which could reasonably be classified as wages to a specialized kind of labor. And, third, Keynes (ibid.: 221) suggests that despite a general risk aversion and hence the necessity to compensate for risk-taking, the eagerness on the part of individual investors to capture the small yields may well result, in the aggregate, in a zero – or even nega- tive – net yield. If so, workers would get all the current income – and possibly a little more!

Although the one-to-one ratio in Panel 3 may seem fanciful, it accords fully with Keynes's observations on the nature of capital. Once again, the similarity of Keynes's vision and Marx's vision is very apparent:

> I sympathize . . . with the pre-classical doctrine that everything is produced by labor, aided by what used to be called art and is now called technique, by natural resources which are free and cost a rent according to their scarcity or abundance, and by the results of past labor, embodied in assets, which also command a price according to their scarcity or abundance. It is preferable to regard labor, including, or course, the personal services of the entrepreneur and his assistants, as the sole factor of production, operating in a given environment of technique, natural resources, capital equipment and effective demand.
>
> (Keynes, 1936: 213–14)

The higher labor income made possible by the socialization of investment is due in part to a higher level of employment ($N°$) and in part to a higher wage rate ($W°$). In effect, by making the use of labor and other factors of production relatively risk-free, the reform measures have increased the demand for labor, allowing workers to move up their supply curves. And as in our depiction of the labor market in the context of the fetish of liquidity, there is no doubt here about the labor market finding its equilib- rium.

We have now identified adjustments in all six panels to incorporate the salutary effects of the centralization of the economy's saving-investment decisions. Still, more adjusting would be required to fully capture Keynes's vision. As in our treatment of the fetish of liquidity, the change in income distribution would have a pronounced effect on consumption and saving propensities. With little or no income going to capitalists and virtually all income going to labor, the post-reform consumption equation would reflect higher consumption propensities. Both the intercept and slope would be greater than in the pre-reform era. This adjustment would entail a still higher level of income and correspondingly higher wage rate and level of employment. Here, as in our treatment of the fetish of liquidity, we gloss over this post-Keynesian flourish. The more salient and fundamental effects of the socialization of investment are shown in Panels 3 and 6: all income goes to labor; the rate of interest is zero.

What counts as "full employment" in Figure 9.3 is $N°$, a level of employ- ment that corresponds to an economy that has achieved "full investment"

I°, which is only possible if the rate of interest is zero. Accordingly, capitalism, whose institutions give rise to an interest rate that is positive and sometimes excessively so, is characterized by a less-that-full-employment level of income. In discussing the secular unemployment associated with the fetish of liquidity (Figure 9.2), we argued that what Keynes called unemployment is more accurately described as a comparative-static employment differential. Now we see that the secular unemployment associated with decentralized decision making (Figure 9.3) is more accurately described as a comparative-institutions employment differential. However, the comparative-institutions analysis of the *General Theory* is woefully lopsided. Keynes continually compares capitalism-as-it-actually-is against the standard of socialism-as-it-has-never-been.

Judging the current system to be both unstable and unjust, Keynes holds out hopes – and is even optimistic about the prospects – for making the transition to something better. He argues from this belief that in a society with ideal economic institutions the rate of interest would be zero to the conclusion that in our society, with its less than ideal economic institutions, the rate of employment is too low. A chain of arguments involving risk, interest investment, capital, output, and labor is tailored to fit each of the two sets of economic institutions and to demonstrate the superiority of the imagined society over the actual one.

In the imagined system of socialism-as-it-has-never-been, risks would be minimized, the rate of interest would be nil, and all investment opportunities would be fully exploited. Capital (whose rental price in equilibrium is the rate of interest) would cease to be scarce, output would be at its maximum, and the labor force would be fully employed. In our current system of capitalism-as-it-actually-is, risks are unnecessarily high, the rate of interest is correspondingly high (read: not zero) and investment is limited to those undertakings whose expected yield exceeds the interest rate. Capital, then, is kept artificially scarce, output is less than its maximum, and the level of employment is below its potential.

To the extent that the central message of the *General Theory* derives from comparative institutions analysis and not from the analysis of cyclical fluctuations, then the decades of difficulties in identifying that message become understandable. Exercises in comparative institutions can have relevance only in the systems being compared are in fact comparable. Actual or possible systems can be compared with one another; ideal or imagined systems can be compared with one another. But a hybrid comparison – between an actual system and an ideal or imagined one – is so biased from the outset in favor of the ideal as to be hardly recognizable as an exercise in comparative institutions analysis.

Further, Keynes provides little or nothing in the way of discussion of the transition from capitalism to socialism. His views are similar to those of Marx (and other socialists) in that both adopt a stages-of-history perspective on capitalism. His outlook is different from that of Marx in that Keynes envisioned the transition to be gradual while Marx called for a revolution. These points of comparison are made clear in a single paragraph in Keynes's final chapter:

> I see . . . the rentier aspect of capitalism as a transitional phase which will disappear when it has done its work. And with the disappearance of its rentier aspect much else in it besides will suffer a sea-change. It will be, moreover, a great advantage of the order of events which I am advocating, that the euthanasia of the rentier, of the functionless investor, will be nothing sudden, merely a gradual but prolonged continuance of what we have seen recently in Great Britain, and will need no revolution.
>
> (Keynes, 1936: 376)

Also, Keynes, like Marx, acknowledged that achieving this state of nonscarce capital would require some sacrifices on the part of the living generation for the benefit of future generations. But Keynes was not quite so sanguine about getting on with the sacrifice. "State action [should] provide that the growth of capital equipment shall be such as to approach saturation-point at a rate which does not put a disproportionate burden on the standard of life of the present generation" (ibid.: 220). Keynes acknowledges in his final chapter that individuals would not voluntarily make these sacrifices under a system of *laissez-faire*, and he leaves the broader questions of political economy unanswered:

> it would remain for separate decision on what scale and by what means it is right and reasonable to call on the living generation to restrict their consumption, so as to establish, in course of time, a state of full investment for their successors.
>
> (ibid.: 377)

At last, we are in a position to offer a comprehensive account of the involuntary unemployment associated with the capitalist system. (1) Capitalism has a lower level of employment that does socialism – the latter term meaning simply capitalism minus its faults. This comparative institutions employment differential is the most fundamental component of Keynes's involuntary unemployment. (2) Capitalism, when plagued with the fetish of liquidity, has a lower level of employment than capitalism-at-its-best. This comparative-static employment differential, whose persistence depends critically on the absence of a real-cash-balance effect, is the second most fundamental component of Keynes's involuntary unemployment. (3) Whether plagued by the fetish or not, capitalism experiences an occasional collapse in investment demand and hence a reduction in the demand for labor. The lower level of employment associated with the lower labor demand – whether or not the fall in the employment level is partially mitigated by a bidding down of the wage rate – counts as the third and least fundamental component of involuntary unemployment. Figures 8.1 through 8.4 are transplanted into Figure 9.2, which is then transplanted into Figure 9.3.

Consideration of comparative institutions, comparative statics, and sluggish market processes are nested into a wheels-within-wheels-within-wheels framework that we call the Keynesian vision.

Part IV

Money and prices

10 Boom and bust in the Monetarist vision

Our treatment of Austrian and Keynesian ideas has been guided by alternative macroeconomic frameworks. The labor-based framework of Chapters 7 through 9 has been contrasted with the capital-based framework of Chapters 3 through 6. In modern pedagogy the more conventional contrast is that between Keynesian ideas and Monetarist ideas. For completeness, we might want to put Monetarism on equal terms by according it its own special framework. If Keynesianism is labor-based, and Austrianism is capital-based, then Monetarism is money-based.

In contemplating a distinct money-based framework, however, nothing quite comparable to the frameworks set out in Chapter 3 and Chapter 7 comes to mind. Dating from the mid-1950s, money-based macroeconomics has blurred the distinction between macroeconomics in general and the more circumscribed monetary theory. Given the general direction of macroeconomic pedagogy over that period (ISLM and Aggregate-Supply/Aggregate-Demand), there is much justification in the claim that the distinction was in need of blurring. But Monetarists have made their case for the significance of money in macroeconomic theorizing without dealing with the capital-based framework of the Austrians and without challenging the labor-based framework of the Keynesians.

The analytical propositions of Monetarism can be set out in terms of the simple and early version of equation of exchange, which expresses a relationship between the volume of transactions T and the quantity of money M available to facilitate those transactions. $MV_T = P_T T$. Buying with money equals money's worth bought. Abstracting from secular growth and hence a secular rise in T and taking the transactions velocity of money V_T to be constant or nearly so, we see a strong positive relationship between the quantity of money M and the mean price P_T at which transactions are made. While conceptually simple and theoretically satisfying (it stresses money as a facilitator of transactions), this version of the equation of exchange features an unconventional reckoning of P. This P includes the prices of financial assets and intermediate goods as well as the prices of final output. Friedman and Schwartz (1982: 20) take note of this "rather special kind of price index" before moving on to what has become the more conventional version.

A broad assumption of near fixity over the relevant time horizon of the structure of the economy and of institutional arrangements allows the equation of exchange to be expressed in terms of final output Q (of both consumption goods and capital goods) rather than in terms of transactions. And owing to the very fact of the economy's circular flow, we can measure real output by the real income Y received by the factors of production. These considerations convert $MV_T = P_T T$ into $MV_Y = P_Y Y$. Monetarists are not bothered, as the Austrians would be, that the conversion eclipses all changes in the intertemporal capital structure, including those that entail a change in the shape of the Hayekian triangle. Downplaying considerations of capital (beyond the basic stock-flow distinction) is very much in the spirit of Monetarism. More importantly, this is the version of the equation of exchange most suitable for empirical research. Its near exclusive use has led to the dropping of the subscripts on V and P. $MV = Py$ has become conventional, the lowercase "y" indicating that income is reckoned in real terms.

"The quantity theory of money," according to Milton Friedman ([1956] 1969a: 52), "is in the first instance a theory of the *demand* for money." Money-based macroeconomics can be set out most straightforwardly as a *pro forma* money-demand equation which includes among its arguments total income, wealth, the yields on bonds and real assets, and expectations about inflation. Money's value, or purchasing power 1/P, then, is determined by the interplay of this money demand and a given – i.e. central-bank governed – money supply. The bulk of the empirical research done under the Monetarist label focuses on the supply and demand for money in many different time periods and in many different countries and demonstrates that, except in special cases (entailing, e.g. hyperinflation or institutional upheaval), money demand exhibits a remarkable degree of stability. This important finding implies that variations in money's purchasing power 1/P and hence in the price level P are attributable largely if not wholly to variations in the money supply. This most fundamental conclusion of Monetarism is captured by Milton Friedman's (1968: 18) memorable refrain, "Inflation is always and everywhere a monetary phenomenon."

The long-run relationship between the quantity of money and the level prices is not in question here. Both theory and evidence are on the side of the Monetarists. However, the short-to-intermediate-run movements of P and Q that are triggered by an increase in M (or in V) are a different matter. The economics underlying the so-called P-Q split has long constituted the soft underbelly of Monetarism. These issues provide the basis for alternative renditions of money-based macroeconomics, each of which can be expressed with the aid of either our labor-based framework or our capital-based framework.

Monetarist frameworks

Rather than create our own money-based macroeconomic framework, we can simply recognize two existing frameworks that feature complementary aspects of the Monetarist vision. One is the four-sector model inspired by Knut Wicksell and developed by Don Patinkin; the other is the short-run/long-run Phillips curve analysis introduced by Milton Friedman and Edmund Phelps. Ultimately, the combining of key features of these two frameworks will allow for a straightforward comparison with corresponding features of our capital-based macroeconomics. Still a third framework, the conventional Aggregate-Supply/Aggregate-Demand analysis that dominated textbooks for years, could be brought into play here. However, tracing out the demand-driven interplay between an upward-sloping short-run aggregate-supply curve and a vertical long-run aggregate-supply curve would serve only to duplicate points made with the aid of Patinkin's model and the expectations-augmented Phillips curve. The two frameworks actually considered identify separately the interest-rate effects and the employment effects of an increase in the money supply.

Patinkin's model

The comparative-statics aspects of the Monetarist vision as well as one aspect of the adjustment process are depicted in Patinkin's four-sector model, which underlies much of the theorizing in his *Money, Interest and Prices* (1965). The four sectors that make up the macroeconomy in his construction are commodities (both consumer goods and investment goods), bonds, money and labor. With the labor market assumed always to be in full-employment equilibrium, the focus of analysis is on the mutual interactions among the remaining three sectors. Macroeconomic equilibrium is defined in terms of the price of bonds and the price of commodities, or, equivalently, the interest rate and the price level. Figure 10.1 shows one such equilibrium as a solid point marking the equilibrium interest rate and the equilibrium price level. The two market-equilibrium curves (CC and BB) that intersect at this solid point identify separately the locus of points that are consistent with an equilibrium interest rate (BB) and the locus of points that are consistent with an equilibrium price level (CC). Drawing from Wicksell, Patinkin identifies the equilibrium interest rate as the natural rate of interest. The corresponding equilibrium price level is in full accordance with the quantity theory of money: P is directly proportional to M.

The CC curve slopes downward and represents combinations of P and i for which there is no excess supply or excess demand for commodities; the BB curve slopes upward and represents combinations of P and i for which there is no excess supply or excess demand for bonds. Points off these curves are characterized by either an excess supply or an excess demand for commodities and/or bonds. In Figure 10.1, the general area characterized

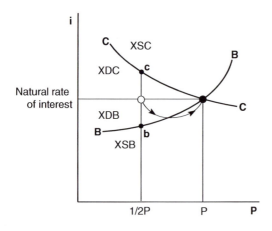

Wicksellian equilibration
in Patinkin's four-sector model
with income fixed at full-employment

Figure 10.1 Monetarist framework (Wicksell–Patinkin).

by an excess demand for commodities is marked XDC; other areas are similarly marked. An LL curve, not shown in Figure 10.1, passes through the
point of macroeconomic equilibrium and represents combinations of P and
i that correspond to the absence of an excess demand or excess supply of
money. This LL curve, which is positively sloped and cuts the BB curve
from below, is redundant in most applications of the Patinkin model.

An appreciation for the respective slopes of CC and BB can be gained
by considering a departure from the combination of P and i that is consistent with equilibrium in both markets. For instance, consider a point lying
directly to the left of the intersection of the market equilibrium curves. At
this point of disequilibrium, the interest rate is still equal to the natural
rate, but the price level is lower, say, by half. The halved price level implies
an excess supply of money (i.e. of real cash balances) and an excess demand
for both commodities and bonds. The slopes of the separate equilibrium
curves are established by the answers to two questions about hypothetical
compensating changes in the rate of interest. (1) How would the interest
rate have to change to eliminate the excess demand for commodities – and
put the economy back on its CC curve? Bond prices would have to fall
enough (the interest rate would have to rise enough) to entice people to
spend their excess money balances exclusively on bonds, increasing the excess
demand for bonds but fully relieving the excess demand for commodities.
Thus, starting from the intersection of the CC and BB curves, a second
point on the CC curve (point c) can be found at a lower price level and a
higher interest rate. The CC curve has a negative slope. (2) How would

the interest rate have to change to eliminate the excess demand for bonds – and put the economy back on its BB curve? Bond prices would have to rise enough (the interest rate would have to fall enough) to entice people to spend their excess money balances exclusively on commodities, increasing the excess demand for commodities but fully relieving the excess demand for bonds. Thus, starting from the intersection of the CC and BB curves, a second point on the BB curve (point b) can be found at a lower price level and a lower interest rate. The BB curve has a positive slope.

To gain an appreciation for the equilibrating process in Patinkin's model, we need only imagine that our point of disequilibrium (at i and ½P) was the previous equilibrium point. Maintaining consistency with the comparative-statics aspects of the quantity theory of money, we can imagine that the money supply was previously just one half of its current magnitude. The central proposition of monetarism is thus illustrated by the ultimate consequences for the interest rate and the price level of a doubling of the money supply (from ½M to M) in a fully employed economy (see Patinkin, 1965: 236–44). With trivial qualifications (and the qualifications are trivial largely because the level of aggregation is so high), the doubling of the money supply doubles the price level and leaves the rate of interest unchanged. The comparative-statics results can be expressed straightforwardly in terms of the equation of exchange: before the doubling of the money supply, $(\frac{1}{2}M)V = (\frac{1}{2}P)y$; after the doubling, $MV = Py$. Neither the real interest rate nor any other real magnitude is affected.

The market process that establishes a new macroeconomic equilibrium is driven by the real-cash-balance effect. When money holdings are doubled, market participants increase their spending on the economy's output. Patinkin's framework allows us to go beyond the simple quantity-theory results and see that at the time of the doubling, there will exist both an excess demand for output and an excess demand for bonds. Because the commodity market fails to clear instantaneously, market participants begin spending more on bonds as well as on output. This spillover effect causes the interest rate to be pushed down as the price level begins to be pushed up. As the price level rises, however, the excess demand for bonds turns into an excess supply. Bond prices are driven back down; the interest rate back up. Note that in Figure 10.1, the adjustment path is horizontal at the point it crosses the BB curve. With the bond market fleetingly in equilibrium, the equilibrating forces impinge on prices only. As a whole, the adjustment process is seen to entail a permanent upward adjustment of the price level and a temporary downward adjustment of the interest rate.

Significantly, Patinkin's choice of aggregates and his assumption that income and output are fixed at their full-employment levels allow for no quantity adjustments to result from the temporarily low rate of interest. Further, theorizing in terms of commodities, which includes both consumer goods and investment goods, means that any such quantity adjustments would take place wholly within the commodities aggregate and hence would be given no play in his framework. Over-investment, as was represented by a movement beyond the PPF in our capital-based framework, and mal-investment, as represented by the interest-rate effect on the mix of consumption and investment, are simply precluded from the outset by construction.

Short-run/long-run Phillips curve analysis

An alternative framework that demonstrates the central proposition of Monetarism features the short-run Phillips curve (SRPC) in its relationship to the long-run Phillips curve (LRPC). As was the case with Patinkin's framework, the comparative-statics results can be expressed straightforwardly in terms of the quantity theory of money. The price level is directly proportional to the money supply. But in contrast to Patinkin's framework, which takes the economy to be operating at its full-employment level throughout the period of adjustment to an increase in the quantity of money, the Phillips curve framework allows for temporary changes in employment and hence in output. In response to an increase in the money supply, the economy experiences levels of real income beyond the full-employment level during the period that prices are adjusting. Employment and output levels first rise and then fall as increased spending bids prices up to a level consistent with the larger money supply. The natural rate of unemployment is a term chosen by Friedman to recognize its analytical kinship to Wicksell's natural rate of interest. This framework, however, simply ignores possible movements in the rate of interest and hence does not allow for – or, at least, does not depict – even a temporary change in the mix of outputs that would be associated with a temporarily low interest rate. As depicted in Figure 10.2, movement along a SRPC in the direction of greater employment and a higher price level eventually resolves itself – by a shift in the SRPC – into an unchanged level of employment (the natural rate) and an increase in the price level fully proportionate to the increase in the money supply.

The sequential adjustments in the labor market that drive the economy along the path shown in Figure 10.2 rely on the real-cash-balance effect but not in the same direct way as in Figure 10.1. An increased quantity of money in the hands of market participants increases spending and causes prices to rise. The rising prices translate into a sequence of changes in the labor market as firms and then workers react. The dynamics in the labor market can be depicted in two (equivalent) ways. Figure 10.3A shows labor demand and labor supply drawn with the vertical axis representing the nominal wage rate W. This construction is directly conformable with our capital-based and labor-based frameworks. Figure 10.3B shows labor supply and labor demand drawn with the vertical axis representing the real wage rate (W/P). This construction is more suitable for a theory that features price-level changes.

In response to an increase in the money supply and consequent bidding up of prices, labor demand shifts ahead of labor supply if only because each

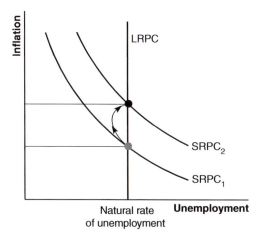

Friedman-Phelps equilibration
in the SRPC/LRPC framework
with no interest-rate considerations

Figure 10.2 Monetarist framework (Friedman–Phelps).

business firm can observe directly and almost immediately the divergence between the price of its output and the costs of its inputs. If output prices rise, then firms increase their demand for labor. As shown in Figure 10.3A, the nominal wage rate rises as workers move up along their supply curves from the initial equilibrium to the hollow point that marks the intersection between S and D′. The nominal wage rate is bid up – though, with the economy still in mid-adjustment, not high enough to match the increased prices. The level of employment and hence the level of output rise above their equilibrium levels.

Full adjustment on the demand side of the labor market – which would bring wages completely back in line with prices – is pre-empted by an adjustment on the supply side of the labor market. The supply-side reaction is somewhat delayed because workers, who, like their employers, are ultimately concerned with real and not nominal wage rates, must assess the increased nominal wage rate in the context of the array of prices of the many goods and services they buy. Although prices generally are moving in an upward direction, owing to the increased money supply, a few prices are actually falling, and the ones that are rising are rising at different rates. That is, the real-cash-balance effect is superimposed upon the ongoing relative-price changes that characterize a healthy market economy. When workers realize that their wage rate, which has risen in nominal terms, has actually fallen in real terms (i.e. that wages are rising more slowly than prices), they negotiate – some collectively, some individually – for higher

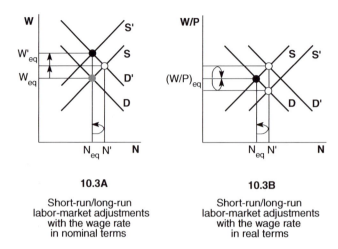

10.3A

Short-run/long-run
labor-market adjustments
with the wage rate
in nominal terms

10.3B

Short-run/long-run
labor-market adjustments
with the wage rate
in real terms

Figure 10.3 Labor-market adjustments to an increased money supply.

nominal wages. The supply of labor shifts from S to S'. The nominal wage rate rises to W'_{eq}, and employment falls to its initial equilibrium level, N_{eq}.

Although Figure 10.3A shows only a single shift of demand followed by a single shift of supply, the actual adjustment path of W and N can be thought of as a consequence of the two curves shifting in small steps or even continuously from D to D' and from S to S' but with the shifting of supply lagging behind the shifting in demand. The intersection of these curves traces out a distinct counter-clockwise path from the initial to the subsequent equilibrium. Reinforcing the shape of the adjustment path are institutional considerations, such as the existence of two-year or five-year labor contracts, which may result in discontinuities and may cause the supply lag to be more pronounced than it would otherwise be.

Figure 10.3B, which duplicates the figure provided by Friedman (1976: 223), shows the same adjustment process in real terms. The nominal wage rate W on the vertical axis is replaced by the real wage rate W/P. The disequilibrium induced by an increase in the money supply is represented in this figure by the two hollow points (the intersections of S and D' and of S' and D). From the firm's point of view, workers are moving downward along the firm's demand curve; from the workers' point of view, the firms are moving upward along the workers' supply curve. Following Friedman and early expositors, the divergence of views is accounted for in terms of the differing "perceptions" of movements in the real wage. Firms perceive the real wage to be falling; workers (initially) perceive it to be rising. Firms and workers, it almost seems, have different perceptive abilities. But as Friedman makes clear, the adjustment process is driven not by differing perceptive abilities, but by a key difference in what employers and employees are separately trying to perceive. To the firm, the "real wage" means the wage rate in comparison to the price of the firm's output. Changes in this classical, or Ricardian, real wage are not difficult to perceive. To the worker, the "real wage" means the wage rate in comparison to the prices of all the goods and services that the workers buy. Changes in this more neoclassical, or Fisherian, real wage are relatively difficult to perceive.

The vertical difference between the two hollow points of Figure 10.3B, then, though commonly seen as stemming from a difference in firms' and workers' abilities to perceive the real wage rate, is more accurately interpreted as stemming from the difference in the Ricardian real wage and the (perceived) Fisherian real wage. In either case, the horizontal difference between the equilibrium level of employment and the supernatural level of employment – Friedman calls it an "overfull" level – corresponding to the two hollow points represent unsustainable increases in the levels of employment and output. A subsequent equilibrium, identical to the initial equilibrium, is established once the vertical disparity is eliminated. During the process of adjustment to the increased money supply, the Ricardian real wage first falls and then rises, while the (perceived) Fisherian real wage first rises and then falls. At the end of the process, both the price level and the nominal wage rate have increased in direct proportion to the money supply, such that the real wage W/P is the same as before.

Resolving a seeming contradiction

Referring the short-run/long-run Phillips curve analysis as UPI (unexpected price inflation) theory, some friendly critics of Monetarism (Birch *et al.*, 1982) see the supposed movements in prices and output spelled out by Friedman as conflicting with one of the most fundamental implications of the quantity theory of money. "It is astonishing that the UPI theory has become so popular even though it *contradicts* the familiar identity MV = PQ" (Birch *et al.*: 211, emphasis mine). In accordance with the equation of exchange, an increase in the money supply in circumstances of an unchanged demand for money implies a corresponding increase in dollar-denominated output. That is, with V constant, an increase in M increases PQ. The seeming contradiction involves the question of the P-Q split. In what proportion does the new money spend itself in bidding up prices as opposed to stimulating real output? Or course, different answers can be given depending upon the state of the economy (Are unemployed workers and idle resources pervasive?) and the nature of expectations (To what extent was the increase in the money supply anticipated?). In the final analysis, however, the equation of exchange, together with a constant velocity of money, imposes an inverse relationship between changes in P and changes in Q. Real output rises to the extent that the price level does *not* rise.

Short-run/long-run Phillips curve analysis, however, seems to impose a direct rather than an inverse relationship between changes in P and changes in Q. Real output increases, at least temporarily, as a result of the differing perceptions of employers and employees of the real wage rate under conditions of price inflation. So, there has to be a (positive) inflation rate *before* the differential perceptions can lead to an increase in real output. That is, an increasing P is prerequisite to – and the proximate cause of – an increase in Q. Real output rises to the extent that the price level *does* rise.

David Laidler (1990: 53) identifies the two views of the relationship between rising prices and rising output by setting them out in Friedman's own words. Echoing Birch *et al.* (though not citing them), Laidler sees these two views as incompatible: the supposed Phillips curve dynamics is not a clarification or elaboration of the process that brings the price level into harmony with real money demand but rather a "fundamental reinterpretation of the labor market behavior underlying [the P-Q split]."

What is seen as a contradiction or incompatibility by the friendly critics is more appropriately seen as a characteristic of the inherent unsustainability of policy-induced movements along a short-run Phillips curve. This inherent unsustainability, of course, is precisely the message contained in Friedman's natural rate hypothesis. A market process involving an increasing M which causes an increasing P which, in turn, causes an increasing Q must contain the seeds of its own undoing. As time goes by, the direction of change in the level of real output must get reversed, and – ultimately – the net change in real output must be zero. Otherwise the final outcome of the process would not square with the kernel of truth in the quantity theory. There is no logical contradiction implied, though, by a market process in which a rising P pulls up Q in an intermediate phase of the economy's adjustment to a monetary injection but in which Q falls back to its initial level as P becomes fully adjusted to the new money supply. (After arguing that there *is* a contradiction here and citing empirical studies that would cast doubts on any P-led market process, Birch *et al.* (1982: 213–19) spell out a more plausible Q-led self-reversing process in the tradition of Clower and Leijonhufvud – anticipating importantly some ideas that now receive attention under the New Keynesian label. These and related issues will be addressed in the following chapter.)

The seeming contradiction is thus resolved by distinguishing between (1) the dynamics of the market's adjustment to a monetary injection, which involves one phase in which P and Q vary directly; and (2) the comparative statics relating money and prices both before and after the increase in money supply. To embrace the ideas represented in (1) and (2) is, of course, to endorse a boom–bust theory of the business cycle. In fact, the Austrian theory of the business cycle and this Monetarist theory of the business cycle can be seen as parallel and complementary theories, each dealing with different but related aspects of a policy-induced artificial boom. The expansion of credit/money according to Austrians/Monetarists sets into motion a market process that has a seemingly positive effect on the performance of the macroeconomy. Those effects are eventually and inevitably nullified, however, by a subsequent phase of that same market process. This statement is deliberately phrased in sufficiently general terms so as to conceal all the differences between the Austrian and Monetarist constructions. The differences stem largely from the fact that Mises and Hayek, influenced by Böhm-Bawerk's theory of capital and interest, focused on the allocation of resources within capital markets as guided by a bank rate of interest that can deviate from the natural rate of interest, while Friedman, influenced by Frank Knight's critical assessment of Böhm-Bawerk, focused on the actual as opposed to the natural level of employment as guided by the employers' and the employees' perceptions of the real wage rate. Bellante and Garrison (1988) demonstrate the large degree of compatibility and mutual reinforcement between the Austrians' capital-market dynamics and the Monetarists' labor-market dynamics.

If we factor in the interest-rate dynamics of the Patinkin model and allow for quantity adjustments during the process of equilibration, we get an account of boom and bust that is similar even in its particulars to the Austrian theory. Employment and output rising above their natural level mean that the economy is pushing beyond its (sustainable) production possibilities frontier, producing more consumption goods *and* more investment goods. As the rate of interest falls below its natural rate during the equilibrating process, resources are allocated away from the production of consumption goods and towards the production of investment goods. The adjustment path has an investment bias to it. Revealingly, the counterclockwise movement in Figure 10.1 and the clockwise movement in Figure 10.2 combine to produce the clockwise movement in the PPF panel of Figure 4.4. Over-investment and malinvestment have a basis in Monetarist as well as in Austrian theory.

To identify a difference, we have to ask why the interest rate falls in response to an increased money supply. In Austrian theory, it falls because of the injection effect: money enters the economy through credit markets. In Monetarist theory, it falls because of a spillover effect: holders of excess cash balances increase their spending on bonds as well as commodities. The consequences of a temporarily lower interest rate are also different. In Austrian theory, a vertically disaggregated structure of production allows scope for nontrivial movements of capital. In Monetarist theory, the adoption of a high level of aggregation implies no movements or trivial movements of resources within the output aggregate. The Monetarist vision, in effect, has the macroeconomy pushing beyond the production possibilities frontier in the early phases of the adjustment process, and then in the late phases, simply falling back to the frontier along the expansion path.

Can we actually take the short-run/long-run Phillips curve and the implicit lag in the adjustment of labor supply to be the Monetarists' theory of the business cycle? Several considerations suggest that we should answer this question in the negative. First, Monetarist empirical studies are concerned almost exclusively with the stability of V and not with the dynamics of P and Q. This narrowly circumscribed research agenda is consistent with early disclaimers concerning the market process that eventually translates a monetary injection into an increase in the overall price level. "We have little confidence in our knowledge of the transmission mechanism, except in such broad and vague terms as to constitute little more than an impressionistic representation rather than an engineering blueprint" (Friedman and Schwartz, [1963] 1969: 222). This lacking was not seen as being unique to the question of the P-Q split: "for both money and most other goods and services, there is as yet no satisfactory and widely accepted description, in precise quantifiable terms, of the dynamic temporal process of adjustment" (Friedman and Schwartz, 1982: 27).

Second, one of the subsidiary – but very explicit – propositions of Monetarism is that "the changed rate of growth in nominal income [induced by monetary expansion] typically shows up *first* in output and hardly at all in prices" (Friedman, 1970c: 23, emphasis mine). Virtually the same statement appears in Friedman's (1987: 17) retrospective on Monetarism and again in Friedman's (1992: 47) encyclopedia entry. Even in the initial casting of his natural rate hypothesis, which eventually evolved into the short-run/long-run Phillips curve analysis – or UPI theory, as Birch *et al.* call it – Friedman ([1968] 1969d: 103) warns against undue emphasis on misperceived wage rates. "To begin with [after the rate of monetary growth is increased], much or most of the rise in income will take the form of an increase in output and employment rather than in prices." Only in a later phase of the expansion do product prices lead factor prices thus giving scope for a difference in the perceptions of the real wage rate and hence an additional boost to output (ibid.). Victoria Chick (1973: 111–15), focusing narrowly on Friedman ([1968] 1969d), in which prices change hardly at all initially but then rise and pull quantities up with them, finds "missing links" in Friedman's argument and concludes that "until the formulation of price and quantity decisions are explained, we have no *theory*." Friedman concurs in his retrospective. Citing himself and others, he notes that:

> A major unsettled issue is the short-run division of a change in nominal income between output and prices. The division has varied widely over space and time and there exists no satisfactory theory that isolates the factors responsible for the variability.
>
> (Friedman, 1987: 17; 1992: 49)

There is a critical distinction here between Friedman, the architect of Monetarism, and Friedman, the critic of Keynesianism. The Keynes-inspired belief that society – or its policy-makers – can choose, at least at the margin, between inflation and unemployment was based on the presumption of a stable and hence exploitable downward sloping Phillips curve. The Phillips curve story as told by Friedman is best understood as a Keynesian story with a Monetarist ending. It was an exercise in immanent criticism. Friedman was simply taking on his adversaries on their own terms. Accordingly, the analysis did not imply his belief that prices, in fact, rise first and then differences in perceptions of the inflation rate lead to a temporary increase in real output. Quite to the contrary, it demonstrated only his willingness to suspend *dis*belief long enough to carry his opponent's argument through to the finish.

We are entitled to ask anew, then, what is the Monetarists' theory of the business cycle? What is the nature of the market process that constitutes the boom–bust sequence? The absence of an obvious and uniquely Monetarist answer to this question is to be attributed partly to that narrowness and agnosticism already mentioned that has come to characterize Monetarism. Sometimes – and particularly in the defensive mode of argument – Monetarism is defined strictly in terms of the empirically demonstrated relationship between the money supply M and *nominal* income Py. The short-run behavior of real income remains an unsettled question. Patinkin's model has real income and real output remaining constant throughout the adjustment process, implying that whatever changes may actually occur are negligible. Friedman, the critic of Keynesianism, allows for rising prices to be a significant proximate cause of increases in real output. Friedman, the architect of Monetarism, has real output rising before prices begin to rise.

The lack of a more definitive answer to the question about the nature of the boom–bust process is to be understood in part, as the following chapter makes clear, to Friedman's judgment that the question itself is irrelevant. The broad empirical evidence suggests to him that there are no significant boom–bust cycles to theorize about. The lack of any satisfying answer by others is explained by the common practice of textbook writers of taking the short-run/long-run Phillips curve analysis as not only a criticism of Keynesian policy schemes but also the actual adjustment mechanism as seen by the Monetarists.

Boom and bust in the labor-based framework

Adopting the common practice ourselves of taking short-run/long-run Phillips curve analysis to be an integral part of Monetarism, we can devise a Monetarist macroeconomics with the aid of our labor-based framework. In Chapters 7 through 9 we were able to depict both cyclical and secular phenomena without taking explicit account of the price level. Downplaying changes in the price level, in fact, helped us remain true to Keynes. Being true to Monetarism, however, requires that the price level be featured. Fortunately, our labor-based framework can be modified so as to bring the effects of price-level changes clearly into view. Figure 10.4 duplicates the labor-based framework presented in Figure 7.1 but tracks all value magnitudes in real terms. W becomes W/P; Y becomes Y/P; and so on. The real rate of interest in Panel 6, i_r, nets out the inflation premium.

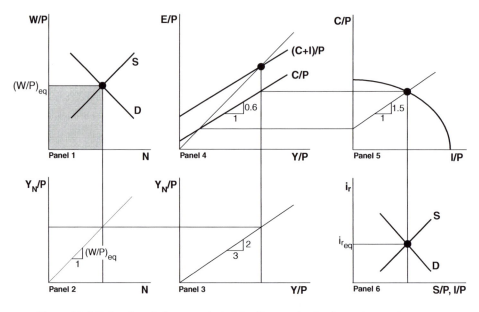

Figure 10.4 Labor-based framework (with all magnitudes in real terms).

Let the initial state of the economy be one of full-employment equilibrium with a stable price level, as represented in the pattern of solid points
in Panels 1, 4, 5, and 6. Both the market for labor and the market for
loanable funds are clearing. Income is equal to expenditures. And the
economy is operating on its production possibilities frontier. In Monetarist
terms, we can simply say that the economy is experiencing the natural rate
of unemployment with and a zero rate of inflation. (It does not actually
matter whether we begin with a zero rate of inflation or with some positive and correctly perceived rate, such as the initial equilibrium depicted
in Figure 10.2. What matters is that the economy has fully adjusted itself
to the ongoing rate of inflation.)

Let the monetary authority increase the money supply by (somehow)
putting money in the hands of the public. Market participants, who now
find themselves with excess cash balances, increase their spending all around.
Let us imagine, however, that the increased spending impinges only on
prices and not at all on quantities. If this is the case, then the solid points
would continue to represent the macroeconomy as it begins to adjust to
the higher money supply. That is, E is rising, but so is P and in the same
proportion; E/P remains unchanged. Similarly for Y/P and the other real
macroeconomic magnitudes. Imagining that the initial phase of the adjustment process involves price changes and not quantity changes, while actually
contrary to the fundamental propositions of Monetarism, is a way of giving

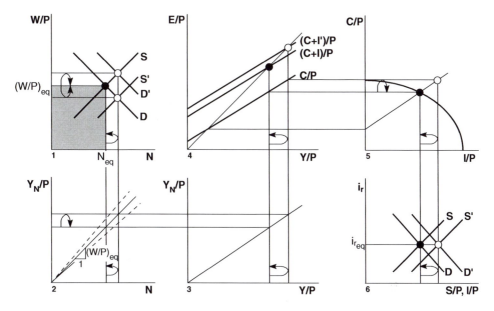

Figure 10.5 Boom and bust (a labor-based view of Phillips curve analysis).

full play to the unexpected price inflation that is integral to the Friedman–Phelps short-run/long-run Phillips curve analysis.

The labor-market adjustments envisioned by Friedman and depicted in Figure 10.3B are simply imported into Figure 10.5 as Panel 1. The two hollow points represent perceptions of the (Ricardian and Fisherian) real wage that separately motivate employers and employees. Panel 2, which depicts the differing perceptions of the real wage rate as dotted-line rotations (clockwise for employers and counter-clockwise for employees), shows that the actual increase in real income to labor is wholly attributable to the increase in employment from N_{eq} to N. With assumed structural fixity, as represented in Panel 3, the increased income to labor implies a proportionally increased total income and total output as marked by the hollow point in Panel 4. The increased income is accompanied by an increase in saving, as shown in Panel 6 by a shift in the supply of loanable funds from S to S'. Treating capital and labor as complements, we see that the increased employment of labor is accompanied by an comparable increase in investment, as depicted in Panel 6 by a shift in the demand for loanable funds from D to D'. The real rate of interest is unaffected. The economy is pushed beyond its PPF along the Keynesian demand constraint, as shown in Panel 5.

The movements from the solid points to the hollow points in Panels 4, 5, and 6 represent real increases in the respective macroeconomic magnitudes.

That is, Y, E, C, S, and I are all increasing; P is increasing too – but to a lesser extent. We have allowed the real component of the increases to be wholly attributable to the temporary but unsustainable increase in the level of employment – an increase which itself is attributable to the workers' misperception of the real wage rate during a period of unanticipated price inflation.

In this reckoning of boom and bust, the artificiality of the boom is clearly registered in both Panels 1 and 5. The account of the self-reversing aspects of the boom – the upper turning point – follows exclusively from the conflicting perceptions registered in Panel 1. When workers eventually realize that prices have risen more than the wage rate has risen, the shifted supply curve S′, as perceived by employers, shifts back. Equivalently, the workers' perception of a shifted labor demand curve D′ is eventually recognized as a misperception. As employment falls back to its natural rate, the economy returns to the macroeconomic equilibrium represented by the solid points of Panels 1, 4, 5, and 6. After the boom and bust, all the real magnitudes are the same as before, while all the nominal magnitudes are increased in direct proportion to the increase in the money supply.

By construction, Figure 10.5 is not true to the Monetarist vision. Identifying the particulars of the unfaithfulness serves to reinforce our reluctance to regard the labor-market dynamics in Panel 1 as a fundamental aspect of Monetarism. Most significantly, we have allowed for no direct cash-balance effect on the output magnitudes. Note that in Panel 4 the increase in consumption spending is strictly an income-induced increase, a movement along an unchanged consumption function. Further, we have allowed for no direct cash-balance effect on the bond market. The supply of loanable funds shifts to the right temporarily only because real incomes rise during the boom. The demand for loanable funds shifts to the right because of increased borrowing to finance the investment goods to complement the increase in the employment of labor.

In one significant respect, this construction is true to the Monetarist vision: it takes movements of the interest rate out of play. That is, neither movements in the real rate of interest nor corresponding relative movements of consumption and investment (along or parallel to the PPF in Panel 5) are any part of the adjustment process that brings the economy back into a macroeconomic equilibrium after an increase in the money supply. Further discussion of this neglected aspect of the adjustment process is facilitated in the following section, which deals with the Monetarist vision in the context of the capital-based framework. Taking interest-rate adjustments out of play – like neglecting the direct cash-balance effect on real magnitudes – serves to focus attention exclusively on the labor market and the supposed misperceptions of the real wage rate: increases in the money supply cause inflation and hence give rise to misperceptions of the real wage rate. The consequent increase in employment increases the output of both consumption goods and investment goods. A subsequent straightening out of those misperceptions causes employment and hence output to fall back to their original levels.

A curious aspect of the money-induced disequilibrium depicted in Figure 10.5 is the separation of the envisioned adjustment process (in Panel 1) from the actual injection mechanism (in Panel 6). Money *enters* the economy through credit markets but *affects* the economy through labor markets. For Monetarists, however, the injection mechanism is wholly irrelevant – a point vividly demonstrated by their common practice of supposing that the increase in the money supply is accomplished by dropping money from a helicopter. Thinking in terms of actual monetary institutions, we have to imagine that the effects of lending money into existence propagate in strictly nominal terms from Panel 6 to Panel 1 and then propagate back in real terms. That is, money-induced increases in prices have to get misperceived by workers before increases in the supply of loanable funds become part of the story.

Despite the problems just noted, a conventional comparison of Monetarism and Keynesianism emerges from the boom–bust process as depicted in Figure 10.5. Panel 5 provides the most fundamental basis for understanding Friedman's oft-quoted remark that "We're all Keynesians now." After being quoted out of context and suspected of endorsing policy activism, Friedman clarified his remark with the claim that "we all use the Keynesian language and apparatus." This claim is readily translatable into the relationships in Panel 5: we all (Keynesians and Monetarists alike – but not the Austrians) confine our attention to possible movements along the demand constraint. Keynes, of course, was concerned about the economy falling permanently inside the PPF, while the Monetarists focus on its rising temporarily beyond the PPF. In the following chapter, we will see an even closer kinship in which the Keynesians and the Monetarists are united in their concern about the economy falling inside the PPF but differ (importantly) as to the cause of the lapse from full employment. However great the difference between the two schools, the presupposed relevance of the demand constraint gives them a strong common denominator and sets them apart from the Austrians, who are largely concerned with sustainable and unsustainable movements along – or parallel to – the PPF.

To correct for the neglect of a direct cash-balance effect on real magnitudes in Figure 10.5 is to cause the effect of misperceived real wages to lose most if not all of its significance. In Figure 10.6 the cash-balance effect by itself accounts for the movements of both real and nominal variables during the adjustment to the increased money supply. In accordance with the fundamentals of Monetarism, the increased expenditures increase demands all around as holders of the new money begin spending their cash balances. People spend more on consumption goods, as depicted in Panel 4 by a shift in consumption spending from C to C′; they spend more on bonds, that is, they save more, as depicted in Panel 6 by a shift in saving from S to S′. With the economy driven partly by the spending of current

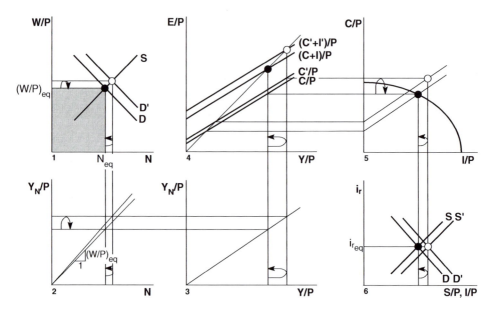

Figure 10.6 Boom and bust (a labor-based view of the real-cash-balance effect).

income and partly by the drawing down of cash balances, the applicable demand constraint in Panel 5 is one that lies above the initial constraint. More specifically, the consumption function shifts upward, raising the demand constraint's vertical intercept, which, as was shown in Chapter 7 (p. 136), is determined by the intersection of the consumption function and the 45° line.

In the initial phases of the boom–bust cycle, the increased demands are almost wholly accommodated in real terms. Initial increases in quantities supplied may require the drawing down of inventories. But with an increased demand for output comes an increased demand for inputs – labor and investment goods. The shift of the demand for labor in Panel 1 from D to D′ follows directly and straightforwardly on the basis of the principle of derived demand. With labor demand shifting rightward, workers move upward along their unshifted supply curve. Investment demand and hence the demand for loanable funds would increases similarly, as depicted in Panel 6 by a shift from D to D′; savers move up their shifted supply curve.

Though markets are clearing all around, the macroeconomy is in disequilibrium, as depicted by the hollow points in Panels 1, 4, 5, and 6. In Figure 10.6 – and in contrast to Figure 10.5 – the difference between the hollow points and the solid points is wholly attributed to the direct cash-balance effect on real magnitudes. The unsustainability of these levels of employment and real output is obvious in Panel 5. Prices and wage rates, slow to rise initially, now begin to rise, putting a damper on the spending out of cash balances. And as the increases in prices and nominal wage rates finally come to match the increase in the money supply, real output and employment, supported only with the spending out of current income, fall back to their original levels. The economy once again settles into the macro-economic equilibrium represented by the solid points of Figure 10.6.

Though we have traced out the equilibrating process with the aid of the labor-based framework, we have added little to the Monetarists' under-standing of the movements of the variables included explicitly in the equation of exchange. $MV = PQ$. When M increases, PQ increases. The increase in PQ initially manifests itself as an increase in Q, but Q falls back to its initial level as P becomes fully adjusted to the increased M.

Figure 10.6 differs from Figure 10.5 largely in terms of our understanding of the roles of labor and of cash balances in adjusting the economy to an increased supply of money. It is possible, of course, that both play an active role. Q rises first. And when P begins rising, workers' misperception of the real wage rate give Q an added boost. But Q finally falls back to its initial level as P rises to match M. We could depict these dynamics by starting from the hollow point in Panel 1 of Figure 10.6 and grafting on the dynamics of Panel 1 of Figure 10.5 and the corresponding changes in the other panels. But with the direct cash-balance effect in play and the conse-quent increase in the derived demand for labor, it is not clear that the possible misperception of the real wage rate has any claim on our atten-tion. Monetarism could easily do without this particular twist.

We might note here that the issue of perceptions can also be raised in connection with the supply of labor in Panel 1 of Figure 10.6. Positively affected by the spending down of real cash balances, the (disequilibrium) real wage rate actually is higher than before the increase in the money supply. Each point along the supply curve for labor presumably represents the quantity of labor workers are willing to supply, *given that they can continue indefinitely to supply that amount at that wage rate*. Suppose, however, that the high real wage rate represented by the hollow point is (correctly) perceived to be temporary. How much labor are workers willing to supply *now* at this high wage rate – that is, given that the wage rate in the near future is expected to be and will be the lower wage rate represented by the solid point? The issue here, of course, is the intertemporal substitution of labor, an effect that has got some attention from the New Classical economists. In fact Robert Lucas (1981: 4) imputes great significance in it: "I see no way to account for observed employment patterns that does not rest on an understanding of the intertemporal substitutability of labor." This effect could be depicted by allowing for a rightward shift in the supply of labor during the adjustment period, a shift that allows for a disequilibrium wage somewhere between the solid point and the hollow point. But, again, with the real-cash-balance effect in play, this aspect of the adjustment process would undoubtedly be of secondary importance.

Boom and bust in the capital-based framework

The Monetarist vision of boom and bust does not entail any essential distinction between consumption and investment. Although investment demand is recognized – by Monetarists and virtually all others – as being generally more volatile than consumption demand, the differential volatility does not come into play in any essential way. Nor does the Monetarist vision entail opposing movements of consumption and investment in response to a change in the interest rate – let alone differential movements within the investment sector. Rather, the two magnitudes move together, both rising during the upswing and then in the downswing falling back to their sustainable levels.

Unlike the Keynesian and Austrian visions, then, the Monetarist vision can be stated in terms of changes in output Q or real income Y/P without special reference to the individual objects of expenditure or components of output C and I. In effect, Monetarism is virtually framework-independent. As long as a framework gives sufficient play to the variables included in the equation of exchange, the Monetarist vision can be expressed in that framework. It is for this reason, presumably, that Friedman (1970a) had no qualms about expressing his ideas with the aid of the Keynesian ISLM apparatus. Interestingly, nearly thirty years after he offered up his own ideas in the Keynesian language, he identified that particular attempt to compromise as his "biggest academic blunder" (Weinstein, 1999: section 3, p. 2).

Friedman has made no similar blunder with respect to the Austrian language, but we can gain insight by making it for him. The boom–bust sequence of Monetarism – in its two different manifestations – was set out in the previous section with the aid of our own labor-based framework and without the framework itself interfering with the telling of the story of boom and bust. Significantly, those same ideas can be set out again – and again in its two different manifestations – with the aid of our capital-based framework. This exercise puts Friedman and Hayek in sharp contrast and provides a basis for reconciling their separate understandings of the market process that turns boom into bust.

Figure 10.7 retains Panels 5 and 6 of the variable-price labor-based framework, but replaces the other panels with the intertemporal structure of production together with the auxiliary labor-market panels, all value magnitudes being expressed in real terms. When we modified the Keynesian framework by dividing all nominal magnitudes by P, we transformed a fixed-price model into a variable-price model. The similar modifications in Figure 10.8, however, simply make explicit the variation in the price level, a variation which was downplayed but (implicitly) allowed for in the capital-based framework.

As in the previous section, we let the initial state of the economy be one of full-employment equilibrium with a stable price level (or with ongoing and fully anticipated inflation), as represented in the pattern of solid points

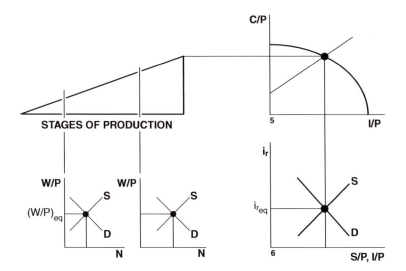

Figure 10.7 Capital-based framework (with all magnitudes in real terms).

in Panels 5 and 6, and in the auxiliary labor-market panels. The markets for labor and the market for loanable funds are clearing. Capital is allocated among the various stages in the structure of production in full accordance with the equilibrium rate of interest. And the economy is operating on its production possibilities frontier.

To set the cyclical process in motion, let the monetary authority increase the money supply by (somehow) putting money in the hands of the public. Market participants, who now find themselves with excess cash balances, increase their spending all around. The increased spending impinges only on prices and not at all on quantities; the solid points of Figure 10.7 continue to represent the macroeconomy as it begins to adjust to the higher money supply. As in Figure 10.5, it is only a misperception of the ongoing inflation that moves the economy away from the solid points.

The labor-market adjustments envisioned by Friedman and depicted in Figure 10.3 are imported into Figure 10.8 as the auxiliary labor markets. Significantly, the two auxiliary labor markets actually shown, though differentiated by their specific temporal locations in the structure of production, experience the same consequences of rising prices. Monetarism does not distinguish between early and late stages of production. Employment increases in both labor markets as does the output in the corresponding stages of production. The increased income is accompanied by an increase in saving, as depicted in Panel 6 by a shift in the supply of loanable funds from S to S'. Additional investment needed to complement the increased employment of labor underlies the shift in the demand for loanable funds from D to D'. Note that the unchanged rate of interest is consistent with

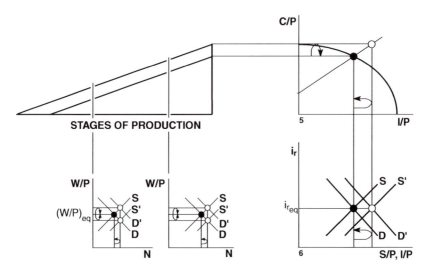

Figure 10.8 Boom and bust (a capital-based view of Phillips curve analysis).

the unchanged slope of the structure of production. The increase in employment serves only to push the economy along the demand constraint beyond its PPF, as shown in Panel 5.

The movements from the solid points to the hollow points in Panels 5 and 6 represent real increases in the respective macroeconomic magnitudes. In this construction, as in Figure 10.5, we have allowed the real component of the increases in C, S, and I to be wholly attributable to the temporary increase in the level of employment – an increase which itself is attributable to the workers' misperception of the real wage rate in conditions of unanticipated price inflation. In this reckoning of boom and bust, the artificiality of the boom is most clearly registered in Panel 5 and in the auxiliary labor-markets. The account of the self-reversing aspects of the boom – the upper turning point – follows exclusively from the conflicting perceptions of employers and employees. When workers eventually realize that prices have risen more than the wage rate, employment once again comes to be governed by the original supply and demand curves, and the macroeconomy once again is represented by solid points of Panels 5 and 6 and the auxiliary labor markets. After the boom and bust, all the real magnitudes are the same as before, while all the nominal magnitudes are increased in direct proportion to the increase in the money supply.

In Figure 10.8, as in Figure 10.5, we neglect the direct real-cash-balance effect on real magnitudes in order to allow the effect of misperceived real wage rates to take center stage. We can move on now to show in Figure 10.9, as in Figure 10.6, the real-cash-balance effect by itself can account for the movements of both real and nominal variables during the

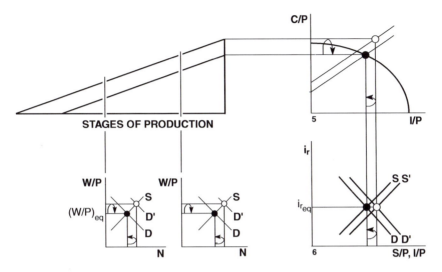

Figure 10.9 Boom and bust (a capital-based view of the real-cash-balance effect)

adjustment to the money supply. When the central bank increases the money supply, the resulting increased expenditures increase demands all around. Initially, the increased demands are almost wholly accommodated in real terms. People spend more on consumption goods, as represented by a lengthening of the vertical leg of the structure of production and by a shifting upward of the demand constraint in Panel 5. They spend more on bonds, that is, they save more, as depicted in Panel 6 by a shift in saving from S to S'. The increased demand for output translates into an increased derived demand for inputs of investment goods, as depicted by a rightward shift in the demand for loanable funds from D to D', and an increased derived demand for labor, similarly represented by rightward shifts in the auxiliary labor markets.

Though markets are clearing all around, the macroeconomy is in disequilibrium, as shown by the hollow points in Panels 5, 6 and the auxiliary labor markets. The unsustainability of these levels of employment and real output are most obvious in Panel 5. Prices and wage rates continue rising, putting a damper on the spending of cash balances. And as the increase in the price level finally comes to match the increase in the money supply, real output and employment, supported now only with the spending of current income, fall back to their original levels. The economy once again settles into the macroeconomic equilibrium represented by the solid points of Figure 10.9.

The contrast between Figure 10.9 and Figure 10.8 is the same as the contrast made earlier between Figure 10.6 and Figure 10.5. And as with the earlier figures, the real-wage misperception effect can be added to the direct cash-balance effect by grafting the labor-market dynamics of Figure 10.8 onto the hollow points in the auxiliary labor markets of Figure 10.9. Similarly, considerations of the intertemporal substitutability of labor, involving a rightward shifting of the labor supply curves, could also be incorporated into this depiction of the economy's adjustment to an increased money supply.

Monetarist and Austrian visions: a reconciliation

Figures 10.5 through 10.9 have facilitated the contrasting of two different versions of Monetarism, each expressed with the aid of our two different frameworks. Figure 10.9 provides a basis for incorporating an often neglected aspect of Monetarism, namely, the interest-rate effect. Attention here to a changing interest rate allows for a revealing comparison between Monetarist views and Austrian views of the market's adjustment to an increased money supply. Patinkin's model, summarized early in this chapter, allows an increase in the money supply to cause changes in both the price level and the interest rate. The economy's adjustment path in Figure 10.1 shows that the change in the price level is permanent while the change in the interest rate is temporary. In Patinkin's model, the interest rate falls because of a spillover effect. In the wake of an increased money supply, people want to spend more on output. But because (1) more output in real terms is not immediately available and (2) the price of output – of commodities in Patinkin's terminology – does not rise immediately and dramatically to clear the market, the increased demand is largely frustrated. As a result, people spend disproportionally on bonds – that is, they save a disproportional part of their excess cash balances – during the early part of the adjustment process. With the spillover effect in play, the interest rate is pushed down as the price level begins to be pushed up. This aspect of the adjustment process could be incorporated into Figure 10.9 by making appropriate modifications in Panel 6. If a portion of the demand for output is frustrated, the corresponding derived demand for inputs, including capital inputs, will be lower than shown in Figure 10.9. The shift in the demand for loanable funds from D to D′ will be less pronounced. If the frustrated demand for output is converted temporarily to demand for bonds, then supply of loanable funds will be greater than shown in Panel 6. The shift in the supply of loanable funds from S to S′ will be more pronounced.

A "long and variable lag" between the increase in the money supply and the full adjustment of prices to the larger money supply has become a key feature of Monetarism. The long lag would surely allow enough time for the low interest rate to have real effects. To keep the spillover effects out of the story of the market's adjustment process would seem to require at least one of several propositions to be true.

First, it could be argued that the spillover effect itself is not great. The adjustment path in Patinkin's model of Figure 10.1 doesn't deviate much at all from the horizontal line that connects the hollow point (the initial monetary disequilibrium) and the solid point (the eventual monetary equilibrium). This proposition implies that there is very little frustrated demand during the adjustment period. But a near absence of an interest-rate effect would seem to have one (or some combination) of three rather implausible implications: (1) the price level would have to adjust fairly quickly to an increased money supply – an implication contrary to the notion of a long lag – or (2) output would have to adjust almost in lockstep with demand, an implication contrary to Friedman's empirical findings to be discussed in the following chapter – or (3) people would have to maintain large idle balances rather than put these funds at interest in the loanable-funds market – an outcome certainly contrary to the spirit of Monetarism.

Second, it could be argued that the capital structure is characterized by such capital specificity that there is simply no scope for moving along the PPF or, equivalently, for changing the shape of the Hayekian triangle. Though Monetarists have long turned a blind eye towards all notions of an intertemporal structure, it is doubtful that their neglect is based on the view that adjustments at the margin are not possible. In fact, Patinkin's model itself did not even distinguish between consumption goods and capital goods, implying that whatever movement of resources there may be between these two subcategories of commodities – and presumably similar for movements *within* the capital goods subcategory – is so efficient as not to impinge even temporarily on the aggregate demand for commodities.

Finally, it could be argued that entrepreneurs, fully anticipating that the low rate of interest is temporary, make their production plans on the basis of the rate of interest that will prevail after the adjustment process. While this rational-expectations view is perfectly consistent with the New Classicism that eventually grew out of Monetarism, it is ill-fitting in Friedman's Monetarism and it is certainly out of place in a model that allows workers to misperceive the wage rate for any extended period of time.

We see at this point that the Monetarists and the Austrians are in disagreement about the role of the interest rate in terms of both nature and significance. The Monetarists' spillover effect with insignificant consequences is contrasted with the Austrians' injection effect with significant consequences. When Friedman himself turned his attention to the question of the significance of injection effects – his own term is "first-round effects" – he blurs a critical distinction. It is one thing to claim that changes in the interest rate are insignificant because they do not change the eventual, or ultimate, equilibrium, i.e. the solid points. It is quite another thing to claim that changes in the interest rate – and consequent changes in the mix of outputs – are an insignificant part of the process that moves the economy away from and then back to the initial equilibrium.

"The basic issue," according to Friedman (1970b: 146), "is ancient – whether the 'first-round effect' of a change in the quantity of money largely determines the ultimate effect." That is, does it matter whether the money enters the economy through credit markets or through markets for output? James Tobin, as quoted by Friedman (1970b: p. 146) believes that "the genesis of the new money makes a difference." Friedman sees that genesis of Tobin's view in the writings of John Stuart Mill (1844: 589): "The issues of a Government paper, even when not permanent, will raise prices; because Governments usually issue their paper in purchases for consumption. If issued to pay off a portion of the national debt, we believe they would have no effect [on prices]." Friedman's use of the term "ultimate effect" together with the supporting passage from Mill confirms that he (Friedman) is dealing with the effect of interest-rate changes on the positions of our solid points.

Friedman goes on, however, to claim that "[James] Tobin's concentration on the first-round effect also parallels the emphasis by von Mises in his theory of the cycle." Here, he refers to Lionel Robbins's "Misesian analysis of the Great Depression." According to Robbins, as quoted by Friedman (1970b: 147):

> In normal times, expansion and contraction of the money supply comes, not via the printing press and government decree, but via an expansion of credit through the banks. . . . This involves . . . a mode of diffusion [of the new money] which may have important effects.

The effects that Robbins – and Mises and Hayek – had in mind, of course, entailed a temporarily low rate of interest and the discoordination of the economy's intertemporal capital structure. These effects, discussed with the aid of the hollow points and adjustment path in Figure 4.4, are seen as an important part of the market's adjustment process and not as having a direct or first-order effect on the ultimate equilibrium. The very fact that Friedman lumped Tobin and Mises together as two economists who focused on first-round effects should tip off any reader that he was painting with too broad a brush; his criticism applies to Tobin and the Keynesians but not to Mises and the Austrians.

When Friedman turns his attention to the issue of why there is such a long lag between the injection of new money into the economy and the full adjustment of the price level, he takes an essentially Austrian view of the interest-rate effects. His own reckoning begins, however, not with the central bank buying government securities, i.e. not with the direct injection effect, but rather with the behavior of the "holders of cash" after the central bank has increased the money supply:

> Holders of cash will . . . bid up the price of assets. If the extra demand is initially directed at a particular class of assets, say, government securities, or commercial paper, or the like, the result will be to pull the prices of such assets out of line with other assets and thus widen the area into which the extra cash spills. The increased demand will spread sooner or later affecting equities, houses, durable producer goods, durable

consumer goods, and so on, though not necessarily in that order. . . . These effects can be described as operating on "interest rates," if a more cosmopolitan [i.e., Austrian] interpretation of "interest rates" adopted than the usual one which refers to a small range of marketable securities.

(Friedman, [1961] 1969b: 255)

Friedman does not incorporate into his treatment of the interest rate effects the notion of an intertemporal structure of production, but he does distinguish between sources and services (stocks and flows) as applied to both producer goods and consumer goods. Nonetheless, Friedman's account allows for a critical process that is inherently self-reversing:

The key feature of this process [during which interest rates are low] is that it tends to raise the prices of sources of both producer and consumer services relative to the prices of the services themselves. . . . It therefore encourages the production of such sources and, at the same time, the direct acquisition of the services rather than of the source. But these reactions in their turn tend to raise the prices of services relative to the prices of sources, that is, to undo the initial effects on interest rates. The final result may be a rise in expenditures in all directions without any change in interest rates at all; interest rates and asset prices may simply be the conduit through which the effect of the monetary change is transmitted to expenditures without being altered at all. . . .

(Friedman, [1961] 1969b: 255–6)

Interest rates being the conduit and the critical self-reversal are, of course, critical features of the Austrian account of boom and bust. All that is lacking is an account of the self-reversing process in the context of an intertemporal capital structure. But even this aspect of the process is brought into view when Friedman abandons his strict stock-flow view:

It may be . . . that monetary expansion induces someone within two or three months to contemplate building a factory; within four or five, to draw up plans; within six or seven, to get construction started. The actual construction may take another six months and much of the effect on the income stream may come still later, insofar as initial goods used in construction are withdrawn from inventories and only subsequently lead to increased expenditure by suppliers.

(Friedman, [1961] 1969b: 256)

Here, a key feature of the Austrian vision becomes evident. People may undertake investment projects as a result of the artificially low interest rates. It is clear in Friedman's own exposition that the self-reversing aspect of the process applies to the building of the factory as much as to the buying of the bonds that financed it. Once prices become more fully adjusted to the increased money supply, some half-built factories will not be completed. Some workers will be laid off. Some time will elapse while this and other malinvestments are liquidated and the laid-off workers are being reabsorbed in other parts of the economy.

Friedman's discussion about the cosmopolitan interpretation of interest rates, demands for sources and their services and, finally, decisions to begin construction of a new factory is not intended to identify the nature of the process through which the economy adjusts to an increased money supply. It is intended instead only to make more plausible why the adjustment tends to take so long. He is only trying to "rationalize a lag in the effects of monetary policy as long as the (observed) twelve to sixteen months . . ." (ibid., 215). The implicit distinction, however, between (1) the nature of the process; and (2) the time required for the process to play itself out is surely a false distinction. It simply makes no sense to claim that (1) the process consists of workers straightening out their perception of the real wage but (2) this process plays itself out slowly because capital is first misallocated and then liquidated in response to an artificially low rate of interest. Replacing the misperception of real wages with the direct cash-balance effect does not improve the logic of Friedman's distinction.

Surely, the aspect of the process that determines the lag is also the aspect that defines the nature of the process. If the misallocation of capital sets the pace, as Friedman's discussion of the lag suggests it well may, then the Monetarist theory of boom and bust becomes one with the Austrian theory. Further, the focus on the misallocation of capital is likely the key to settling the major unsettled issue in Monetarism mentioned earlier. The issue of the short-run division of a change in nominal income between output and prices is essentially the issue about the lag. That is, a long lag means that quantities move first and prices move much later. Paraphrasing Friedman's statement of the unsettled issue, we can say that "The lag has varied widely over space and time and there exists no satisfactory theory that isolates the factors responsible for the variability."

Our suggestion here, of course, is that the particulars of the intertemporal capital structure have varied widely over space and time and these particulars may well explain the variability of the lag. The Austrian theory of the unsustainable boom implies, for instance, that such booms will last longer in a capital-intensive economy than in a labor-intensive one. This implication squares nicely with casual observation. Nothing quite like the boom of the 1920s and subsequent bust could have happened in a labor-intensive economy.

With a given capital intensity, credit-driven booms will last longer if speculators in financial markets are largely unattuned to the role of the central bank. This implication, too, has its obvious empirical counterpart. There weren't many savvy Fed watchers in the 1920s, but there were many of them by the time that the political business cycle had become conventional wisdom. Any attempt to understand the financial markets of the earlier period or to understand the corresponding allocation of resources within the intertemporal capital structure in terms of modern notions of rational expectations would be hopelessly anachronistic. A more healthy assessment of the role of expectations makes it plausible that a credit-driven boom in the early years of the Federal Reserve's existence could last for years and that qualitatively similar booms in later years could last eighteen months or so.

Morphing from Friedman to Hayek

If Friedman's discussion of the misperception of the real wage rate is taken to be a questionable and, in any case, an inessential part of Monetarism, then our understanding of the Monetarist vision is best depicted by Figures 10.6 or 10.9 and not by 10.5 or 10.8. If Friedman's speculation about the length of the lag is to be taken seriously, then the Monetarist vision is best depicted by Figure 10.9, modified to take the nature of the lagged adjustment of prices into account.

As already suggested, the modifications would begin with the loanable-funds market and would systematically affect all other aspects of the macroeconomy during the boom–bust cycle. There are four specific modifications: (1) a temporary reduction of the interest rate should be shown in Panel 6 – to reflect either the spillover effects identified in the Patinkin model or the injection effects that follow straightforwardly from institutional considerations. (2) There should be an investment bias in the disequilibrating forces in Panel 5 to show that an artificially low rate of interest has real consequences. The movement from the solid point on the PPF to the hollow point on the shifted demand constraint should give way to a clockwise rotation of the adjustment path to show that a low rate of interest favors investment spending over consumption spending. (3) The slope of the Hayekian triangle should become flatter than the slope associated with the natural rate of interest. Starting construction on a new factory on the basis of cheap credit is represented by a shifting of resources from late stages of production to earlier stages of production. And finally, (4) the auxiliary labor markets should be modified to show that changes in the demand for labor are very much stage-specific. Workers employed to build that new factory were bid away from other activities that were less sensitive to the change in the interest rate. No Figure 10.10 showing all these modifications is provided here. The reader is simply referred to Figure 4.4.

For the fullest understanding of boom and bust, we can simply envision the two adjustment processes – of Figures 4.4 and 10.9 – working simultaneously. The Austrian economists certainly do not deny the operation of the real-cash-balance effect. Quite to the contrary, Mises was an early contributor to our understanding of this effect. Rather, the Austrians deliberately kept movements of the price level in the background in order to call attention to the more consequential effects of injecting money through credit markets. The Monetarists, by contrast, feature the real cash balance effect and emphasize the temporariness of the increase in real output. But since actual boom–bust episodes seem to involve real effects that are more enduring than the real-cash-balance effect would suggest, they point to capital allocation effects as a possible explanation for the otherwise implausible lag.

11 Monetary disequilibrium theory

Beyond the simple truth of the quantity theory of money, Monetarism has many faces. As demonstrated in the previous chapter, the market process that translates boom into bust can be conceived as one that entails systematic misperceptions of the real wage rate in circumstances of unexpected price inflation. Alternatively, a direct real-cash-balance effect associated with an increase in the money supply may fully account for a real but temporary increase in output and incomes. A broad reading of Monetarism suggests that the market process may involve both aspects (real-wage-rate misperceptions and a direct real-cash-balance effect) while considerations of capital and interest govern the lag structure. With almost any interpretation, temporary changes in real magnitudes eventually give way to purely nominal changes in a sequences of phases that can be depicted in both our labor-based framework and our capital-based framework. After the boom–bust episode, MV still equals PQ – with Q determined once again by non-monetary considerations, V determined by the preferences of money holders in the context of given institutional considerations, and P standing in direct proportion to M.

The present chapter deals with still another face of Monetarism. Empirical findings that predate the introduction of short-run/long-run Phillips curve analysis serve as the basis for a wholesale rejection of boom–bust theorizing. The timing of these findings together with both early and recent interpretations of their significance lend support to our claim that misperceptions of the real wage rate are not and never have been an essential part of Monetarist doctrine. Similarly, the scope for upward movements in real output and real incomes above the levels associated with the economy's natural rate of employment is judged, on the basis of these empirical findings, to be negligible. It is as if combinations of consumption and investment beyond the production possibilities curve are not merely unsustainable; they are, or so the data suggest, no part of our macroeconomic experience. Alternatively stated, if potential output is set by an unyielding supply-side constraint, then variation around this potential is sharply asymmetrical: output can rise only negligibly above it but can fall dramatically below it.

Friedman's Plucking Model

In a report on research in progress issued more than three decades ago and again in a recent article consisting largely of excerpts from the earlier report, Milton Friedman ([1964] 1969c; 1993) called into question the entire class of business cycle theories that treat boom and subsequent bust as a logical and chronological sequence. The report, published in 1969 as "The Monetary Studies of the National Bureau," was drawn from the National Bureau's 1964 *Annual Report*.

All boom–bust theorizing entails an endogenous upper turning point: what goes up must come down. Although flippant, this quip captures the essence of the theories that Friedman summarily rules out of consideration. His objections are not confined to the bust's alleged inevitability. Replacing the "must come down" with "regularly or usually does come down" makes the claim no more acceptable to him. The chronology itself is being challenged on the basis of macroeconomic data available since the mid-1960s.

The data, according to Friedman, suggest that busts are related chronologically if not logically to *succeeding* booms. What goes down must come up – or, at least, regularly does come up. The "Plucking Model," so named by Friedman, is not actually a model (as that term has come to be used) but rather a convenient and memorable way of describing the temporal pattern in the macroeconomic data. Imagine a piece of string glued to the underside of an inclined plane. The inclined plane itself represents the economy's potential; the string tracks its actual performance. If the string were glued fast at each and every point, then the economy being modeled is one that fully and continuously realizes its potential – the degree of incline representing its rate of secular growth. With actual levels of employment, income and output coinciding with their respective natural, or potential, levels, there are no recessions, depressions, or cycles of any sort.

To get the flavor of the Plucking Model, we must imagine that the string, though not at all elastic (it doesn't spring back when plucked), is stretchable to a considerable extent. It has the consistency of taffy. With this imagery we can depict an economy that does not always realize its full potential. Imagine that our taffy-like string is plucked down at random intervals and to various extents. The string now sags – more seriously over some segments than over others – in each instance where plucked loose from the plane. The vertical distance between string and plane represents the shortfall of the macroeconomic aggregates – all of them – from their potential levels. Figure 11.1 shows three such pluckings over a span of years. The down-sags in Friedman's verbal rendition of the Plucking Model are identified as busts, the up-sags as booms.

In what sense and to what extent would the entire string, made up of still-glued segments alternated with sagging segments, portray the cyclical pattern of output, income and employment of market economies? In a no-growth economy (represented by a horizontal plane), each down-sag would,

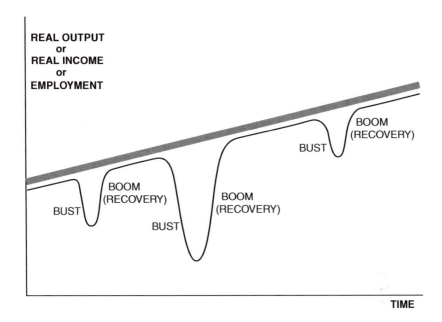

Figure 11.1 Collapse and recovery (Friedman's Plucking Model).

of necessity, be perfectly correlated with the *succeeding* up-sag and, by construction, uncorrelated with the *preceding* up-sag. Allowances for a positive rate of growth and for random disturbances to the growth path weaken this contrast between perfect correlation and no correlation, but data for the United States (1867–1960) suggest that bust–boom correlation is much stronger than boom–bust correlation. In Friedman's judgment, then, explanations of how an economic boom gives way to a bust are not so much incorrect as irrelevant. We need instead a bust–boom theory, an explanation of how market or extra-market forces that pluck the aggregates below their trend line are subsequently overcome by market forces that return them to trend.

The alternatives considered both here and in Friedman's discussion of the Plucking Model are not exhaustive. To contrast boom–bust with bust–boom is to suggest that the business cycle has only one endogenous turning point, and that the relevant question is: Which one? The macroeconomic data considered by Friedman seem to weigh in favor of an endogenous lower turning point and against an endogenous upper turning point. A comprehensive treatment of the alternatives would have to recognize the possibilities of oscillations, in which both turning points are endogenous, and random shocks, which involve no endogeneity. (This latter alternative, of course, characterizes so-called Real Business Cycle Theory, according to which neither string nor plane have any claim on our attention.) Ruling out full endogeneity and no endogeneity, however, allows for a sharp contrast between theories compatible with Friedman's Plucking Model and the theories he summarily dismisses, which include, of course, the capital-based account of boom and bust presented in Chapter 4.

Friedman issues a challenge to anyone willing to accept it to provide empirical evidence bolstering his Plucking Model using data from other countries and more recent data from the United States. Goodwin and Sweeney (1993) take up the challenge and are able to provide some weak support for Friedman's asymmetry hypothesis, as they call it. In a more recent study Kim and Nelson (1999: 317) ran tests on the basis of a formal model and found that "GDP is well characterized by the plucking model . . . [and that there is] no role for symmetric cycles." But does the asymmetry exhibited by, say, output and/or real income actually weigh against our capital-based theorizing about boom and bust? We will argue (1) that even strong empirical support for asymmetry, if based upon conventional macroeconomic aggregates, would not rule out boom–bust theories in general; (2) that the particular theory in this general class of theories that Friedman singles out – that of Ludwig von Mises and the other Austrians – offers special insights as to how a boom–bust market process leaves a trail of bust–boom aggregates; (3) that the asymmetry actually suggests a first-order distinction between Keynesian theory and a class of theories that includes both Monetarism and Austrianism; (4) that Friedman's recent reaffirmation of the Plucking Model confirms our perspective on his own boom–bust theorizing; and (5) that the specific strands of theory most compatible with Friedman's empirical work are Monetary Disequilibrium Theory and some aspects of the seriously misnamed New Keynesian Theory, both of which are compatible with and even complementary to the Austrian theory.

Levels of aggregation

As Friedman (1993: 172) recognizes, the asymmetry that he identifies derives from the fact that there are strict limits to how far the economy's level of employment and inflation-adjusted aggregates (real output and real income) can rise above trend but not so strict limits to how far they can fall below it. The asymmetry does not hold, as he also recognizes, for prices and other dollar-denominated aggregates. We will argue that the production possibilities frontier – or, equivalently, the constraint depicted by the inclined plane of the Plucking Model – implies almost trivially the time pattern of broad-based aggregates that Friedman observes but without the significance that he seems to attach to this asymmetry.

Prerequisite to characterizing different business cycle theories as involving either boom–bust or bust–boom is identifying the level of macroeconomic aggregation at which cyclical patterns are thought to exist. As an empirical matter, a bust–boom pattern at one level of aggregation may entail – but conceal – a boom–bust pattern at another level of aggregation. As a theoretical matter, identifying the appropriate aggregation scheme is as significant as theorizing in terms of the chosen aggregates. The choice of aggregates, in fact, hints importantly at the vision of the macroeconomy that underlies the theory. Implicitly, a macroeconomic modeler is asserting that relationships *within* the chosen aggregates have little claim on our attention in comparison to relationships *among* those aggregates.

On the issue of aggregation, Friedman's own Monetarism deviates in one direction from the conventional Keynesian framework, while Austrianism, which Friedman calls into question, deviates in the other. As discussed in Chapter 2, total spending in the private sector was disaggregated by Keynes into two components – consumption spending and investment spending. The basis for this now-conventional construction is the contrasting stability characteristics of the two components. Consumers are such creatures of habit that current consumption spending is almost wholly predictable on the basis of current income. Investors, who must cope with the "dark forces of time and ignorance that envelop our future" (Keynes, 1936: 155) are almost wholly unpredictable. The stability of consumption spending and the instability of investment spending, thought to be inherent in decentralized decision making, underlies the division of the spending on these two categories of goods into two separate aggregates.

Contemporaneous criticism of the Keynesian construction from the Austrians and the eventual counter-revolution of the Monetarists took exception to the Keynesian vision – but on different grounds. Although investment spending is widely recognized as being a relatively volatile in comparison with consumption spending, Monetarists have always downplayed the distinction between a stable and an allegedly unstable component of private spending. Market forces in both product and factor markets work to keep prices and wages from getting too far out of line with underlying economic realities.

Central to Austrian theorizing is a recognition of the potential for investment decisions getting out of line with underlying economic realities but a denial that the systematic deviations are inherent in the market process. As spelled out in Chapter 4, credit expansion engineered by the central bank can distort the pattern of intertemporal resource allocation. A policy-induced boom, in the Austrian vision, is inherently unsustainable and inevitably ends in a bust as the underlying economic realities do eventually assert themselves.

The Monetarists' and Austrians' choice of aggregation schemes can be traced to the earliest writings of the two schools, where theorizing is based upon a higher (Monetarists) and a lower (Austrians) level of macroeconomic aggregates. The Monetarist vision of macroeconomic relationships suggests the appropriateness of a single aggregate that tracks output or, equivalently, income. The intertemporal allocation of resources and even the division in the current period between consumption and investment spending are thus downplayed as microeconomic issues by the near-exclusive attention to the relationship between the money supply and the general level of prices. The equation of exchange gives little or no play to the relationships of interest to the Austrians or even to those of interest to the Keynesians.

In the judgment of the Austrians, Keynes had disaggregated enough to reveal potential problems in the macroeconomy but not enough to allow for the identification of the nature and source of the problems and the prescription of suitable remedies. By contrast the Monetarists, in the Austrians' judgment, have not disaggregated enough even to reveal the potential problems.

Macroeconomic data and microeconomic doubts

If further substantiated empirically, Friedman indicates, the lack of boom–bust correlation "would cast grave doubt on those theories that see as a source of a deep depression the excesses of the prior expansion [The Mises cycle theory is a clear example]." The bracketed reference to Mises was added by Friedman in 1993. He qualifies his implicit (in [1964] 1969c) and explicit (in 1993) dismissal of Mises's theory with a footnote indicating that "Proponents of the view cited might well argue that what matters is the cumulative effect of several expansions, as we define them, and that the relevant concept of expansion is of a 'major' expansion or a phase of a long cycle." The more relevant qualification, however, would be one that distinguishes not between longer and shorter expansions but rather between expansions discernible at higher and lower levels of macroeconomic aggregation.

Although Friedman (1993: 172) points to Austrian business cycle theory – specifically "the Mises cycle theory" – as a clear example of the class of theories on which his own Plucking Model casts "grave doubt," the data described by the Plucking Model are, in fact, wholly consistent with the Austrian theory. The Austrians – and particularly Mises – always emphasized the *mal*investment that characterizes an artificial boom, the differential effect as between early and late stages of production. Investment in the relatively early stages of production is excessive in that resources are drawn away (by an artificially low rate of interest) from the relatively late stages of production. Empirically, then, the boom would be but weakly reflected in the conventional investment aggregate and hardly at all – except in comparison to periods of economy-wide resource idleness – in an aggregate that also included consumption spending.

The absence of any obvious and dramatic movement beyond the production possibility frontier does not imply that *over*-investment (as contrasted to *mal*investment) is no part of the Austrian account of boom and bust. In fact, the arguments in Chapter 4 suggest that modern Austrians have been too dismissive of this aspect of the account – presumably in their zeal to highlight malinvestment as the unique feature of the Austrian theory. An increased demand for consumption goods can be expected to follow quickly on the heels of the initial increased spending in the early stages. As discussed in Chapter 4, Mises himself refers to the early part of the boom as a period of malinvestment *and* over-consumption. Some period of over-production (unsustainably high levels of both consumption goods and investment goods) is a virtual prerequisite for there being scope for malinvestment (a greater expansion of early-stage production at the expense of later-stage production). Were there no scope at all for a general over-production (a movement beyond the PPF), then the re-equilibrating market forces identified by the Austrians would make themselves felt almost simultaneously with the disequilibrating forces. The boom would be nipped in the bud; the self-reversing process would become, in effect, a self-precluding process.

The issue, however, is not the magnitude of the over-production as compared with possible levels of underproduction. The changing pattern of production during the boom–bust cycle shown in Figure 4.4 is not to be taken as representing the typical or even potential magnitude of over-production. The path undoubtedly hugs the PPF to a much greater extent than shown. Essential to the Austrian theory is the notion that there is a bubbling up beyond the frontier during the boom and a falling below the frontier after the bubble breaks. The potential magnitude and in many cases the actual magnitude of the fall is unquestionably greater than the magnitude of the bubbling up – for the very reasons that Friedman mentions. Further, the magnitude of the bubbling up may not be significantly greater than the irregular expansions of the frontier itself. That is, movements beyond the PPF due to monetary shocks and the expansion of the PPF due to technology shocks are intermingled. Though the two types of movements differ greatly in terms of their economic significance, highly aggregated macroeconomic data, which do not distinguish between them, are bound to make even their combined effect seem small in comparison with the occasional dramatic lapses from full employment.

The self-reversing process highlighted in Austrian theorizing refers to something going on *within* the output aggregate. It is represented in Friedman's Plucking Model not by the preceding up-sag but rather by some portion of a segment of string that Friedman, operating at a higher level of aggregation, identifies as trend-line growth. The bust, even in Austrian theorizing, can affect both the composition and magnitude of the economy's output. Hayek referred to the possible spiraling downwards of demand in all stages, as distinguished from the reallocation of resources among the stages, as a "secondary contraction." But this spiraling downward into "deep depression," to use Friedman's terms, is ultimately linked to the "excesses of the prior expansion," though this latter term, for the Austrians, refers to the policy-induced and hence unsustainable capital restructuring that immediately preceded the bust.

By contrast, the "excesses of the prior expansion," for Friedman, is the preceding up-sag in his Plucking Model. Surely this segment of the string is more accurately described as representing recovery from a prior deep depression. It almost goes without saying that the eventual recovery from Hayek's secondary contraction, matches in magnitude the extent of the contraction measured as an aggregate. Friedman would qualify this match with considerations of secular growth and random shocks; the Austrians would accept these qualifications and add two of their own: first, a full recovery is precluded because some capital is irretrievably lost during the period of intertemporal misallocation, i.e. committed to projects that were eventually abandoned and, to the (limited) extent possible, liquidated. And, second, the redistribution of wealth during the boom–bust cycle can have an effect on the natural rate of interest and hence on the economy's growth rate.

In sum, a boom–bust theory in the sense of policy-induced malinvestment followed by an inevitable capital restructuring and complicated by a secondary contraction leaves, at a higher level of aggregation, a data trail that suggests bust–boom cycles. Friedman's Plucking Model provides no evidence against the Austrians. Ironically, it does provide evidence against the boom–bust theory based on short-run/long-run Phillips curve since that theory adopts the same high level of macroeconomic aggregation depicted by the Plucking Model.

The Plucking Model itself does allow for a key distinction, implicit already in the contrasting of the two schools, as to the perceived nature of the downturn. The focus of the Monetarists is on the exogenous force that does the plucking. A period of presumably healthy economic growth, as represented by a glued section of string, is interrupted by some extra-market force, namely, an inept central bank that allows the money supply to contract, plucking real output loose from its growth path. The focus of the Austrians is on the make-up of the string and the consistency of the glue that holds it to the inclined plane. The string, aggregate output, is made up of diverse resources allocated among the stages of production; the glue can represent the pattern of wage rates and resource prices that holds this intertemporal capital structure together. If an artificially low rate of interest creates a pattern of wage rates and resource prices inconsistent with inter-temporal consumption preferences, the string – and the capital structure – are destined to come unglued. The central bank plays a central role for both Austrians and Monetarists, but while the Monetarists fault it for precipitating the bust through monetary contraction, the Austrians fault it for igniting the boom through credit expansion.

The clearest contrast of monetary histories is that between the Austrian-oriented Benjamin Anderson ([1949] 1979) and Friedman and Schwartz (1963). Judicious application of Austrian and Monetarist theory to central banking history would undoubtedly allow for instances in which one or the other and sometimes both come into play. For instance, Austrian theory may best account for some nineteenth-century downturns and for the downturn at the end of the 1920s easy-money boom; Monetarist theory may best account for the prolonged contraction that followed the initial downturn in 1929 and for the subsequent downturn in 1937, which seems to be wholly attributable to an unexpected and ill-advised monetary contraction.

Ceilings and asymmetries

Goodwin and Sweeney (1993: 178) interpret Friedman as claiming to have identified *two* empirical regularities in the early macroeconomic data: (1) the asymmetry and (2) the ceiling effect. It is not clear, however, that there are two separate effects here. Is it the case that output exhibits an asymmetrical pattern *and* bumps up against an effective ceiling of some sort or that output exhibits an asymmetrical pattern *because* it bumps up against that ceiling? The answer to this question depends, in the first instance, upon whether the effective ceiling is imposed by supply-side or demand-side considerations. On this issue, both the Monetarists and the Austrians take the supply-side, as represented by the production-possibilities frontier, to be the binding constraint. The supply-side orientation is evidence of both schools' general belief in the efficacy of market forces and especially in the Austrians' theorizing about the market process triggered by cheap credit: the early stages are expanded *at the expense of* the late and final stages. There is only limited scope for a simultaneous expansion of all stages – as would be possible under conditions of a general deficiency of effective demand.

If the effective constraint were imposed by demand-side considerations, then the two hypotheses identified by Goodwin and Sweeney would in fact be separable. A demand-side constraint would allow for plucking in both directions – and would leave as an open question whether and how up-side plucking compares to down-side plucking. Keynes's major concern with the market system was precisely that the economy usually finds itself on the demand constraint some distance below the supply constraint, causing employment and output to be chronically below their potential levels. He allowed for some fluctuation of employment and output around their average levels but believed cyclical unemployment to be of minor importance relative to the underlying secular unemployment. The contrast between cyclical unemployment and secular unemployment and the relationship between them was the focus of Chapters 8 and 9.

Keynes's description of the interplay between cyclical and secular components of employment and output suggest symmetry rather than asymmetry. Identifying a fetish-related high interest rate as the proximate cause of the secular problem (decentralized decision making in the face of uncertainty was the ultimate cause), Keynes indicates that "the rate of interest . . . may fluctuate for decades about a level which is chronically too high for full employment" (1936: 204). And the interest rate, according to Keynes, is "subject . . . to fluctuations for all kinds of reasons" (ibid.: 203). There is no hint of asymmetry here. In his stocktaking Chapter 18, Keynes concludes that:

the outstanding features of our actual experience [are that] we oscillate, avoiding the gravest extremes of fluctuation in employment and
in prices in *both* directions, around an intermediate position appreciably
below full employment and appreciably above the minimum employment a decline below which would endanger life.

(ibid.: 254, emphasis mine)

Unlike Friedman (and the Austrians), Keynes sees no need to distinguish
between the temporal pattern of a real magnitude (employment) and that
of a nominal magnitude (prices). Although some special theory might be
added to Keynes's general theory so as to square the Keynesian vision
with the Plucking Model, there is a strong presumption that a demand-
side constraint entails symmetry and that asymmetry implies a supply-side
constraint.

Institutional barriers, such as the imposition of a minimum wage or labor
legislation that gives extra-market powers to unions, can give play to a
demand-constrained process and allow for plucking in the upward direction. Mises ([1958] 1962: 153–5) spelled out a process in which monetary
inflation, in circumstances where the nominal wage rate is held above its
market-clearing level, erodes the real wage rate, thereby permitting an
increase in employment. But the increase is only temporary, Mises points
out, if unions and other special interest groups have the political power to
increase the nominal wage rate so as to compensate for the decrease in the
purchasing power of money. Instances of this and other such politico-econ-
omic boom–bust sequences, should be evident even at the Monetarists' level
of aggregation and may account for some of the weakness of the multi-
country tests for asymmetry.

However, given the general relationship between the nature of the ceiling
and the pattern of macroeconomic variation, the tests performed by Goodwin
and Sweeney and by Kim and Nelson help to determine whether total
output is effectively constrained by a demand-side ceiling or by a supply-
side ceiling. If we can neglect the union-power/minimum-wage episodes
just mentioned, where institutional barriers make the demand-side constraint
binding, these tests help us choose between Keynesianism, on the one hand,
and Monetarism or Austrianism, on the other. They do not help us choose
between Monetarism and Austrianism. That is, the Plucking Model with
its asymmetric variation suggests that Keynes's vision does not fit the facts
but that the facts are consistent with the visions of both Mises and Friedman.

More generally, instances of built-in ceiling effects and the consequent asymmetries are probably all too common – both inside and outside
economics – to be used as an acid test separating theories that square with
reality from those that do not. The limited significance of Friedman's
Plucking Model is suggested by a frivolously analogous model in the field
of medicine. Consider an individual whose health is generally good but who
suffers on occasion from the common cold. Some colds are worse than others,

and our representative individual catches one at random intervals. Bouts of illness in general allow for both major and minor departures from good health in a negative direction, but there are no offsetting bouts of super-health, steroids *et al.* aside, that produce significant departures in the positive direction. The implied temporal pattern of health might even be depicted by what we could call a Sneezing Model. It follows trivially, though, that improvements in healthiness attributable to recovering from a cold corre-late better with the severity of that cold than with the severity of the next cold. But neither noting this fact nor demonstrating it empirically for different countries and different time periods would result in a publication in the *New England Journal of Medicine*. Nor would the time pattern of healthiness have implications for the relevance of explanations that identify cause and effect. Researchers, presumably, are as interested – if not more so – in how a healthy individual catches a cold as in how he or she shakes one off. Excesses in exertion or exposure during a preceding period of apparent good health may figure importantly in our understanding the episodes of poor health despite their non-appearance in the summary reck-oning of healthiness over time. Kim and Nelson (1999: 318) also hit upon this same analogy, but they use it to strengthen the plausibility of the Plucking Model rather than doubt its significance: "Thus, recessions are like the common cold: they come on suddenly and recovery follows a fairly predictable course, but the time that has passed since the last cold is of no use in predicting when the next will occur, or its severity."

Depressions as monetary disequilibrium

It was argued in Chapter 10 that Monetarism in its own boom–bust mode of theorizing can be saved from contradiction by carefully observing the analytical distinction between statics and dynamics. That is, the (static) equation of exchange can be squared with the (dynamic) economic process in which a rising price level (P) gives a boost to real output (Q). Further, the boom–bust theory of Chapter 10 can be squared with the bust–boom data of the present chapter by carefully distinguishing between criticism and advocacy. To show, with special attention to expectations, that policy-induced movements along a short-run Phillips curve would cause the curve itself to shift is not to claim that such movements and counter-movements are the essence of cyclical episodes in the Monetarists' view.

But what is, after all, Friedman's theory of the business cycle? We know that a monetary contraction is what throws the macroeconomy below its supply-side ceiling. But what is the nature of the market process, or trans-mission mechanism, that constitutes the bust–boom sequence? Its general nature is clear from the fundamental and subsidiary propositions of Monetarism. In the beginning, prices adjust hardly at all; in the end, prices adjust fully to the money supply. The theory, then, has to explain what facts of reality preclude instantaneous price adjustments, what factors govern the rate that adjustment takes place, and possibly whether and how some prices adjust more quickly than others. Theoretically satisfying answers to these questions together with some allowance for transient changes in the velocity of money imply the time pattern of quantity adjustments. But explaining non-instantaneous price adjustments in the face of an economy-wide change in nominal demand is precisely the research agenda of so-called New Keynesianism. Such considerations as decision costs and menu costs as well as overlapping contracts and the staggering of wage adjustments are factored into the firm's maximizing behavior to explain how prices eventually get adjusted to a change in market conditions.

The name New Keynesian was first suggested by Michael Parkin (Gordon, 1990: 1115) and accepted by Ball *et al.* (1988). The name is intended to capture in several ways the idea that this school is a hybrid of sorts made up partly of Keynesianism, partly of New Classicism. It shares with New Classicism a commitment to a certain modeling technique. (The "fully articulated artificial economies" are choice-theoretic and mathematically tractable models whose dynamic operating characteristics are often explained – somewhat apologetically – in the form of other-worldly parables.) It shares with Keynesianism the rejection of the idea of continuously clearing markets – as either an approximate fact of reality or a fruitful modeling technique. The "New" does double duty. While juxtaposing technically similar models, one that assumes instantaneous market clearing and the other, non-instantaneous market clearing, it distinguishes models that incorporate non-instantaneous clearing as an *ad hoc* assumption (Old Keynesianism) from those that offer a theoretical explanation for the sluggishness of prices and wages. (In fairness, we should recognize that Keynes offered plenty of reasons for downward price and wage stickiness – but none, apparently, that measure up to the standards of rigor imposed *ex post facto* by the New Keynesians.)

Although the name New Keynesianism appears to be a studied choice, almost engineered to maximize the information content, it is, in the broader sweep of things, a misnomer. (The inappropriateness of the New Keynesian label was first pointed out to me by Leland Yeager.) The alleged link to Keynes (the rejection of instantaneous market clearing) is, in fact, a link also to every other school of thought except for the one idiosyncratic school (New Classicism) that embraces the notion of instantaneous market clearing – which is to say, it is no link at all. Further, the clear focus on the equation of exchange and particularly on the P-Q split – as opposed to a focus on the difference between consumption spending and investment spending – makes it much more appropriate to designate this school as New Monetarism rather than New Keynesianism. But here the "New," as appended to Monetarism, is in partly literal and partly tongue-in-cheek. New Monetarism can be distinguished from Friedman's Monetarism by the change in the locus of agnosticism. From its beginning the New Keynesianism has been concerned almost exclusively with the question of the P-Q split and not at all with the specific source of the change in MV. Answers given are largely independent of whether a change in the money supply or a change in the velocity of circulation underlies the change in nominal demand. But at the same time we must recognize the similarity between the modern modeling of the P-Q split and pre-Friedman analysis of Monetary Disequilibrium as offered by Warburton (1966) and developed more recently by Yeager ([1968] 1997c, [1986] 1997c). What is new here are the standards of rigor that constrain the theorizing about overall price and wage adjustments. In terms of the substantive propositions, however, much of New Keynesianism is a reincarnation of Old Monetarism.

This perspective is almost fully in accord with that of Gregory Mankiw and David Romer, two of the early promoters of New Keynesianism:

> An economist can be a monetarist by believing that fluctuations in the money supply are the primary source of fluctuations in aggregate demand and a new Keynesian by believing that microeconomic imperfections lead to macroeconomic price rigidities. Indeed, since monetarists believe that fluctuations in the money supply have real effects but often leave price rigidities unexplained, much of new Keynesian economics could also be called new monetarist economics.
>
> (Mankiw and Romer, 1991: 3)

Here, the term "microeconomic imperfections" is undoubtedly intended to mean "anything less than perfect price and wage flexibility." Friedman and other Monetarists of his day can be forgiven for not explaining why instantaneous market clearing is not a universal feature of the market economy. Only with the dominance of New Classical thinking and the assumption of "microeconomic perfection" did it become incumbent on those not invoking this assumption to explain why. In the 1960s Friedman and others took rigidities – in the sense of less than perfect flexibility (and with some prices more rigid than others) – to be a well-recognized feature of the market economy. And while Friedman may have left price rigidities unexplained, the still-older Monetarists focused their attention on this very issue – though, again, without the rigor that would satisfy a New Keynesian.

Leland Yeager (1997d: 285–8) reminds us that Old Monetarism has its origins in Richard Cantillon and David Hume and traces to, among others, Harry Gunnison Brown and Clark Warburton. The Old Monetarists' explanation for less-than-perfect price and wage flexibility is not offered in the form of maximizing profits with respect to menu costs or in some other instance of maximization-subject-to-constraint. Rather, price and wage rigidities follow from a few commonplace observations about decentralized decision making in a money-using economy. Money is (rightly) seen as fundamentally a facilitator of exchange and as an institution without which few of the potential gains from trade could be exploited. The social benefits that flow from the existence of a commonly accepted medium of exchange are not to be underestimated. The Old Monetarists are not disputing the overall benefits of money, then, when they also single out the medium of exchange as both the source of economy-wide disequilibrium and as an impediment to a quick and painless return to equilibrium.

Money is the source: "For nothing other than the medium of exchange," according to Yeager (1997d: 229), "could an excess demand be so pervasively disruptive." Logically, the excess demand could arise either from an decrease in the money supply (M) in circumstances where money demand is unchanging or an increase in money demand (1/V) in circumstances where money supply is unchanging. On the basis of historical experience the Old Monetarists, especially Warburton, held that it is a collapse in M and not a fall in V that brings on depression. They recognize, however, that people's reaction to monetary disequilibrium may entail a fall in V – a scramble for liquidity – which, of course, adds to the problems caused by the decrease in the money supply. Yeager (1997d: 219) expresses the possible plunge into deep depression with a mixed metaphor uncharacteristic of his writing: "The rot can snowball." This phase of the cycle is partially captured by the (old) Keynesian idea that the economy spirals downward as the decline in (aggregate) income and declines in (aggregate) expenditures are mutually reinforcing. We can note here that on the issue of cyclical downturns, scrambling for liquidity is seen as (logically) a secondary problem by Monetarists, by Austrians, and even by Keynes. (But, of course, Keynes's notion of an ongoing fetish of liquidity and the associated secular unemployment is quite another matter.)

Money is the impediment to recovery: "the medium of exchange," Yeager (ibid.: 228) points out, "lacks a price and market of its own." This unique characteristic of money is reported by Yeager as a "banal but momentous fact." Imbalances in supply and demand for ordinary goods, such as shoes or shotguns, impinge primarily on the market in which those goods are bought and sold. Although there may be some secondary effects – on the markets for shoelaces and shotgun shells – there are no significant macroeconomic effects. In great contrast, an imbalance in the supply and demand for money impinges on all markets. An excess demand for money (due, say, to a decrease in the money supply) puts downward pressure on all prices. For equilibrium to be re-established, all prices and wages have to adjust downward and can do so only on a piecemeal basis. Complex and far-reaching interdependencies among individual prices and wages, combined with what Yeager (ibid.: 228 and *passim*) calls the who-goes-first problem, preclude a quick and smooth adjustment in their general level. Quantity adjustments on an economy-wide scale, i.e. depression, characterize the period of slow and ragged adjustments in prices and wages. This is Monetary Disequilibrium Theory.

Is this theory suspect on methodological grounds? More specifically, does the lack of "rigor" – as defined by New Keynesians or New Classicists – stand in the way of our accepting any of the these propositions as true and paying due attention to them? Yeager characterizes the claims of Monetary Disequilibrium Theory as:

> propositions for which empirical evidence keeps pressing itself upon us every day in such abundance that only with effort can we even imagine a world where those propositions are not true ... No one will make a scientific reputation by discovering [e.g. that money has no market of its own] of course, but it hardly follows that inescapably familiar facts are by that very token unimportant and deserving of neglect.
>
> (Yeager, 1997d: 245)

There is irony in the fact that an insistence on rigor – in the sense of a fully articulated artificial economy – can easily eclipse the very features of actual economies (i.e. complexity, decentralization, and interdependence) that make the Warburton–Yeager perspective most fully in accord with reality.

Surely, though, Monetary Disequilibrium Theory, as spelled out by Warburton and Yeager, is precisely the theory that best complements Friedman's Plucking Model. The initiating cause of the bust is a decrease in the money supply. The resulting monetary disequilibrium can provoke a scramble for liquidity, intensifying the economy-wide disequilibrium. All the while, piecemeal adjustments in individual prices and wages do nonetheless actually get made. Monetary equilibrium does eventually get re-established as such adjustments have their own effects throughout the economy. The recovery, misidentified by Friedman as a boom, takes the economy back to its potential level of output.

Plucking in the Keynesian and Austrian frameworks

The pattern of macroeconomic variation described by Friedman's Plucking Model and Monetary Disequilibrium Theory as set out by Yeager are wholly compatible. Both make the critical distinction between real and nominal magnitudes that accounts for the general nature of the variation; both adopt a high level of abstraction, giving little or no play even to the division of output between consumption and investment. In Monetary Disequilibrium Theory, an excess demand for money impinges on consumption and investment alike. The piecemeal nature of price and quantity adjustments in both components of output gets an emphasis that overshadows any distinction between the two components. Nevertheless, the bust–boom cycle depicted by the Plucking Model and explained by Monetary Disequilibrium Theory can be traced out using either of our analytical frameworks. Articulating this Old-cum-New Monetarist view of cyclical variation in the contexts of the labor-based and capital-based frameworks helps to illuminate its contrast with (old) Keynesian and Austrian views.

Figure 11.2 shows the macroeconomy in an initial equilibrium as represented by the four solid points – and as would be represented in Friedman's

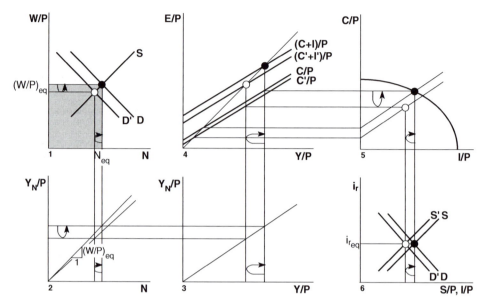

Figure 11.2 Monetary disequilibrium (in the labor-based framework).

Plucking Model by a point somewhere along a portion of the string that is glued fast to the inclined plane. The only plausible source of economy-wide disequilibrium is a decrease in the money supply – stemming most likely from an inept policy move by the central bank. (The argument holds, of course, for circumstances in which it is appropriate to measure the decrease in the money supply relative to established trend line money growth or, more generally, relative to widely held expectations about money growth.) The fact that neither the decrease in the money supply nor the consequent excess money demand are explicitly depicted in Figure 11.2 is consistent with the central feature of the Monetarist vision: money has no market of its own.

Absent perfect wage and price flexibility, quantity adjustments take the economy into the interior of the PPF, as shown in Panel 5 of Figure 11.2. The string in Friedman's Plucking Model has come unglued. Although the plunge into depression has a distinct self-aggravating quality about it, it differs from the Keynesian spiraling down in several ways. First and already noted, the cause of the downward movement is a change in the money supply and not some waning of business confidence. Second, the attempt of market participants to maintain or re-establish their real cash balances impinges directly on consumption as well as on investment. The consumption function of Panel 4 shifts downward as does the demand constraint in Panel 5.

Third, there are no significant interest-rate effects – either as a cause or as a consequence of the lapse into depression. Even a scramble for liquidity that may well accompany – and worsen – the plunge into depression does not impinge in the first instance on interest rates. People achieve greater liquidity partly by reducing their purchases of interest-earning assets (as depicted by a leftward shift in the supply of loanable funds) and partly by reducing their purchases of consumer goods. In turn, the weakened demand for consumer goods weakens the demand for the corresponding investment goods (as depicted by a leftward shift in the demand for loanable funds.) As a first approximation, the interest remains unchanged. Reasons can be offered for actual movements in the interest rate during the bust–boom cycle and for greater variation in investment spending than in consumption spending, but these aspects of the cycle are not at all central to Monetary Disequilibrium Theory.

Fourth, the decrease in the demand for labor, which reflects both a direct real-cash-balance effect and a derived-demand effect, is accompanied by a decrease in the real wage rate. The generally lower real wage rate depicted in Panels 1 and 2 is not meant to suggest a uniform and instantaneous change in the real wage rate. Quite to the contrary, the piecemeal nature of the adjustment process, so central to the Monetarist vision, implies that changes in actual real wage rates will depend on the sequence and extent of decreases in nominal wage rates and in individual prices. Falling prices in the face of nominal wage inflexibility will cause some real wage rates to rise. Considerations of union power, labor legislation and/or market structure may affect the particular pattern of real wage rates over the course of the bust–boom cycle, but such considerations are incidental to the general theory of depression and recovery.

Finally, the depth of the depression is marked in Figure 11.2 by four hollow points – indicating disequilibrium and not some unemployment equilibrium as would characterize the (old) Keynesian vision. The equilibrating process, though piecemeal and therefore sluggish, continues to work. Real cash balances are eventually replenished through decreases in nominal wages and prices while the initial patterns of real wages and relative prices are re-established. The economy returns to it full-employment level, as depicted by the solid points. The string eventually reglues itself to the inclined plane.

The Monetarist story of bust and boom can be told just as well in an Austrian venue. Figure 11.3 allows us to track depression and recovery in the context of a capital structure and stage-specific labor markets. Here the initial macroeconomic equilibrium has the economy on its production possibilities frontier. The intertemporal structure of production involves a discounting of inputs at the various stages that is consistent with the interest rate that equilibrates the market for loanable funds. That is, the slope of the hypotenuse of the Hayekian triangle reflects the equilibrium rate of interest. And labor markets representing early-stage employment and late-stage employment are separately characterized by equilibrium.

Aspects of the process of depression and recovery depicted with the aid of the production possibilities frontier and the market for loanable funds

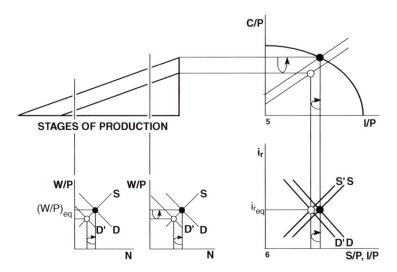

Figure 11.3 Monetary disequilibrium (in the capital-based framework).

are the same as in our discussion of the Monetarist vision as set out in the labor-based framework. Retaining in Panel 5 of Figure 11.3 the initial and shifted (Keynesian) demand constraint emphasizes this equivalence. The remaining elements of Figure 11.3, which feature the intertemporal capital structure, are significant in this application for the absence of any essential relative changes. An unchanged rate of interest in the market for loanable funds implies a Hayekian triangle whose hypotenuse has an unchanged slope. The quantity adjustments that take the economy into depression exhibit no systematic bias with respect to early or late stages of production. The Hayekian triangle shrinks in size but, at least as a first approximation, retains its shape. Accordingly, there are no differential effects on the labor markets in the various stages of production. The extent of the decreases in labor demand, which reflect both a direct real-cash-balance effect and a derived-demand effect, are not systematically stage specific.

The hollow points in Figure 11.3 are intended to indicate the general nature of the economy's movement into depression. They fully allow, however, for the piecemeal nature of the adjustments and hence for the non-uniformity of price, wage-rate, and interest-rate changes. The Monetarist vision can even allow, as an incidental effect, for some changes one way or the other in the shape of the Hayekian triangle and for corresponding changes in the stage-specific labor market. Just as investment spending in general is more volatile than consumption spending, investment spending in the early stages may be more volatile than investment spending in the late stages. But to allow for such changes is not to identify these changes as an essential aspect of the market process that takes the economy into depression and back to its full-employment potential. The essential aspect of the process is the replenishing of real cash balances through wage and price reductions. Once this aspect of the process has played itself out, the economy has recovered from depression. The string and the inclined plane are together again.

It would be possible to retell the story of depression and recovery factoring in misperceptions of the real wage rate during an early phase of the cycle and the correcting of those perceptions in a later phase. That exercise would serve only to reinforce the our claim that the short-run/long-run Phillips curve analysis is an nonessential aspect of the Monetarist vision.

It is fair to say that putting the labor-based framework and then the capital-based framework through their paces to trace out depression and recovery in the Monetarist vision tells us more about what is not happening – or about what possible happenings are inessential – than about what actually does happen. The truth is that the equation of exchange, which is surely the simplest and most abstract reckoning of macroeconomic relationships, is perfectly adequate for understanding the Monetarist vision. Interest rates aside, differences between consumption and investment aside, notions of an intertemporal structure of production aside, $MV = PQ$. A decrease in M in the face of an unchanging V means a downward movement in PQ. To the extent that P does not fall uniformly and in proportion to M (and how could it?), Q falls instead. A falling Q may well cause V to fall, as people aim for abnormally high levels of cash balances. This scramble for liquidity causes PQ to fall even further – again, with Q falling to the extent that the downward adjustment in P is sluggish. Eventually, the decrease in M gets fully translated into decreases in P, and Q rebounds to its full potential. These movements in each of the variables that make up the equation of exchange are perfectly consistent with Friedman's Plucking Model, and the idea that this process is more likely to take eighteen months than to take eighteen days or eighteen minutes is made plausible by the commonplace propositions of Monetary Disequilibrium Theory.

Rival theories?

Is there any sense in which the Austrian theory of the business cycle is a rival of Monetary Disequilibrium Theory? Yeager, who offers an exceedingly harsh appraisal of the Austrian theory, clearly thinks so. "Some economists," Yeager (1997d: 230) writes, "may consider [the Austrian theory of the business cycle] too unfamiliar, outmoded, or preposterous to be worth any further consideration." He does offer a few considerations, however, with the aim of supporting Austrianism generally by "helping rid it of an embarrassing excrescence."

Our own understanding of Austrianism and Monetarism suggests that there is no direct rivalry between a theory of the unsustainable boom and a theory of depression. Yeager (1997d: 254), however, takes the Austrians and the Monetarists as offering rival theories of depression. "[The Austrian theory] blames recession or depression on a preceding excessive expansion of money and credit." Here we see that while Friedman misidentified the Austrians' understanding of the cause of cyclical downturns, taking the recovery from the previous depression as the boom, Yeager misidentifies the proximate consequence of credit expansion, taking the depression itself (rather than the intertemporal discoordination and hence the inevitable crisis and downturn) to be the focus of the theory. It is true that the depression that is likely to ensue can be deeper and longer-lasting than the initiating cause would imply. But this is only to say that the Austrian theory is not a theory of depression *per se* but rather a theory of the unsustainable boom. Lionel Robbins's *Great Depression* (1934) was written well before the depression had run its course. And significantly, Rothbard's *America's Great Depression* ([1963] 1972), despite its title, dealt with events only through 1932.

When Yeager (1997: 232) does recognize that the Austrian theory is not a theory of depression, he seems to fault it for not being one.

> It does not explain and hardly even purports to explain the ensuing depression phase. . . . Austrian economists can explain the continuing depression only lamely, mentioning maladjustments being worked out painfully over time – unless they invoke a "secondary deflation," meaning monetary factors going beyond their own distinctive theory.

Undoubtedly, the fact that Keynes was (in Hayek's view) over-emphasizing the self-aggravating downward spiral into depression explains why Hayek and other Austrians tend to de-emphasize it – except in explaining how a bad situation could get worse. More to the point, we can acknowledge that the Austrian theory is a distinctive one – and that it is distinctive in a way that complements – rather than rivals – Monetary Disequilibrium Theory.

Yeager's own understanding of the source of macroeconomic disequilibrium provides a basis for establishing the complementarity. As quoted earlier, he simply asserts: "For nothing other than the medium of exchange . . . could an excess demand be so pervasively disruptive." For theories based narrowly on the equation of exchange and its summary accounting for output, Yeager's "nothing other" might seem plausible. But capital-based macroeconomics takes one step in the direction of disaggregation and finds something else – a general mismatch between intertemporal preferences and intertemporal production plans – that can be "pervasively disruptive." An artificially low interest rate during the boom implies an excess demand for investment goods (the excessiveness being particularly pronounced in the earlier stages of production). The market process that gives play to this excess demand but eventually eliminates it generates a pattern of boom and bust. But rather than recognize the process identified by the Austrians as a plausible and (at least sometimes) significant aspect of cyclical episodes, Yeager dismisses the theory as "conceivable but incomplete" and "unnecessarily specific" – and then goes on to invoke Occam's razor as a basis for rejecting the Austrian theory and reaffirming Monetary Disequilibrium Theory (1997d: 232).

Interlocking pieces of the macroeconomic puzzle

Drawing from both economics and political science, we have a firm basis for distinguishing allies and rivals in macroeconomics. Some macroeconomic theories reflect the belief that the market system doesn't work – or that it works perversely or too sluggishly. The economy generally finds itself inside the production possibility frontier. At the very least, activist macroeconomic policy is required to drive the economy to its full-employment level of output, after which stabilization policy is essential to keep the economy from overheating or lapsing into depression. At most – following Keynes into his final chapter of the *General Theory* – the decentralized decision making of the market must be replaced by centralized decision making in order to put an end once and for all to the instabilities associated with the private pursuit of profits in a economic environment where uncertainties about the future and interdependencies among selfishly motivated economic actions dominate.

Other macroeconomic theories reflect the belief that the market system does work. The interplay among individual decision makers, each of whom is striving to make the fullest use of his or her own resources and capabilities, generates and continually updates the needed information – in the forms of prices, wage rates, and interest rates – that can guide the economy along a sustainable growth path. Left to its own devices, the market economy will generally find itself on the production possibility frontier and producing a combination of consumption goods and investment goods that are consistent with people's willingness to save. The market economy is vulnerable, however, to ill-conceived macroeconomic policy. Policies that affect markets on an economy-wide scale – such as unanticipated changes in the money supply or monetary manipulations of the rate of interest – rarely if ever affect it for the good. The economy does good enough on its own. It is already on the PPF and is producing the appropriate combination of consumption and investment goods – or at least its market forces were already pushing in that direction. Activist macroeconomic policy, then, is likely to be counterproductive. It may push the economy beyond the frontier or into the interior. Macroeconomists who share this general view of market forces and policy activism are – should be – natural allies.

Differences among the macroeconomic theories that are consistent with this general view stem partly from differences in views about the particular nature of the economy-wide disturbance. A price level not in accord with the existing money supply has one set of implications; an interest rate not in accord with people's saving preferences has another. Differences in theories can also stem from a difference in focus. A boom–bust theory need not be in competition with a bust–boom (or depression–recovery) theory.

A comparison of Austrian and Monetarist views suggests strong elements of complementarity. Possibly the most obvious comparison (taking for the sake of comparison Chapter 10, rather than the present chapter, to be the essence of Monetarism) is one that focuses on the initial movement of the economy beyond the PPF during the early phase of a boom–bust cycle. Here we compare the Austrian theory of the business cycle as depicted in Figure 4.4 with the Monetarist theory as depicted in Figures 10.5 and 10.6. Both theories identify monetary stimulation as the cause of the artificial boom; both identify a self-reversing market process that turns boom into bust. The key differences are in terms of the focus and applicability. The Austrians focus on the distortion of the interest rate that monetary expansion entails. That is, the money is injected through credit markets and impinges in the first instance on interest rates and hence on the inter-temporal pattern of investment. The Monetarists focus on the effects of excessive cash balances first on output and then on the price level and on the scope for disequilibrium in labor markets, where workers may be slow to perceive changes in the real wage rate in an inflationary environment.

In many boom–bust episodes, the Austrian theory and the Monetarist theory may both be applicable. The market may have to adjust simultaneously for misperceived wage rates, for excessively large real cash balances, and for excessively cheap credit. It seems implausible, for that matter, that there could be significant scope for the economy to be pushed beyond the PPF (as shown, for instance, in Figure 10.6) without there being at the same time significant scope for the economy to be pushed away from the preferred mix of consumption and investment (as shown in Figure 4.4). But in some episodes, imagined or real, it is possible that only one of the theories would be applicable. For instance, if the injection of money did not involve credit markets (Friedman's fanciful assumption of money being dropped from a helicopter comes to mind here), then Monetarist theory would apply but the Austrian theory would not.

Suppose, however, that monetary stimulation occurs during a period that was already experiencing rapid growth due to technological advance. Rising cash balances, then, would not necessarily be excessive; the price level may rise but little if at all and hence would not be a source of real-wage-rate misperception. Nonetheless, if money was lent into existence during this period, credit would be artificially cheap and the pattern of investment would be affected accordingly. The Austrian theory would apply but the Monetarist theory would not. The primary example of these circumstances is the 1920s, a period during which the Federal Reserve first turned its attention to the business of fostering prosperity in a peacetime economy. Bellante and Garrison (1988), Sechrest (1997) and Horwitz (2000) further explore similarities and differences between the Austrian theory of the business cycle and the corresponding Monetarist theory.

When the focus shifts to the issues of depression and recovery, we continue to see Austrians and Monetarists largely as allies. At the highest level of aggregation, apparent bust–boom cycles – or, more accurately, depression and recovery – tend to dominate the time-series data. The proximate cause of a deep depression is likely to be a collapse of the money supply. But did the collapse occur (a) in the midst of a period of healthy growth because of sheer ineptness of the central bank or (b) near the end of a policy-induced boom that was unsustainable in any event and in the midst of confusion about just what the problem was and how best to deal with it? This is the question that separates the Monetarists (a) from the Austrians (b).

Monetarists have documented the centrality of money in explaining the dramatic downturns observed in different countries and in different time periods. The common pattern of the downturns themselves formed the empirical basis for Friedman's Plucking Model. However, the theory of just how reductions in the money supply have dramatic and lasting real effects must be drawn from the Monetarism of Warburton and Yeager, as discussed earlier in the present chapter, or even from the Austrian ideas about capital that Friedman uses to account for the otherwise implausible lags.

Markets work but can be disrupted by ill-conceived macroeconomic policy. Both the Austrians and the Monetarists provide insights about just how. Raburn Williams tells "the stories," as he calls them, in his *Politics of Boom and Bust in Twentieth-Century America: A Macroeconomic History* (1994). He draws appropriately from Benjamin Anderson's *Economics and the Public Welfare* ([1949], 1979), which takes an Austrian point of view, and from Friedman and Schwartz's *Monetary History of the United States, 1867–1960* (1963). He weaves together a coherent account of the various cyclical episodes (including consecutive chapters on "The Great Bull Market" and "The Great Depression" – and thereby demonstrates the essential compatibility of Austrian and Monetarist ideas. Historian Paul Johnson (1997), who has a full appreciation of Monetarism, adds further to the plausibility of the Austrian theory by weaving the story of credit expansion during the inter-war period into his *History of the American People*.

Part V

Perspective

12 Macroeconomics

Taxonomy and perspective

Capital-based macroeconomics in perspective

The macroeconomics of capital structure is not intended as a substitute for all other macroeconomic constructions. But the issues highlighted by it do deserve attention both in elementary treatments of macroeconomic relationships and in advanced theorizing. Any theoretical construction that makes a first-order distinction between consumption and investment is fundamentally deficient if it does not recognize the teleological and temporal relationships between these two magnitudes: we invest now in order to consume later. No school of thought actually denies this means-ends connection. Even Keynes (1936: 104) writes, "Consumption – to repeat the obvious – is the sole end and object of all economic activity." Similarly, no school can deny that production takes time. But does the existence and variability of production time have a first-order claim on our attention? This is the issue that separates the schools of thought. Conventional macroeconomics makes the assumption that this time dimension can safely be ignored in dealing with short-run variations in output and employment; Austrian macroeconomics takes production time to be a foundational concern. The implications of a variable production time and of the possibility of a mismatch between intertemporal production decisions and preferred intertemporal consumption patterns give both substance and flavor to capital-based macroeconomics.

Figure 12.1 offers a six-panel reckoning of the contrasting treatments of the relationship between consumption and investment. The significance of the production possibilities frontier is traced from the Classical thought that served as a foil for Keynes to so-called New Classical thought, which has turned foil into high theory. Arranged in rough chronological order, panels A through F are laid out in a lazy-S sequence to facilitate groupings and comparisons.

Panel A depicts the Classical vision – a vision in which a fully employed economy experiences secular growth. In each period, the economy is on its production possibilities frontier; in the current period it has the potential (as indicated by the arrows) of moving along the frontier. This is the severely

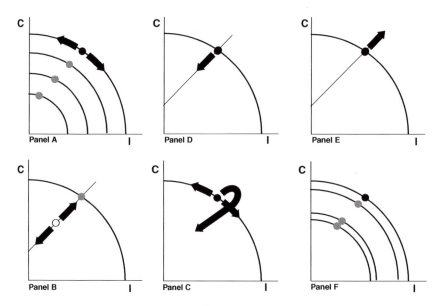

Figure 12.1 A graphical taxonomy of visions.

Panel A: The Classical vision (secular growth with full employment); Panel B: The Keynesian vision (cyclical variation of resource idleness); Panel C: The Austrian vision (preference-based and policy-induced variatons); Panel D: The Monetarist vision (depression as monetary dis-equilibrium); Panel E: The Monetarist/New Classical vision (money-induced misperceptions); Panel F: The New Classical vision (growth without trends or cycles).

over-simplified portrayal of Classical thinking that best served Keynes's purposes. It is true, however, that the long-run orientation of the classical economists caused them to downplay the unemployment and other inefficiencies associated with the market process that adjusts prices and wages in the face of changes in the underlying economic conditions. They focused instead on the factors that affect the economy's long-run growth rate.

Much of the writing of the quintessential Classical economists (Smith, Ricardo, and Mill) dealt directly or indirectly with possible movements along the production possibilities frontier. Smith's distinction between productive and unproductive labor, for instance, is best understood as a distinction between capital-creating labor (i.e. investment) which can move the economy clockwise along the frontier and enable more rapid growth, and service-rendering labor (i.e. consumption), which can move the economy counter-clockwise along the frontier, retarding its growth. In his treatment of the substitutability of machinery and labor, Ricardo argued to similar effect. Machinery represents the long-term factor that permits production for the distant future; labor represents the short-term factor aimed at more immediate consumption. A change in the rate of interest will change the optimal mix of machinery and labor. A lower interest rate will favor machinery over labor, which will enable the economy to grow at a more rapid rate.

The variability of the time element in the production process underlies Mill's Fourth Fundamental Proposition respecting capital: "Demand for commodities is not demand for labour" (Mill, [1848] 1895: 65). His elaboration of this cryptic aphorism links his ideas to Ricardo's and Smith's. Today's demand for commodities, i.e. for consumption goods, "determines the direction of labour; but not the more or less of labour itself." The market process transforms a reduction in the demand for current consumption into an increase in the demand for productive capacity and hence an increase in the supply of future consumption goods. In other words, a change in the demand for current consumption moves the economy *along* the production possibilities frontier.

Panel B depicts the Keynesian vision and the double contrast between the *General Theory* and the theories of Smith, Ricardo, and Mill: (1) the economy is *generally* not on the production possibilities frontier; and (2) consumption and investment *generally* move together rather than in opposition. The assumption of a fixed structure of industry, invoked in Keynes's Chapter 4, effectively overturned Mill's Fourth Fundamental Proposition. With clockwise and counter-clockwise movements ruled out, the demand for commodities *is* the demand for labor. Or less cryptically, the assumption of structural fixity implies – almost trivially – that the demand for labor moves in lockstep with the demand for final output. Keynes squared his vision with the classical vision by making a sharp distinction between the short run, during which all the pressing policy issues arise, and the long run, in which the classical theory "comes into its own." If well-chosen monetary and fiscal policies can move the economy to the frontier and keep it there, then classical theory can account for movements, if any, along the frontier.

Panel C depicts the Austrian vision, which allows for a contrast between preference-based and policy-induced variations in consumption and investment. Arguments employed by the Austrians draw importantly from the classical school. Hayek (1942), for instance, elaborated upon Ricardo's insight about the substitutability of machinery and labor in the context of early and late stages of production. He dubbed the reallocation of resources during the course of the business cycle the "Ricardo Effect." During the upswing of the cycle, an artificially low rate of interest favors machinery over labor. Using the Austrian construction, Hayek would say that the low interest rate favors early-stage activities over late-stage activities. As the production process moves forward in time, capital shortages are experienced in the late stages of production – shortages that eventually bring on the downturn and reverse the direction of resource allocation.

The problem of policy-induced intertemporal discoordination can easily get compounded by a loss of business confidence and/or by a collapse of the banking system. These complicating factors can cause the economy to suffer a general economic contraction. The Austrian theory, then, can serve as a bridge between the classical and Keynesian visions. That is, it shows how a misguided – or politically-motivated – macroeconomic policy can cause an economy that initially is functioning in accordance with the classical vision to become dysfunctional in the very sense envisioned by Keynes.

Comparisons of "Keynes and the Classics" that are based on the competing visions depicted in Panels A and B inevitably favor Keynes. His view of the relationship between consumption and investment seems to be both descriptive (of an economy suffering from depression) and relevant (to prescribing policy for restoring prosperity). Smith and Ricardo – especially if we capsulize their ideas as Panel A – seem largely irrelevant. It is well known, however, that Keynes applied the term "classical" in the broadest possible sense. As used in his *General Theory* the term readily translates as "pre-Keynesian" or "non-Keynesian" and certainly includes Keynes's contemporaries, such as Mises and Hayek. Comparisons of "Keynes and the Classics" that are based on the competing visions depicted in Panels B and C cannot help but put Keynes in an unfavorable light. In fact, the Austrian theory has the stronger claim to being the more "general," showing how, in the absence of disruptive policy, the economy can function as depicted in Panel A and how, in the aftermath of a policy-induced boom–bust episode, the economy can function as depicted in Panel B. Keynesian theory, then, becomes a special case of Austrian theory. Keynes, by contrast, could not incorporate the movements depicted in Panel C into his own theory. Consumption and investment simply do not move in opposite directions in his vision. When specifically contemplating the possibility of forced saving being attributable to an artificially low rate of interest, Keynes (1936: 183) could only borrow some imagery from Ibsen and write:

> [A]t this point we are in deep water. The wild duck has dived down to the bottom – as deep as she can get – and bitten fast hold of the weed and tangle and all the rubbish that is down there, and it would need an extraordinarily clever dog to dive down and fish her up again.

His own framework was simply not up to the task of analysing policy-induced changes in resource allocation that are inconsistent with intertemporal preferences.

Panel D depicts one aspect of the Monetarists' vision. A decrease in the money supply – or, much less likely, an increase in the demand for money – can cause the economy to sink into depression. That is, except in the implausible case in which prices and wages adjust downward quickly and smoothly to conform to the lower money supply, the economy will experience quantity adjustments. Output and employment will fall. The economy can eventually recover on its own as prices and wages do eventually adjust, but the recovery may be a slow and painful one. In some quarters of the greater Monetarist school, countercyclical monetary and fiscal policies may be worthy of consideration. A comparison of Panels B and D shows why the economists of the early Chicago School were not particularly impressed with Keynes (Davis, 1971). They believed themselves to be fully capable of recognizing depressed conditions when they saw them and even of prescribing the right medicine for recovery. Differences seemed to be confined to the issue of which conditions were considered "normal" and which "abnormal".

A comparison of Panels C and D helps to put this aspect of the Monetarists' vision into perspective. Under what conditions is the money supply likely to fall? Panel D gives us no hints: if, *for whatever reason*, the money supply falls, so too will output and employment. Panel C suggests that the money supply is particularly susceptible to collapse when policy-makers are trying to cope with the final throes of a policy-induced artificial boom. Intertemporal discoordination of economic activity, waning confidence on the part of the business community, and indecision of the monetary authority can set the stage for a collapse of the money supply. And the decrease in the quantity of money, which puts downward pressure on all prices at the very time that systematic adjustments in relative prices are underway, can make the depression much more severe than would otherwise have been.

Panel E depicts the aspect of the Monetarists' vision that became dominant in the late 1960s, when attention had shifted from depression to inflation. Monetary expansion can push the economy beyond the production possibilities frontier. The increased spending manifests itself initially as an increase in real output and employment but ultimately as an increase in prices and nominal wage rates. The slow-but-sure adjustment in price-level expectations held by the worker/consumer governs the labor-market dynamics of the boom–bust cycle. With capital theory no part of the analysis, the division of output between consumption and investment is largely beside the point. The economy experiences an unsustainable boom by (1) pushing beyond the frontier (with both investment and consumption increasing) and then (2) retracing its steps back to the frontier.

A comparison of Panels B, D, and E allows us to tease out the various meanings of Friedman's oft-quoted remark that "We're all Keynesians, now." The "all" especially in the context of the late 1960s, when the remark was made, should be interpreted as "all mainstream macroeconomists." Panels B, D, and E each feature the Keynesian demand constraint, which defines the domain over which macroeconomic variation can take place. Totally missing from these panels – along with capital theory in general – are the Ricardo Effect, Mill's Fourth, Mises's malinvestment, and Hayek's forced savings. Friedman intended by his remark to embrace the Keynesian framework while leaving room for disagreement on several key issues – the reasons that the economy might sometimes not be at full employment, the ability of the market to get the economy back to full employment, and the advisability of activist fiscal and monetary policy.

By making a minor – but telling – qualification, Panel E can also depict the monetary misperception theory of business cycles put forth by Robert Lucas's New Classicism. With the maturing of Monetarism, expectations –

about movements in the general price level – had become the whole story. The increasingly narrow focus on expectations allowed the distinction between consumption and investment to drop out of the picture altogether. Interpreted in New Classical terms, then, the movement shown in Panel E is significant only for the temporary departure from the economy's sustainable level of output and not at all for the mix of investment and consumption. The so-called Lucas supply curve allows the economy's output (conceived as a single service indistinguishable from the labor that renders it) to respond positively to an increase in the price of output during the period that the suppliers are determining whether the price increase reflects a real increase in demand or only an increase in the money supply. The similarities of Monetarism (in the form of adaptive expectations in labor markets) and New Classicism (in the form of monetary misperceptions) serve to emphasize the irrelevance to either theory of the trade-off between consumption and investment.

Finally, Panel F depicts the New Classical vision in the form of real business cycle theory. Markets are assumed always to be in equilibrium. And possible movements along the frontier are typically ruled out of consideration by construction. This theory assigns little or no role to money in explaining observed variations in output and employment. Instead of explaining apparent departures from the production possibilities frontier in terms of monetary misperceptions, it simply denies that there are any actual departures. Outward movements that look like boom–bust cycles are to be accounted for by a frontier that itself shifts in irregular increments. The adherence to a particular modeling technique and the focus on an undifferentiated output variable have precluded any attention to the ideas that separate Keynesian views from Austrian and (old) Classical views.

Not all Monetarists have followed the research program from Panel E to Panel F. Friedman in particular has found the New Classical constructions less than satisfying. Largely on the basis of time series data, he has reaffirmed the vision of the economy depicted in Panel D by reintroducing his Plucking Model of business cycles. Meanwhile, the so-called New Keynesians have modified the New Classical constructions by jettisoning the assumption of continuous market clearing. By allowing for certain price and wage rigidities, this diverse school has been able to rescue at least some of the substantive issues.

But the issues that were dominant in the debate between Keynes and Hayek are no less relevant today. Unfortunately, the development of macroeconomics – from Panel C to Panels D through F – has had the effect of de-emphasizing and then precluding altogether the relative movements in consumption and investment. Allowing even for the possibility that disequilibrium between these two magnitudes – and within the investment magnitude – can help account for cyclical variation requires that we back track to the capital-based macroeconomics of the Austrian School.

Visions, frameworks, and judgments

After having identified and depicted a half-dozen different visions of the relationship between consumption and investment, we can return to the broader distinction between capital-based analytical frameworks (Panels A and C) and labor-based analytical frameworks (Panels B, D, E, and F). Note that only Panels A and C feature movements along the production possibilities frontier. If we narrow our focus to the visions that feature cyclical variation as disequilibrium phenomena, our distinction is one that separates the Austrian vision (Panel C) from the Keynesian and Monetarist visions (Panels B, D, and E); this is the distinction that separates the analytics in Chapters 3 through 6 from the analytics in Chapters 7 through 11.

But if we turn from the question "What market forces are in play?" to the question "Are those market forces prone to fail?," we get a different categorization. On the issue of the general efficacy of decentralized decision making, the most obvious contrast is the one that pits the Keynesians against the Austrians and Monetarists. The questions pertaining to analytical orientation and to broad judgments about the efficacy of market economies can be transformed into two sentence-completion statements to give us a two-by-two matrix. (1) The issues of macroeconomic coordination are best analyzed by focusing on the market mechanisms governing (capital, labor); and (2) decentralized decision making is likely to result in macroeconomic (coordination, discoordination).

Figure 12.2 shows that we have a full complement of positions. The names that appear in the individual cells are chosen to epitomize the particular combination of choices in the sentence-completion exercise. In three of the four instances, however, these individuals have plenty of cellmates. Hayek represents Austrians generally – with the exception of Lachmann. Friedman enjoys the company of most all other monetarists as well as the older monetary disequilibrium theorists (Warburton) and some New Classical economists (Lucas). Keynes represents Keynesianism in most all its modern manifestations. And Lachmann shares his cell with Shackle.

**BROAD JUDGMENTS
ABOUT MARKET ECONOMIES**

Decentralized decisionmaking is
likely to result in macroeconomic:

		COORDINATION	DISCOORDINATION
ANALYTICAL ORIENTATION The issues of macroeconomic coordination are best analyzed by focusing on the market(s) for:	CAPITAL	**HAYEK**	**LACHMANN**
	LABOR	**FRIEDMAN**	**KEYNES**

Figure 12.2 A matrix of frameworks and judgments.

We can make several comparisons on the basis of our two-way distinction, some of which are well established and some of which become apparent – or, at least, more apparent – with the aid of the arguments presented in this book.

First, we note that the columns contain political allies; the rows contain analytical allies. When Friedman remarked that "We're all Keynesians now," he meant that he and Keynes were rowmates. He later complained of being misinterpreted, indicating, in effect, that he was taken to mean that he and Keynes were columnmates. By contrast, when Richard Nixon made essentially the same remark in the early 1970s, he did mean that he and, more broadly, the macroeconomic policy-makers of both the Democratic and Republican Parties were columnmates to Keynes – that they all were committed to using fiscal and monetary policies to shore up the otherwise unstable macroeconomy.

Second, we see how Lucas can credit his columnmate Hayek with conceiving of the price system as a communication network, identifying the signal-extraction problem, and pioneering the monetary-misperception theory of business cycles, yet ally himself (implicitly) with his rowmate Keynes: "I see no way of explaining the cyclical variation of output except in terms of the intertemporal substitutability of labor." Had Lucas been Hayek's rowmate as well as columnmate, he might have considered an explanation in terms of the intertemporal substitutability (and complementarity) of capital.

Third, we see how Lachmann can be categorized as an Austrian ("The production process is facilitated by a structure of heterogeneous capital goods") and at the same time a Keynesian ("We live in a kaleidic society"). A long-time admirer of Keynes, Lachmann never tired of repeating his claim that "the future is unknowable but not unimaginable." He refrained from imagining away the problem of intertemporal coordination and from asserting the inherent perversity of the market process. He simply left us with the open question of whether or not we can count upon equilibrium forces to coordinate intertemporally. The flavor of his writings, however, suggests that this question will remain an open one for some time to come: even the assertion of a 'tendency' towards equilibrium has to be qualified in his view with understanding that this tendency is one among others. But the final chapter of his *Capital and Its Structure* reads like a program for policy activism. Are we to believe that the future is a little less unknowable to Keynesian policy-makers than to market participants?

Finally, we can see why the early as well as the ongoing debates between the Austrians and the Keynesians have proven so difficult to resolve. Diagonally opposed in our two-by-two reckoning, Hayek and Keynes argued about whether or not markets work and at the same time about just which markets were the most appropriate focus for settling their differences. On reflection, we may be grateful that the economics profession was not treated to similarly protracted debates between, say, the diagonally opposed Friedman and Lachmann.

While these comparisons and observations tend to be mutually reinforcing, they are not individually novel. They conform to common perceptions of the relationships among these different schools of thought. However, the capital-based macroeconomics presented in Chapters 3 and 4 and the comparison of frameworks facilitated by Chapters 7 and 8 allow for an observation that conflicts with the common perception. It is the common view that the Monetarists reach their conclusions on the basis of scientific (i.e. empirical) investigations while the Austrians' conclusions derive largely from their ideology. In fact, the opposite view is more nearly correct. By adopting the Keynesian labor-based framework, the Monetarists are hardly in a position to dispute with the Keynesians about the market mechanisms that keep the macroeconomy on track. The Austrians are in much the better position to identify the relevant market forces that underlie their judgment that decentralized decision making facilitates coordination – including especially intertemporal coordination – and that government policies aimed at "growing the economy" lead to discoordination. While it is appropriate to contrast the Monetarists and the Keynesians, as Leijonhufvud (1981a: 297ff.) does, in terms of their respective "belief systems," it is appropriate to contrast the Austrians and the Keynesians in terms of their respective understandings of the nature of market process.

Bibliography

Anderson, B. ([1949] 1979) *Economics and the Public Welfare: A Financial History of the United States, 1914–1946*, Indianapolis: Liberty Press.

Ball, L., Mankiw, N., and Romer, D. (1988) "The New Keynesian Economics and the Output-Inflation Trade-Off," *Brookings Papers on Economic Activity*, 1, 1–65.

Barro, R. (1974) "Are Government Bonds Net Wealth?" *Journal of Political Economy*, 82(6), 1095–117.

—— (1981) *Money, Expectations and Business Cycles*, New York: Academic Press.

Bellante, D. and Garrison, R. (1988) "Phillips Curves and Hayekian Triangles: Two Perspectives on Monetary Dynamics," *History of Political Economy*, 20(2), 207–34.

Birch, D., Rabin, A., and Yeager, L. (1982) "Inflation, Output, and Employment: Some Clarifications," *Economic Inquiry*, 20(2), 209–21.

Birner, J. (1990) "Strategies and Programmes in Capital Theory: A Contribution to the Methodology of Theory Development," doctoral dissertation, University of Amsterdam.

Böhm-Bawerk, E. ([1884, 1889, and 1909] 1959) *Capital and Interest*, 3 vols, South Holland, IL: Libertarian Press.

Brenner, R. (1994) "Macroeconomics: The Masks of Science and Myths of Good Policies," in D. Colander and R. Brenner (eds) *Educating Economists*, Ann Arbor, MI: University of Michigan Press, 123–51.

Brimelow, P. (1982) "Talking Money with Milton Friedman," *Barron's*, 25 October, 6–7.

Buchanan, J. (1976) "Barro on the Ricardian Equivalence Theorem," *Journal of Political Economy*, 84(2), 337–42.

Butos, W. (1997) "Toward an Austrian Theory of Expectations,"*Advances in Austrian Economics*, 4, 75–94.

Budget of the United States: Historical Tables, Fiscal Year 1998, Washington, DC: US Printing Office

Butos, W. and Koppl, R. (1993) "Hayekian Expectations: Theory and Empirical Applications," *Constitutional Political Economy*, 4(3), 303–29.

Caldwell, B. (1995) "Introduction," in B. Caldwell (ed.) *Contra Keynes and Cambridge*, Chicago: University of Chicago Press, 1–48.

Cassel, G. (1903) *The Nature and Necessity of Interest*, London: Macmillan.

Chick, V. (1973) *The Theory of Monetary Policy*, London: Gray-Mills Publishing.

Cochran, J. and Glahe, F. (1999) *The Hayek-Keynes Debate: Lessons for Current Business Cycle Research*, Lampeter, Wales: Edwin Mellen.

Coddington, A. (1982) "Deficient Foresight: A Troublesome Theme in Keynesian Economics," *American Economic Review*, 72(3), 480–7.

Cowen, T. (1997) *Risk and Business Cycles: New and Old Austrian Perspectives*, London: Routledge.

Davis, J. (1971) *The New Economics and the Old Economists*, Ames, IA: Iowa State University Press.

Figgie, H. (1992) *Bankruptcy 1995: The Coming Collapse of America and How to Stop It*, Boston: Little, Brown and Co.

Foss, N. (1994) *The Austrian School of Modern Economics: Essays in Reassessment*, Copenhagen: Handelshojskolens.

Friedman, M. (1968) *Dollars and Deficits: Living with America's Economic Problems*, Englewood Cliffs, NJ: Prentice Hall.

—— ([1956] 1969a) "The Quantity Theory of Money: A Restatement," in M. Friedman, *The Optimum Quantity of Money and Other Essays*, Chicago: Aldine, 51–67.

—— ([1961] 1969b) "The Lag Effect in Monetary Policy," in M. Friedman, *The Optimum Quantity of Money and Other Essays*, Chicago: Aldine, 237–60.

—— ([1963] 1969) "Money and Business Cycles," in M. Friedman, *The Optimum Quantity of Money and Other Essays*, Chicago: Aldine, 189–235.

—— ([1964] 1969c) "Monetary Studies of the National Bureau," in M. Friedman, *The Optimum Quantity of Money and Other Essays*, Chicago: Aldine, 261–184.

—— ([1968] 1969d) "The Role of Monetary Policy," in M. Friedman, *The Optimum Quantity of Money and Other Essays*, Chicago: Aldine, 95–110.

—— (1970a) "A Theoretical Framework for Monetary Analysis," in R. Gordon (ed.) *Milton Friedman's Monetary Framework: A Debate with His Critics*, Chicago: University of Chicago Press, 1–62.

—— (1970b) "Comments on the Critics," in R. Gordon (ed.) *Milton Friedman's Monetary Framework: A Debate with His Critics*, Chicago: University of Chicago Press, 132–72.

—— (1970c) *The Counter-Revolution in Monetary Theory*, London: Institute of Economic Affairs.

—— (1976) "Wage Determination and Unemployment," in M. Friedman, *Price Theory*, Chicago: Aldine, 213–37.

—— (1987) "The Quantity Theory of Money," in J. Eatwell, M. Milgate, and P. Newman (eds) *The New Palgrave: A Dictionary of Economics*, London: Macmillan, 4: 3–20.

—— (1992) *Money Mischief: Episodes in Monetary History*, New York: Harcourt Brace Jovanovich.

—— (1993) "The 'Plucking Model' of Business Cycle Fluctuations Revisited," *Economic Inquiry*, 31(2), 171–7.

Friedman, M. and Schwartz, A. (1963) *A Monetary History of the United States, 1867–1960*, Princeton, NJ: Princeton University Press.

—— (1982) *Monetary Trends in the United States and the United Kingdom: Their Relation to Income, Prices and Interest Rates, 1867–1975*, Chicago: University of Chicago Press.

Frisch, R. (1933) "Propagation Problems and Impulse Problems in Dynamic Economics," *Economic Essays in Honour of Gustav Cassel*, London: Allen and Unwin, 171–205.

Garrison, R. (1978) "Austrian Macroeconomics: A Diagrammatical Exposition," in L. Spadaro (ed.) *New Directions in Austrian Economics*, Kansas City: Sheed, Andrews and McMeel, 167–204.

—— (1982) "Austrian Economics as the Middle Ground: Comment on Loasby," in I. Kirzner (ed.) *Method, Process, and Austrian Economics: Essays in Honor of Ludwig von Mises*, Lexington, MA: Lexington Books, 131–8.

—— (1984) "Time and Money: The Universals of Economic Theorizing," *Journal of Macroeconomics*, 6(2), 197–213.

—— (1985a) "Intertemporal Coordination and the Invisible Hand: An Austrian Perspective on the Keynesian Vision," *History of Political Economy*, 17(2), 309–21.

—— (1985b) "A Subjectivist View of a Capital-Using Economy," in G. O'Driscoll, Jr. and M. Rizzo with R. Garrison, *The Economics of Time and Ignorance*, Oxford: Basil Blackwell, 160–87.

—— (1986a) "The Hayekian Trade Cycle Theory: A Reappraisal," *Cato Journal*, 6(2), 437–53.

—— (1986b) "From Lachmann to Lucas: On Institutions, Expectations and Equilibrating Tendencies," in I. Kirzner (ed.) *Subjectivism, Intelligibility and Economic Understanding: Essays in Honor of Ludwig M. Lachmann on his Eightieth Birthday*, New York: New York University Press; London: Macmillan and Co., 87–101.

—— (1987) "The Kaleidic World of Ludwig Lachmann." Review article: Ludwig M. Lachmann, *The Market as an Economic Process*, *Critical Review*, 1(3), 77–89.

—— (1989) "The Austrian Theory of the Business Cycle in the Light of Modern Macroeconomics," *Review of Austrian Economics*, 3, 3–29.

—— (1990) "Austrian Capital Theory: The Early Controversies," in B. Caldwell (ed.), *Carl Menger and his Legacy in Economics*, Durham, NC: Duke University Press, 133–54.

—— (1990a) "Is Milton Friedman a Keynesian?" in M. Skousen (ed.) *Dissent on Keynes*, New York: Praeger Publishers, 131–47.

—— (1991a) "Austrian Capital Theory and the Future of Macroeconomics," in R. Ebeling (ed.) *Austrian Economics: Perspectives on the Past and Prospects for the Future*, Hillsdale, MI: Hillsdale College Press, 303–24.

—— (1991b) "New Classical and Old Austrian Economics: Equilibrium Business Cycle Theory in Perspective," *Review of Austrian Economics*, 5(1), 93–103.

—— (1992b) "The Limits of Macroeconomics," *Cato Journal*, 12(1), 165–78.

—— (1993a) "Keynesian Splenetics: from Social Philosophy to Macroeconomics." Review article: Allan H. Meltzer, *Keynes's Monetary Theory: A Different Interpretation*, *Critical Review*, 6(4), 471–92.

—— (1993b) "Public-Sector Deficits and Private-Sector Performance," in L. White (ed.) *The Crises in the Banking Industry*, New York: New York University Press, 29–54.

—— (1994a) "Hayekian Triangles and Beyond," in J. Birner and R. van Zijp (eds) *Hayek, Coordination and Evolution: His Legacy in Philosophy, Politics, Economics, and the History of Ideas*, London: Routledge, 109–25.

—— (1994b) "The Roaring Twenties and the Bullish Eighties: The Role of Government in Boom and Bust," *Critical Review*, 7(2–3), 259–76.

—— (1995a) "Linking the Keynesian Cross and the Production Possibilities Frontier," *Journal of Economic Education*, 26(2), 122–30.

—— (1995b) "The Persistence of Keynesian Myths: A Report at Six Decades," in R. Ebeling, (ed.) *Economics Education: What Should We Learn About the Free Market?* Hillsdale: Hillsdale College Press, 109–36.

—— (1996a) "Central Banking, Free Banking, and Financial Crises," *Review of Austrian Economics*, 9(2), 109–27.

—— (1996b) "Friedman's 'Plucking Model': Comment," *Economic Inquiry*, 34(4), 799–802.

—— (1997) "The Lachmann Legacy: An Agenda for Macroeconomics," *South African Journal of Economics*, 65(4), 459–81.

—— (1998a) *Chronically Large Federal Budget Deficits*, FMF Monograph 18. Sandton, South Africa: The Free Market Foundation.

—— (1998b) "The Intertemporal Adam Smith," *Quarterly Journal of Austrian Economics*, 1(1), 51–60.

—— (1999) "The Great Depression Revisited," *The Independent Review*, 39(4), 595–603.

Goodwin, T. and Sweeney R. (1993) "International Evidence on Friedman's Theory of the Business Cycle," *Economic Inquiry*, 31(2), 178–93.

Gordon, R. (1990) "What Is New Keynesian Economics?" *Journal of Economic Literature*, 28(3), 1115–71.

Hall, R. and Rabushka, A. (1995) *The Flat Tax*, 2nd edn, Stanford, CA: Hoover Institution Press.

Hayek, F. A. (1928) "Das Intertemporale Gleichgewichtssystem der Preise und die Bewegungen des Geldwertes," *Weltwirtschaftliches Archiv*, 2, 33–76.

—— (1931) "Reflections on the Pure Theory of Money of Mr J. M. Keynes," *Economica*, 11(31), 270–95.

—— (1941) *The Pure Theory of Capital*, Chicago: University of Chicago Press.

—— (1942) "The Ricardo Effect," *Economica*, N.S. 9(34), 127–52.

—— (1945a) "Time Preference and Productivity Reconsidered," *Economica*, N.S. 12(45), 22–5.

—— (1945b) "The Use of Knowledge in Society," *American Economic Review*, 35(4), 519–30.

—— (1952) *The Sensory Order*, Chicago: University of Chicago Press.

—— (1955) *The Counter-Revolution of Science*, New York: Free Press of Glencoe.

—— ([1935] 1967) *Prices and Production*, 2nd edn, New York: Augustus M. Kelley.

—— ([1928] 1975a) *Monetary Theory and the Trade Cycle*, New York: Augustus M. Kelley.

—— ([1933] 1975b) *Collectivist Economic Planning: Critical Studies on the Possibilities of Socialism*, Clifton, NJ: Augustus M. Kelley.

—— ([1937] 1975c) "Investment that Raises the Demand for Capital," in F. A. Hayek, *Profits, Interest, and Investment*, Clifton, NJ: Augustus M. Kelley, 73–82.

—— ([1939] 1975d) "Price Expectations, Monetary Disturbances and Malinvestments," in F. A. Hayek, *Profits, Interest, and Investment*, Clifton, NJ: Augustus M. Kelley, 135–56.

—— (1975e) *Full Employment at Any Price?*, Occasional Paper 45, London: Institute of Economic Affairs.

—— ([1969] 1978) "Three Elucidations of the Ricardo Effect," in F. A. Hayek, *New Studies in Philosophy, Politics, Economics and the History of Ideas*, Chicago: University of Chicago Press, 165–78.

—— (1984) *Money, Capital and Fluctuations*, R. McCloughry (ed.), Chicago: University of Chicago Press.

—— (1994) *Hayek on Hayek: An Autobiographical Dialogue*, S. Kresge and L. Wenar (eds), Chicago: University of Chicago Press.

Hazlitt, H. (1959) *The Failure of the "New Economics"*, Princeton, NJ: D. Van Nostrand Co., Inc.

Hicks, J. (1937) "Mr Keynes and the 'Classics': A Suggested Interpretation," *Econometrica*, 5, 147–59.

—— (1939) *Value and Capital*, Oxford: Clarendon Press.

—— (1967) "The Hayek Story," in J. Hicks, *Critical Essays in Monetary Theory*, Oxford: Clarendon Press, 203–15.

—— (1976) "Some Questions of Time in Economics," in A. Lang *et al.* (eds) *Evaluation, Welfare and Time in Economics*, Lexington, MA: D. C. Heath and Co., 135–51.

Horwitz, S. (2000) *Microfoundations and Macroeconomics: An Austrian Approach*, London: Routledge.

Jevons, W. ([1871] 1965) *The Theory of Political Economy*, New York: Augustus M. Kelley.

Johnson, P. (1997) *A History of the American People*, New York: HarperCollins.

Keynes, J. M. (1936) *The General Theory of Employment, Interest, and Money*, New York: Harcourt, Brace, and Company.

—— (1937) "The General Theory of Employment," *Quarterly Journal of Economics*, 51, 209–23.

Kim, C. and Nelson, C. (1999) "Friedman's Plucking Model of Business Fluctuations: Tests and Estimates of Permanent and Transitory Components," *Journal of Money, Credit and Banking*, 31(3) 317–34.

Kirman, A. (1992) "Whom or What Does the Representative Individual Represent?" *Journal of Economic Perspectives*, 6(2), 117–36.

Kirzner, I. (ed.) (1994) *Classics in Austrian Economics: A Sampling in the History of a Tradition*, London: William Pickering.

—— (1996) *Essays on Capital and Interest: An Austrian Perspective*, Brookfield, MA: Edward Elgar.

—— (1997) "Entrepreneurial Discovery and the Competitive Market Process: An Austrian Approach," *Journal of Economic Literature*, 35(1), 60–85.

Koppl, R. (1998) "Lachmann on the Subjectivism of Active Minds," in R. Koppl and G. Mongiovi (eds) *Subjectivism and Economic Analysis: Essays in Memory of Ludwig M. Lachmann*, London: Routledge, 61–79.

Krugman, P. (1994) *Peddling Prosperity: Economic Sense and Nonsense in the Age of Diminished Expectations*, New York: W. W. Norton and Co.

Lachmann, L. (1945) "A Note on the Elasticity of Expectations," *Economica*, N. S. 12(48), 249–53.

—— (1976) "From Mises to Shackle: An Essay on Austrian Economics and the Kaleidic Society," *Journal of Economic Literature*, 14(1), 54–62.

—— ([1943] 1977) "The Role of Expectations in the Social Sciences," in W. Grinder (ed.) *Capital, Expectations, and the Market Process*, Kansas City: Sheed, Andrews and McMeel, 65–80.

—— ([1956] 1978) *Capital and Its Structure*, Kansas City: Sheed, Andrews and McMeel.

—— (1986) *The Market as an Economic Process*, New York: Basil Blackwell.

Laidler, D. (1990) "The Legacy of the Monetarist Controversy," *Federal Reserve Bank of St. Louis Review*, 72(2), 49–64.

Leijonhufvud, A. (1968) *On Keynesian Economics and the Economics of Keynes*, New York: Oxford University Press.

—— ([1976] 1981a) "Schools, 'Revolutions,' and Research Programmes in Economic Theory," in A. Leijonfufvud, *Information and Coordination*, Oxford: Oxford University Press, 291–345.

—— (1981b) "The Wicksell Connection: Variations on a Theme," in A. Leijonhufvud, *Information and Coordination*, Oxford: Oxford University Press, 131–202.

—— (1984) "What Would Keynes Have Thought about Rational Expectations?," in D. Worswick and J. Trevithick (eds) *Keynes and the Modern World*, Cambridge: Cambridge University Press, 179–205.

—— (1986) "Real and Monetary Factors in Business Fluctuations," *Cato Journal*, 6(2), 409–20.

—— (1998) "Three Items for the Macroeconomic Agenda," *Kyklos*, 51(2), 197–218.

—— (1999) "Mr Keynes and the Moderns," in L. Pasinetti and B. Schofeld (eds) *The Impact of Keynes on Economics in the 20th Century*, Cheltenham: Edward Elgar.

Long, J. and Plosser, C. (1983) "Real Business Cycles," *Journal of Political Economy*, 91(1), 39–69.

Lucas, R. (1981) *Studies in Business Cycle Theory*, Cambridge, MA: MIT Press.

—— (1987) *Models of Business Cycles*, Oxford: Basil Blackwell.

McColloch, J. (1981) "Misintermediation and Macroeconomic Fluctuations," *Journal of Monetary Economics*, 8(1), 103–15.

Machlup, F. (1976) "Hayek's Contribution to Economics," in F. Machlup (ed.) *Essays on Hayek*, Hillsdale, MI: Hillsdale College Press, 13–59.

Maddock, R. and Carter, M. (1982) "A Child's Guide to Rational Expectations," *Journal of Economic Literature*, 20(1), 39–52.

Mankiw, N. and Romer D. (1991) "Introduction," in N. Mankiw and D. Romer (eds) *New Keynesian Economics: Imperfect Competition and Sticky Prices*, Cambridge, MA: MIT Press, 1–26.

Meltzer, A. (1988) *Keynes's Monetary Theory: A Different Interpretation*, Cambridge: Cambridge University Press.

Menger, C. ([1871] 1981) *Principles of Economics*, New York: New York University Press.

Mill, J. S. (1844) Reviews of books by Thomas Tooke and Robert Torrens, *Westminster Review*, 41, 579–93.

—— ([1848] 1895) *Principles of Political Economy*, London: George Routledge and Sons.

Mises von, L. (1943) "Elastic Expectations and the Austrian Theory of the Trade Cycle," *Economica*, N. S. 10(39), 251–2.

—— ([1922] 1951) *Socialism: An Economic and Sociological Analysis*, New Haven, CT: Yale University Press.

—— ([1912] 1953) *The Theory of Money and Credit*, New Haven, CT: Yale University Press.

—— ([1958] 1962) "Wages, Unemployment and Inflation," in L. Mises, *Planning for Freedom*, 2nd edn, South Holland, IL: Libertarian Press, 150–61.

—— (1966) *Human Action: A Treatise on Economics*, 3rd rev. edn, Chicago: Henry Regnery.

—— (1969) *Theory and History: An Interpretation of Social and Economic Evolution*, New Rochelle, NY: Arlington House.

—— ([1919] 1983) *Nation, State, and Economy: Contributions to the Politics and History of Our Time*, trans. L. Yeager, New York: New York University Press.

——, Haberler, G., Rothbard, M., and Hayek, F. ([1978] 1996) *The Austrian Theory of the Trade Cycle and Other Essays*, Auburn, AL: Ludwig von Mises Institute.

Muth, J. (1961) "Rational Expectations and the Theory of Price Movements," *Econometrica*, 29(3), 315–35.

Nelson, C. and Plosser C. (1982) "Trends and Random Walks in Macroeconomic Time Series: Some Evidence and Implications," *Journal of Monetary Economics*, 10(2), 139–62.

O'Driscoll, G. (1977a) "The Ricardian Non-Equivalence Theorem," *Journal of Political Economy*, 85(1), 207–10.

—— (1977b) *Economics as a Coordination Problem: The Contributions of Friedrich A. Hayek*, Kansas City: Sheed, Andrews and McMeel.

O'Driscoll, G. and Rizzo, M. with Garrison, R. (1985) *The Economics of Time and Ignorance*, Oxford: Basil Blackwell.

Patinkin, D. (1965) *Money, Interest, and Prices*, 2nd edn, New York: Harper and Row.

Phelps, E. (1970a) "The New Microeconomics in Employment and Inflation Theory," in E. Phelps *et al.*, *Microeconomic Foundations of Employment and Inflation Theory*, New York: Norton, 1–23.

—— (1970b) "Money Wage Dynamics and Labor Market Equilibrium," in E. Phelps *et al.*, *Microeconomic Foundations of Employment and Inflation Theory*, New York: Norton, 124–66.

Prescott, E. (1986) "Theory Ahead of Business Cycle Measurement," *Federal Reserve Bank of Minneapolis Quarterly Review*, Fall, 9–22.

Reekie, W. (1984) *Markets, Entrepreneurs and Liberty: An Austrian View of Capitalism*, New York: St Martin's Press.

Ricardo, D. ([1817] 1911) *The Principles of Political Economy and Taxation*, London: J. M. Dent and Sons.

Robbins, L. ([1934] 1971) *The Great Depression*, Freeport, NY: Books for Libraries Press.

Robinson, J. (1975) "What Has Become of the Keynesian Revolution?," in M. Keynes (ed.) *Essays on John Maynard Keynes*, Cambridge: Cambridge University Press, 123–31.

Rock, J. (ed.) (1991) *Debt and the Twin Deficits Debate*, Mountain View, CA: Mayfield Publishing.

Rothbard, M. ([1963] 1972) *America's Great Depression*, 3rd edn, Kansas City: Sheed and Ward.

Samuelson, P. (1962) "Parable and Realism in Capital Theory: The Surrogate Production Function," *Review of Economic Studies*, 39(3), 193–206.

—— (1964) *Economics*, New York: McGraw Hill, Inc.

—— ([1966] 1971) "A Summing Up," in G. Harcourt and N. Laing (eds) *Capital and Growth*, Harmondsworth: Penguin Books, 233–50.

Sargent, T. and Wallace, N. (1975) "'Rational' Expectations, the Optimal Monetary Instrument, and the Optimal Money Supply Rule," *Journal of Political Economy*, 83(2), 241–54.

—— (1976) "Rational Expectations and the Theory of Economic Policy," *Journal of Monetary Economics*, 2(2), 169–83.

Schumpeter, J. (1954) *History of Economic Analysis*, New York: Oxford University Press.

—— ([1911] 1961) *The Theory of Economic Development: An Inquiry into Profits, Capitalism, Credit, Interest, and the Business Cycle*, trans. R. Opie, New York: Oxford University Press.

Sechrest, L. (1997) "Austrian and Monetarist Business Cycle Theories: Substitutes or Complements?," *Advances in Austrian Economics*, 4, 7–31.

Selgin, G. (1991) "Monetary Equilibrium and the 'Productivity Norm' of Price-Level Policy," in R. Ebeling (ed.) *Austrian Economics: Perspectives on the Past and Prospects for the Future*, Hillsdale, MI: Hillsdale College Press, 433–64.

Shackle, G. (1967) *The Years of High Theory: Invention and Tradition in Economic Thought, 1926–1939*, Cambridge: Cambridge University Press.

—— (1974) *Keynesian Kaleidics*, Edinburgh: Edinburgh University Press.

Skousen, M. (1990) *The Structure of Production*, New York: New York University Press.

Smith, A. ([1776] 1937) *An Inquiry into the Nature and Causes of the Wealth of Nations*, New York: Modern Library.

Snowden, B., Vane, H., and Wynarczyk, P. (1994) *A Modern Guide to Macroeconomics: An Introduction to Competing Schools of Thought*, Aldershot: Edward Elgar.

Solow, R. (1997a) "Is There a Core of Usable Macroeconomics We Should All Believe In?," *American Economic Review*, 87(2), 230–2.

—— (1997b) "Trevor W. Swan," in T. Cate (ed.) *An Encyclopedia of Keynesian Economics*, Aldershot: Edward Elgar, 594–7.

Spadaro, L. (ed.) (1978) *New Directions in Austrian Economics*, Kansas City: Sheed, Andrews and McMeel.

Stanley, T. (1998) "New Wine in Old Bottles: A Meta-Analysis of Ricardian Equivalence," *Southern Economic Journal*, 64(3), 713–27.

Tullock, G. (1987) "Why the Austrians are Wrong about Depressions," *Review of Austrian Economics*, 2, 73–8.

Vaughn, K. (1994) *Austrian Economics in America: The Migration of a Tradition*, Cambridge: Cambridge University Press.

—— (2000) "The Rebirth of Austrian Economics: 1974–1999," *Economic Affairs*, 20(1), 40–3.

Warburton, C. (1966) *Depression, Inflation, and Monetary Policies: Selected Papers: 1945–53*, Baltimore: Johns Hopkins University Press.

Weinstein, M. (1999, section 3, p. 2) "Milton Friedman: My Biggest Mistake," *New York Times*, 4 July.

Wicksell, K. ([1898] 1962) *Interest and Prices: A Study of the Causes Regulating the Value of Money*, trans. R. Kahn, New York: Augustus M. Kelley.

Williams, R. (1994) *The Politics of Boom and Bust in Twentieth-Century America: A Macroeconomic History*, St Paul, MN: West Publishing.

Yeager, L. ([1968] 1997a) "Essential Properties of the Medium of Exchange," in L. Yeager, *The Fluttering Veil: Essays on Monetary Disequilibrium*, Indianapolis: Liberty Fund, 87–110.

—— ([1973] 1997b) "The Keynesian Diversion," in L. Yeager, *The Fluttering Veil: Essays on Monetary Disequilibrium*, Indianapolis: Liberty Fund, 199–216.

—— ([1986] 1997c) "The Significance of Monetary Disequilibrium," in L. Yeager, *The Fluttering Veil: Essays on Monetary Disequilibrium*, Indianapolis: Liberty Fund, 217–51.

—— (1997d) *The Fluttering Veil: Essays on Monetary Disequilibrium*, Indianapolis: Liberty Fund.

Index

3089130